The Fury of
Men's Gullets

The Fury of Men's Gullets

Ben Jonson and the Digestive Canal

Bruce Thomas Boehrer

PENN

University of Pennsylvania Press

Philadelphia

Copyright © 1997 University of Pennsylvania Press
All rights reserved
Printed in the United States of America on acid-free paper

10 9 8 7 6 5 4 3 2 1

Published by
University of Pennsylvania Press
Philadelphia, Pennsylvania 19104-6097

Library of Congress Cataloging-in-Publication Data

Boehrer, Bruce Thomas.
    The fury of men's gullets : Ben Jonson and the digestive canal / Bruce Thomas Boehrer.
      p.   cm.
    Includes bibliographical references and index.
    ISBN 0-8122-3408-1 (alk. paper)
    1. Jonson, Ben, 1573?–1637—Knowledge—Anatomy. 2. Body, Human, in literature. 3. Jonson, Ben, 1573?–1637—Knowledge—Manners and customs. 4. Literature and society—England—History—17th century. 5. Literature and science—England—History—17th century. 6. Dinners and dining in literature. 7. Alimentary canal in literature. 8. Food habits in literature. 9. Digestion in literature. I. Title.
PR2642.B58B64   1997
822'.3—dc21   97-11661
                                                                                                                      CIP

For my mother,
Katherine Hamner Boehrer

Contents

Acknowledgments ix

Introduction: Jonson and Alimentary Theory 1

1. The Genealogy of Manners 42

2. Renaissance Overeating 80

3. A Well-Digested Work 112

4. The Ordure of Things 147

5. Jonson's Crudities 176

Conclusion 202

Notes 209

Bibliography 223

Index 235

Acknowledgments

THIS STUDY HAS EARNED the generous attention of some outstanding scholars, each of whom has helped raise it above its humble gastrointestinal origins. Laura Rosenthal, Diane Roberts, Jeff Tatum, Stephen Greenblatt, Valerie Traub, and Robert Watson all read the manuscript either in its entirety or in large part. Karen Cunningham, Julie Solomon, Kim Hall, Peter Stallybrass, Bill Kelly, Stephen Orgel, Margreta de Grazia, and David Lee Miller generously shared their own work with me, offered valuable research suggestions, and gave me encouragement along the way. Jerry Stern, David Kirby, Hunt Hawkins, Ralph Berry, Joe McElrath, and Susan Seeley all offered me valuable out-of-field assistance. Pam Ball and Gary White taught me volumes about fine cooking and congeniality.

The research for this book has been conducted at a variety of libraries and archives, including the Folger Library, the Huntington Library, the British Library, the London Public Record Office, the London Guildhall Library, the Gorgas Library of the University of Alabama, and the Strozier Library of Florida State University. Thanks to the impeccable professionalism and courtesy of the staff at all these institutions, the book could almost have written itself. I am also deeply grateful to the National Endowment for the Humanities and to my home institution, Florida State University, for funding that has enabled me to conduct my research on such a far-flung basis.

I presented a piece of Chapter 3 of this book at the annual SAMLA proceedings for 1992, a piece of Chapter 4 to the University of Florida Group for the Applications of Psychoanalysis in 1995, and a piece of Chapter 5 within the Florida State University Literature Colloquium series for 1995. All of these audiences were forthcoming and gracious in their questions and comments. An early draft of Chapter 2 first appeared in *PMLA* 105.5 (October 1990); part of Chapter 3 saw print in *Philological Quarterly* 72.3 (Summer 1993); and an early version of Chapter 4 appeared in *New Perspectives on Ben Jonson* (Fairleigh Dickinson University Press, 1997). I am grateful to these publications for giving me a forum within which to develop my work, and I am especially indebted to Marshall Brown, William

Kupersmith, and James Hirsh for their editorial advice and assistance. Jerry Singerman and the staff of the University of Pennsylvania Press took a chance on my first book and now, five years later, seem not to have repented their heresy. I am thankful for all their help.

My fearless and loving wife, Barbara DeMent, not only has assisted with my research but also has gracefully suffered my many and varied eccentricities in the process. My family and friends have politely endured hours of hypnotic conversation on such subjects as dyspepsia, bowel disorders, and the invention of the flush-toilet. My students and colleagues have been more supportive than was strictly necessary, or perhaps even wise. And there is my mother, to whom this book is dedicated. O wonderful son, that can so 'stonish a mother.

Textual Note

All textual references to Ben Jonson's works are drawn from C. H. Herford and Percy and Evelyn Simpson, eds., *Ben Jonson* (Oxford: Clarendon Press, 1925–1952), 11 vols.

Introduction: Jonson and Alimentary Theory

BEN JONSON KNEW THE FATE of failed books as well as anyone. At the start of his *Epigrams* (1612–1613), he advises his bookseller to send remaindered copies of his verse to the London grocers' district, where they will be popular as wrapping paper: "If . . . [my book] will not sell, / Send it to *Bucklersbury*, there 'twill, well" (*Epigrams* 3.11–12). In *The Staple of News* (1626), on the other hand, Jonson envisions a different but parallel end for the author's labor. There he describes the Spanish ambassador, Count Gondomar, conjuring up a peculiar employment for Middleton's famous satire of him, *A Game at Chess*:

> LIC[KFINGER]. What news of *Gundomar*?
> THO[MAS BARBER].   A second *Fistula*,
>   Or an *excoriation* (at the least)
>   For putting the poore *English-play*, was writ of him,
>   To such a sordid vse, as (is said) he did,
>   Of cleansing his *posterior's*.
>   (3.2.207–211)

Again and again, Jonson conceives of books as having this sort of alimentary character, subject to processes of selection, preparation, ingestion, digestion, and excretion that mimic—and ultimately merge with—the literal functions of the digestive tract. This view of literature is not unique to Jonson, but in Jonson's hands it becomes a particularly flexible instrument of professional and social self-construction. To this extent, he is one of its outstanding modern exponents.

In fact, Jonson knew that books could literally be of culinary value. When he describes his ideal supper in Epigram 101, he promises his prospective guests that they will not have to endure bad poetry, but his promise is a slyly qualified one:

> Ile professe no verses to repeate:
> To this, if ought appeare, which I know not of,
> That will the pastrie, not my paper, show of.
> (*Epigrams* 101.24–26)

As Roger Gognard has pointed out, the bad poetry threatens to appear anyway, lining the bottoms of Jonson's pie-pans (3–4),[1] and as Sara van den Berg has remarked of this passage, Jonson may "subordinate his verse to pastry," but "no pastry can appear apart from the paper of this poem" (62). Despite—or more precisely, *through*—his suppression of verse's character as dinner entertainment, the poet self-consciously allows the repressed material to return to the table in another form.

I like to think of these lines as having a further valence. In an age during which few dramatists bothered to oversee the publication of their work, Jonson was notorious for intervening in the business of his printers (Riggs 220–224; Donovan 24; Herford, Simpson, and Simpson 9:45). He can hardly have failed to notice the signature odor of the Renaissance printing-house, which was the pervasive stench of urine (Gaskell 37). At least once—often twice—a day, the printers unbound the leather balls that they used to ink their presses, and, in order to keep the leather supple, they soaked it in open bowls of their own stale. The ink balls, thus permeated with the printers' urine, must have introduced some minute chemical residue of the digestive tract into the ink absorbed by the paper of Jonson's books. That paper, in turn, would have been exactly what returned to Jonson's party as the nonstick lining of his pastry tins. The poet's imaginary supper is an event where verse demands to appear at the table, and where piss insists upon mingling with food, despite the severest of official restrictions.

In *Bartholomew Fair* (1614), again, Jonson makes clear and deliberate use of this same alimentary circularity. When Justice Overdo arrives at the play's fair ground in order to chastise the local criminals, he halts proceedings with a grandiose temperance speech:

> Thirst not after that frothy liquor, Ale: for, who knowes, when hee openeth the stopple, what may be in the bottle? hath not a Snaile, a Spider, yea, a Neuft bin found there? . . . Neither doe thou lust after that tawney weede, tabacco . . . whose complexion is like the Indians that vents

it! . . . And who can tell, if, before the gathering, and making vp thereof, the *Alligarta* hath not piss'd thereon?

(2.6.11–27)

Overdo's rhetorical slide from ale to tobacco is similar to the more familiar movement from drink to food. Tobacco is well known among European writers as a substitute for food and drink;[2] European explorers of the New World noted that tobacco was both smoked and chewed by the indigenous peoples they encountered (Brooks 15); and the customary Jacobean verb for smoking—a verb that, according to Frances Teague, is used by later authors in allusion to *Bartholomew Fair* (55–56)—was "to drink." The alligator piss on Overdo's tobacco, like the newt in his beer bottle (the small animal itself inevitably depositing its excrements into the ale), serves as another reminder of how difficult it can be to keep alimentary processes separate, to impose a system of external conceptual distinctions on the body's necessarily interlinked metabolic processes. Likewise, just as the categories of ingestion and excretion interpenetrate, so Jonson's literary activities are pervaded with an unmistakable digestive character. As urine mingles with food, food amalgamates with poetry; the poet's ink bears the imprint of the alimentary canal whereas his pies preserve the marks of the printing press. This is a consistent and distinctive pattern in Jonson's work.

Jonson and Alimentary Transformation

This book aims to understand Jonson's enduring fascination with alimentary matters. To that end, it also deals with what one could call the sociohistorical significance of food. I assume, in other words, that Jonson's preoccupation with the digestive tract must be considered in light of what alimentation could mean for writers and readers in early seventeenth-century England. The historically specific range of meanings within which early modern alimentation could appear is, of course, never fully recuperable, and to that extent any work that aims at a completely historicized analysis of this subject matter is always already and must remain, by the largest possible definition of its project, a failure. On a more immediate and modest level, the present work can at least hope to provide a reasonably comprehensive account of the primary textual materials relevant to its agenda, and I hope it will be judged in light of its ability to perform this more limited task. In any event, the present study makes itself up from the artifacts of an irrecoverable past, which it can itself only approximate or at best supplant. No other procedural choice is available.

In the process of examining the historical particularities of Jonson's alimentary discourse, I have chosen to draw heavily on the theoretical work of Gilles Deleuze and Felix Guattari. Deleuze and Guattari, although not the most fashionable of recent theoretical writers, offer a uniquely useful avenue of approach to Jonson's discourse of alimentation precisely because the characteristics of their work often place them at odds with current academic trends. Their writing focuses at great length on a retheorization of the body—a retheorization that emphasizes fluidity, exploration, and transformability, while working very hard to break down the notions of anatomical categoricity that have influenced much recent writing on ideas of the body. Deleuzian theory also tends to render the interplay between classical and popular cultural canons particularly kinetic and ambiguous. Still further, the work of Deleuze and Guattari proceeds largely by processes of historical analysis and commentary, embracing everything from felting to recent cinema, and therefore arguably complementing the historicist bent of the present study. In short, Deleuze and Guattari offer a theoretical perspective that is particularly well adapted to a study of cultural transitions and metamorphoses, uncertainties and opportunities. If, as Alexander Leggatt has observed, "the public Jonson . . . is not a single character but a complex variety of roles, seemingly inconsistent at times but ultimately interconnected" (215), the study of Jonson may well be enhanced by a theoretical approach that emphasizes multiplicity and transformability over univocality and consistency. Such a body of theory may help us to appreciate the uncanny flexibility that pervades Jonson's language and writing.

In fact, the literary and cultural artifacts that provide the subject of this book are distinguished by their deep involvement in ongoing processes of social, and even physical, metamorphosis. Making themselves out of the residual materials of a past from which, by definition, they differ, they too impose their difference on the past, estranging it from itself and remaking it in the service of present needs. That process of estrangement arguably furnishes the raw substance of social change, and in early modern Europe such change encompasses many of the material terms of modern existence, from the most portentous to the most trivial. Thus when Christopher Hill surveys the cultural legacy of the seventeenth century, he nicely elides the global and the domestic, matters of state and matters of the table:

The England of 1603 was a second-class power; the Great Britain of 1714 was the greatest world power.... Englishmen's diet was transformed in this century by the introduction of root crops, which made it possible to have meat in winter. Potatoes and many new vegetables were added to it, as were tea, coffee, chocolate, sugar, and tobacco.... The modern arrangement of meals—breakfast, lunch, and dinner—dates from the seventeenth century.... By the end of the century pottery and glass had replaced pewter and wood at table. (2–3)

And so forth. Nor are the broad processes of such cultural transformation alien to the material of individual biography, although in individual cases the transformation takes a predictably less schematic form. One reason to study Ben Jonson is that his personal history interacts clearly, and in many cases decisively, with the larger cultural trends Hill and other historians seek to describe. To this extent, Jonson becomes an important test case for the signifying capacities of his society as a whole.

In keeping with this view of matters, the poet's life-records reflect an intense, ongoing campaign of self-refashioning, and Jonson's sustained effort to remake himself arguably both derives from and contributes to larger processes of social transformation. When conversing with William Drummond at the top of his career, he looks back on his childhood and early employment history with a fascinating selectivity of vision:

His Grandfather came from Carlisle & he thought from Anandale to it, he served King Henry 8 & was a Gentleman.... He himself was Posthumous born a moneth after his fathers decease, brought up poorly, putt to school by a friend (his master Cambden) after taken from it, and put to ane other Craft (I thinke was to be a Wright or Bricklayer) which he could not endure, then went he to ye low Countries but returning soone he betook himself to his wonted studies. (Drummond 234–243)

David Lee Miller has put memorable emphasis on the equivocal phrase "Posthumous born," which locates Jonson's own identity in a belatedness—a born-deadness—central to Lacanian concepts of ego construction (234–241). As Jonson describes his childhood to Drummond, a necessary rhetorical fissure opens within the idea of the poet himself, between Jonson the subject of the childhood narrative and Jonson the narrator; the distance between these two selves is then patched over with virtuoso narrative improvisations. Jonson makes a point not to remember the exact character of his first job, which "he could not endure"; yet in almost the same breath he identifies himself by tracing his ancestry a hundred years back to a "Gentleman" of Henry VIII; he describes scholarship as his "wonted" activity, that to which he was accustomed, the manner to which he was born;

and in doing so he characterizes his military service in the low countries as a moment of vagrancy from an already established career path. The poet reconstructs his past in order to make himself into a single, rhetorically stable, self-consistent person: the *doctus poeta* of James I's court. Yet the energy with which he effects this retroactive self-reconstruction helps reveal it as only one among various available interpretive strategies, some of which (e.g., the poet's proud occasional identification with the military profession) receive greater emphasis at other moments. Moreover, the same self-transformational energy that goes into the conversations with Drummond arguably helps turn Jonson into one of England's first modern literary professionals.

The present work must begin by noting that Jonson's much celebrated self-transformation occurs very largely in alimentary terms. David Riggs has recently emphasized the character of the poet's childhood home on Hartshorn Lane, Westminster, in a neighborhood whose "distinctive feature" was "the sewage ditch that ran along the premises of [his stepfather's] cottage" (10). As Riggs observes, "during Jonson's lifetime, Hartshorn Lane would become one of the major sewage canals in the greater London area" (10); moreover, the poet's stepfather, following a common practice of early modern Londoners, constructed a "little garden"—almost certainly a kitchen garden—over the sewage ditch that abutted his cottage (10). The alimentary circularity that invests *Bartholomew Fair* and Epigram 101 thus emerges from Jonson's childhood as a pattern not merely of aesthetic but also of biographical determination, coextensive with the childhood circumstances against which the poet rebelled so bitterly. Inserted into the metaphorical anus of greater London, Jonson begins his life by eating self-consciously recycled excrement.

The poet's childhood circumstances also lead to a further observation. Scholars have often focused on the long, concerted spiral of upward social mobility that characterizes Jonson's career; as far as I know, however, no one has concentrated on the digestive troping of this mobility. In fact, Jonson's career can be described as a kind of inverted figurative peristalsis. The life that begins so inauspiciously atop a Westminster sewage conduit in time attaches itself to the preeminent aesthetic and culinary monument of early Stuart culture: the royal banqueting house at Whitehall. In the process, Jonson crafts himself into a regular fixture of Jacobean and Caroline royal culinary entertainment. The masques he composes with Inigo Jones, Alphonso Ferrabosco, and others are regularly described as composite productions, but only recently, in the work of scholars like Patricia

Fumerton,[3] has this insight been extended to encompass culinary presentation and behavior at the table.

In fact, I suspect that the masque's status as an element of culinary ritual helps to explain certain features of both Jonson's literary artistry and of his career as a whole. In the former instance, Jonson's work repeatedly conflates or contrasts the office of poet with that of chef; examples of this gesture include (but are by no means limited to) the prologue to *Epicoene* (1609), the prologue to *The New Inn* (1629), and the antimasque to *Neptune's Triumph for the Return of Albion* (1624). In terms of the larger structure of Jonson's career, the same juxtaposition or conflation occurs repeatedly: there are the dining-club-cum-literary-society Jonson and his followers established at the Devil and Saint Dunstan Tavern; the public feasting and drinking during Jonson's Scottish journey; the pension of canary wine Jonson received late in life from the Crown (Herford, Simpson, and Simpson 1:247); and the poet's infamous girth, which increased with (and through) his reputation, transforming him from a "leane . . . hollow-cheekt Scrag" (Dekker, *Satiromastix* 5.2.263) into a living literary monument with a "mountaine belly and . . . rockie face" (*Underwood* 9.17). Again and again, in a manner that is at once jovial and a bit invidious, Jonson seeks to incorporate the office of chef into the body of his work, while his work, in turn, runs the risk of being translated into a subsidiary element of culinary presentation. This tension not only makes sense in terms of Jonson's proprietorial attitude toward his masque productions; it also conforms to the larger emphasis on individual creativity and ownership of literary property that is a distinctive feature of the poet's overall career.

The following chapters must therefore deal not only with the alimentary troping of Jonson's work, but with the alimentary troping of his life as well. Any such project will be rendered more difficult by the great potential indecorum of its subject matter, for any scholarly study that focuses on Jonson's treatment of alimentation necessarily complicates efforts to present the poet as an austere classicist or rigorous reformer of morals. To this extent, the present work risks charges of character assassination; certainly one of the earliest efforts to come to grips with Jonson's use of alimentary motifs—Edmund Wilson's famous essay on Jonsonian anality—has incurred such charges (see, e.g., Pearlman 365–366). Yet a supreme irony of Jonson's fixation on digestive matters is that it derives in large part from the very classicism that it would seem to disturb. As Robert Watson has noted, Jonson's classicism has the effect of "subverting the usual boundaries between works and between genres" even as it aligns Jonson himself with "traditional values" (13); the poet's use of classical alimentary and convivial themes provides a case in point. Thus I hope that the present study might provide a useful adjunct to the important recent work on Jonsonian classicism by scholars like Katharine Maus, Richard Peterson, Thomas Greene, and Douglas Duncan. In the process, this book might be able to shed some light on the way in which Jonson's alimentary references provide material for personal and cultural transformation—for negotiating the distance between a classical past and a postmodern future. With such an aim in mind, the remainder of this introduction is devoted to two issues: first, to examining the major theoretical models that have been established in the postmodern present to account for the significance of alimentation; and second, to introducing one extended instance of the alimentary complexities that Jonson's work exploits—complexities that derive, in large part, from the poet's treatment of the classical past.

Theory and the Belly

Twentieth-century writers have used three major theoretical models to analyze the presence of alimentary motifs in early modern English drama: the Freudian, the Bakhtinian, and what I call the anthropological. From each standpoint, Jonson's work has earned considerable local scrutiny.

Freud

Edmund Wilson's "Morose Ben Jonson" made the definitive early psychoanalytic statement about Jonson's life and work, arguing that "Jonson seems an obvious example of a psychological type which has been described by Freud and designated by a technical name, *anal erotic*" (217). As Wilson understands it, this character type is marked by a preoccupation with "orderliness . . . ; parsimony; . . . [and] obstinacy" (218). It is subtended by an extreme emotional aloofness, even impoverishment (220), and it manifests itself in adult behavior through a fixation on various symbolic substitutes for fecal matter—most particularly money. Jonson exhibits this anal fixation, according to Wilson, through his repeated use of motifs of hoarding (218–219); through his treatment of fecal release as an act of aggression (228); and through his personality, which was viewed by at least some of his contemporaries as distinctively grudging and ungenerous (220–221). The result is a Freudian interpretation that sees Jonson's work as impaired by its author's psychological morbidity and that disparagingly contrasts Jonson's "glaring defects" (215)—in perhaps predictable fashion—with the free, gentle, and generous accomplishments of Shakespeare. In short, Wilson refers to anal eroticism as a "psychological type," but his description of the type and his application of it to Jonson's case clearly indicate that he regards it as an emotional infirmity.

More recently, Wilson's reading of Jonson has incurred some telling censure. E. Pearlman has put the counter-case most cogently:

> [Wilson's] picture of Jonson, though unattractive and harsh, is not entirely untrue. . . . But Wilson's version of Ben Jonson is neither a complete nor a fecund truth. If the retentive character is defined by stinginess, to what do we attribute the extraordinary abundance—plays, poems, masques, translations, a grammar, criticism—of Jonson's creativity? And what accounts for a play like *Bartholomew Fair*, which not only celebrates the anus, but is a paean to every orifice, every bodily fluid, every quiddity of man's [sic] animal nature. . . . Clearly, Jonson possessed, and was perhaps even handicapped by, a retentive streak. But it is mean to let a part of a complex individuality stand for the whole. Wilson's analysis is a partial truth, a psychological synecdoche. (366)

Pearlman's remarks are admirable for at least two reasons: they nicely distinguish the characteristics of Jonson's work that Wilson has trouble explaining, and yet they acknowledge the limited validity of Wilson's reading. Pearlman's is a revisionist Jonson, but a selectively revisionist one, in whom the theory of anality still plays an important, albeit restricted, role.

More recently still, David Riggs has revived the psychoanalytic approach to Jonson's work, correlating anal motifs with patterns of oedipal aggression. The fecal references of *The Case Is Altered* (1597), for instance, thus metamorphose into a version of "archetypal family romance" (30) in which the wicked stepfather Jacques de Prie buries his personal treasure in a dung heap. Hence, Riggs concludes, "The scenes in which Jacques builds his cache . . . appear . . . to be the work of a man who suffers from [analerotic neurosis]. Since Jonson never proceeded through the stage at which the child learns to cope with intergenerational conflict, when he fantasized about stepfathers, he instinctively regressed to the anal stage and soiled his foster parent with excrement" (31). But Riggs, like Pearlman, carefully circumscribes this reading by calling attention to its limitations: "it is inadequate," he continues, "to conclude that Jonson 'was' an anal-erotic personality. . . . The author of *The Case Is Altered* had infantile wishes, but he also had found a creative way of gratifying those wishes" (31). In effect, like his garden-planting stepfather, "Jonson had discovered how to turn manure into a valuable commodity" (31), and for Riggs this discovery saves the poet from charges of anal eroticism.

Each of the foregoing treatments of Jonsonian anality is admirable in its own right, and the present work is deeply indebted to them all. But because none of them devotes much attention to Freud's own writings on the subject of anality, all three works incline toward an unnecessarily narrow—and unnecessarily pejorative—understanding of anal eroticism.[4] In fact, the early statements made by Freud and his followers on the subject of anality are by no means entirely disparaging or restrictive. When Freud introduces the topic in 1908, he presents anal eroticism not as a psychological ailment, but as "a certain set of character-traits" ("Character" 169) whose bearing on particular varieties of neurosis deserves exploration. He then defines the central characteristics of anal eroticism in a way that needs to be quoted at length:

The people I am about to describe are . . . especially *orderly, parsimonious* and *obstinate*. Each of these words actually covers a small group or series of interrelated character-traits. "Orderly" covers the notion of bodily cleanliness, as well as of conscientiousness in carrying out small duties and trustworthiness. . . . Parsimony may appear in the exaggerated form of avarice; and obstinacy can go over into defiance, to which rage and revengefulness are easily joined. . . . It is easy to gather from these people's early childhood history that they took a comparatively long time to overcome their infantile *incontinentia alvi*. . . . [Hence] we infer that such people are born with a sexual constitution in which the erotogenicity of the anal zone is exceptionally strong. But . . . the anal zone had lost its erotogenic significance in the course of development; and it is to be suspected that the regularity with which this triad of properties is present in their character may be brought into relation with the disappearance of anal erotism. ("Character" 169–170)

The first thing to be noted in this account of anal eroticism is the extreme variety of attitudes and behaviors it incorporates under the rubrics of order, parsimony, and obstinacy. Whereas Wilson invoked these three terms to define the anal-erotic personality *tout court*, for Freud they function as a tentative means of organizing a wide range of potentially contradictory character traits. Moreover, the focus on morbidity so evident in Wilson's account of the anal Jonson takes less clear shape in Freud. The English word *orderly* is largely neutral in its moral and clinical connotations, and if placed properly within the Teutonic cultural context, the German equivalent *ordentlich* actually emerges as a term of high praise. *Parsimony*, too, tries to stake out a kind of semiotic middle ground; it can be either a grim form of thrift or avarice with a happy face, depending on how one chooses to view it. As for obstinacy, one need only recall the proverbial declension "I am firm; thou art obstinate; he is pigheaded" to note how precariously this term mediates between competing extremes of laudable and reprehensible behavior. In short, Freud at least attempts to construct the anal-erotic personality as bearing the virtues of its defects and the defects of its virtues. Wilson, Pearlman, and Riggs all have greater or lesser trouble accepting this characterization of matters. Thus Wilson's account of Jonson is largely condemnatory, whereas Riggs and Pearlman proceed as if Jonson's praiseworthy qualities placed him by definition beyond the purview of anal eroticism.

In addition, Freud's account of the anal-erotic character offers a remarkably capacious explanation of how anal eroticism is assimilated into the subject's adult personality. The principal mechanism in this process is apparently social condemnation, which encourages the subject to repress the erotogenicity of the anal zone; however, the forms adopted by such repression are necessarily various and ongoing, involving reaction formation, a wide range of possible sublimations, and the continued existence of unsublimated drives, all in more or less variable admixtures. Thus, although the origins of anal repression may be located in the infantile processes of toilet training, to characterize anality as a purely "infantile" mode of experience (Riggs 31), and to describe anal behavior exclusively as a function of psychological "regression" (Riggs 31), is not entirely fair. On the contrary, Freud ends his earliest discussion of anality by musing on the relative force of repressed and unrepressed anal eroticism in the formation of adult character:

If there is any basis in fact for the relation posited here between anal erotism and this triad of character traits, one may expect to find no very marked degree of "anal character" in people who have retained the anal zone's erotogenic character in adult life, as happens, for instance, with certain homosexuals. ("Character" 175)

From a late twentieth-century perspective, Freud's eagerness to speculate on the "anal character" of homosexuals may seem offensive, at the very least. But at moments like this Freud is clearly committed to the complementary propositions that anal eroticism exerts an ongoing influence on adult behavior through a whole series of possible accommodations to social repression, and that the study of anal eroticism thus functions primarily as a study of character formation and only secondarily as a classification of neurosis.

This early document on anal eroticism provoked an immediate and violent reaction. As the editors of Freud's *Complete Works* observe, "the theme of this paper has now become so familiar that it is difficult to realize the astonishment and indignation which it aroused on its first publication" ("Character" 168). The source of this indignation was nicely summarized by Ernest Jones as "the discovery that certain traits of character may become profoundly modified as the result of sexual excitations experienced by the infant in the region of the anal canal" (413). The objectionable point, in other words, was the interconnection between character development and anal sexual experience. Perhaps naturally, therefore, Freud's next statement on the subject tended to focus upon the psychopathology of anal eroticism. His 1913 paper on "The Disposition to Obsessional Neurosis" sought, in a highly overdetermined manner, to distinguish between character and neurosis by restricting the play of anal eroticism to the latter:

> In the field of the development of *character* we are bound to meet with the same instinctual forces which we have found at work in the neuroses. But a sharp theoretical distinction between the two is necessitated by the single fact that the failure of repression and the return of the repressed—which are peculiar to the mechanism of neurosis—are absent in the formation of character. In the latter, repression either does not come into action or smoothly achieves its aim of replacing the repressed by reaction-formations and sublimations. Hence the processes of the formation of character are more obscure and less accessible to analysis than neurotic ones. ("Neurosis" 323)

This passage seeks, among other things, to impose a "sharp theoretical distinction" on processes of character formation, which, given the very terms whereby Freud initially introduces them, are unavoidably multivalent and complex. In a still later work, *Civilization and Its Discontents* (1930), the fuzziness of the distinction between character and neurosis becomes obvious. There Freud observes that the primary qualities of the anal personality—"parsimony, a sense of order and cleanliness"—are not only "valuable and welcome in themselves" but are also "important requirements of civilization" that erupt into neurosis only when "they become markedly dominant" within the individual character (96–97). Thus, despite the effort to define healthy character development and anal neurosis as separate nosological animals, the difference between them that finally emerges is one of degree, not of kind. Anal eroticism does inform healthy character after all, simply in "more obscure and less accessible" ways than it does neurosis. The resulting argument is vaguely reminiscent of a Monty Python comedy routine; there is no anal eroticism in the well-adjusted character, Freud insists, and by none he means that there is a certain amount. It is small wonder, given such theoretical complexities, that Norman O. Brown has called anal eroticism "the most paradoxical of psychoanalytical specifications of sublimation" (177). The scholarship on anality in Ben Jonson's work, as outstanding as it is, might reasonably be extended to account for this complexity; I believe the result could be both a richer understanding of the functions of anality in the poet's work and a less severe appraisal of the poet's own character.[5]

Condemnatory appropriation of the theory of anal eroticism may in fact say less about Jonson's own life and work than about the critical tradition to which that life and work have been assimilated. Moreover, the view of Jonsonian anality as consonant with neurosis also leads to various ironies within the critical tradition itself. For one example, Wilson carefully contrasts Jonson with Shakespeare on the ground that the former exhibits characteristics of anal eroticism absent from the life and work of the latter: "Shakespeare . . . has an immense range. . . . To an intelligent and sensitive man of any school of thought, Shakespeare appears sensitive and intelligent. But Ben Jonson, after Shakespeare, seems neither. Though he attempts a variety of characters, they all boil down to a few motivations" (215)—motivations consistent with the author's own character as an anal neurotic. In the past decade, however, Anne Barton has argued lengthily and persuasively that Jonson's career actually charts a course of accommodation to the principles of Shakespearean comedy. This rapprochement, according to Barton, begins to emerge clearly in *Bartholomew Fair* and becomes increasingly pronounced in Jonson's later plays. These later works betray "an alteration in Jonson's attitude toward . . . the Elizabethan literature he had treated earlier as negligible" (*Jonson* 210); one index of this alteration is Jonson's increasing interest in personal relations, personal transformation, and personal trust. The last of these terms is crucial. According to Barton, "personal loyalty" emerges as a major theme of *Bartholomew Fair* (*Jonson* 205–206); it becomes, if anything, still more important in *The Devil Is An Ass* (1616), a play in which "'trust' is the most important word" (*Jonson* 229); and by *The Magnetic Lady* (1632), Barton declares, "the word 'trust' is . . . such a resonant monosyllable in Jonson's vocabulary that it can carry almost the same weight of feeling as a declaration of love" (*Jonson* 296). Yet this emphasis on trust, coextensive with Jonson's increasing respect for Shakespearean comedy, is also an emphasis on one of the qualities specifically identified by Freud as a major sublimation of anal eroticism ("Character" 169). In short, the very thing that Wilson views as crucially distinguishing Jonson from Shakespeare—the former's sublimation of anal eroticism—emerges, for Barton, as an index of the two playwrights' developing aesthetic solidarity.

I note this contradiction not out of any desire to censure Wilson or Barton—both of whose works greatly overshadow the present study—but in order to note the impasse into which even the most sophisticated of critics can be driven by the multivalence of Jonson's anality. Finally, I would also add that it is not exactly—or at least not simply—*Jonson*'s anality that is at stake here. Riggs suggests this latter point when he characterizes *The Case Is Altered* as "an adaptive, rather than a neurotic" work (31). The scatology of that play—and most of Jonson's others—could not succeed dramatically if it were the manifestation of a single dysfunctional personality. In an age when Shakespeare's Malvolio could remark on the greatness of Olivia's P's, when John Ford could laugh at a character who has been beaten till his "feet capered in the kennel" (*'Tis Pity She's a Whore* II.vi.75), and when Sir John Harington could predict that his invention of the flush-toilet would earn him an appointment to Queen Elizabeth's "privy . . . council" (61), Jonson's preoccupation with excretory processes should arguably be viewed as culturally paradigmatic rather than individually neurotic. In later pages, this view of matters leads us into the sewage system of Jacobean London. For now, however, it leads us to Bakhtin.

Bakhtin

Few authors have exerted a more powerful influence over late twentieth-century political criticism than Mikhail Bakhtin. Unlike Freud, whose work on anality has often been appropriated to the study of individual neurosis, Bakhtin's expansive theories emphasize the social collectivity; moreover, in studying the forms of early modern European festival behavior, Bakhtin has touched on numerous issues of interest to Jonson scholarship. Ian Donaldson, for one, has read Jonson's work in light of rituals of misrule such as those examined by Bakhtin and others;[6] Peter Womack has studied Jonson in terms of the Bakhtinian notion of dialogism—"discourse . . . which adopts language, not simply as an instrument of representation, but also as an object of representation" (7). But more immediately relevant to the present study, Leah Marcus, Peter Stallybrass, and Allon White have employed quasi-Bakhtinian theories of popular humor and the grotesque body in ways that touch on the issue of alimentary representation in Jonson's work.

Focusing on the holiday practices of the early Stuart court, Marcus sees Jonson's work as implicated in those practices and in the paradoxical theory that motivated the Stuart monarchs' advocacy of them. For James I and Charles I, Marcus argues, "festival freedom was seen as a sign of submission to power" (8), and the contradictorily stoic and saturnalian impulses of Jonsonian drama may thus be read as an attempt to negotiate between the opposed terms of freedom and subjection encompassed within the holiday pastimes themselves. Unlike Marcus, Stallybrass and White center their analysis on the politics of the commonalty rather than of the nobility. Examining the history of fair and market activity in western Europe, they see Jonson's work in general—and *Bartholomew Fair* in particular—as an expression of uneasy psychic dependence on structures of popular festivity from which Jonson, in his professional capacity as *doctus poeta*, felt it increasingly necessary to dissociate himself. Thus, in writing about popular institutions such as Bartholomew Fair, Jonson attempted to "rewrite the social and economic relations which determined his own existence; in the fair he could stigmatize the voices which competed against his own and reveal just how 'dirty' were the hands which sullied his 'pure' wares" (77).

Both of these arguments represent carefully conceived improvements on a largely Bakhtinian model of popular festivity, a model that regards the festival behavior of the commonalty as all-inclusive, celebratory, and politically liberating. For both Marcus and Stallybrass and White, festival activity necessarily impinges upon the protocols of dining; likewise, Bakhtin devotes a chapter of *Rabelais and His World* to the banquet imagery of *Gargantua and Pantagruel*. In the process, Bakhtin carefully defines that imagery as an expression of "the unique yet complex carnival experience of the people" (10):

The banquet images—food, drink, swallowing—are closely linked in Rabelais' novel with the popular-festive forms. . . .This is no commonplace, privately consumed food and drink, partaken of by individuals. This is a popular feast, a "banquet for all the world." The mighty aspiration to abundance and to a universal spirit is evident in each of these images. (278)

Indeed, Bakhtin continues, Rabelaisian food and drink "are one of the most significant manifestations" of a particular way of thinking about the body—a way that Bakhtin himself has famously labeled as "grotesque":

The distinctive character of this body is its open unfinished nature, its interaction with the world. These traits are most fully and concretely revealed in the act of eating; the body transgresses here its own limits: it swallows, devours, rends the world apart, is enriched and grows at the world's expense. . . .Man's encounter with the world in the act of eating is joyful, triumphant; he triumphs over the world, devours it without being devoured himself. The limits between man and the world are erased, to man's advantage. (281)

In a world dominated by the conceptual canon of the grotesque body—a world that celebrates the openness and communality of the social group—dining constitutes a reaffirmation of society's collective health. Moreover, it is a reaffirmation "in flagrant contradiction with the literary and artistic canon of antiquity" (28), which conceives of the body as "isolated, alone, fenced off from other bodies" (29).[7] Thus Bakhtin traces Rabelaisian images of eating through medieval Latin and vernacular recreational texts, concluding that "It is in this sphere that we must seek the main source of Rabelais' banquet images. The influence of the ancient symposium is of secondary importance" (282).

Despite its value as an analysis of Rabelais, Bakhtin's formulation will clearly not quite do for Jonson. Jonson's classicism is sufficiently aggressive, consistent, and self-conscious to resist relegation to the status of "secondary" influence. Michael Bristol has identified Jonsonian drama as "an effort to oppose and displace a theater already practiced and appreciated throughout plebeian culture" (119), and although the present study would like to complicate this view of matters, it surely contains an element of truth. Moreover, as Richard Peterson has pointed out, a number of Jonson's prominent alimentary images actually constitute appropriations of similar imagery from the classical canon (Peterson 6–9, 14–17). Such appropriations do not necessarily negate the influence of popular festivity on Jonson's work, but they certainly render it ambiguous; indeed, one can easily come away from Jonson's work with the sense that such ambiguities are the essence of the poet's project.

Still further, the complications attendant upon Jonson's use of popular and classical festivity generate additional problems in the realm of sociopolitical analysis. The robust optimism of Bakhtin's theory is famous, and it has invited a good measure of rethinking. Neither Marcus nor Stallybrass and White can quite accept the triumphant, celebratory view of popular festivity proposed in *Rabelais and His World*. Just as one can question the strict separation of popular from classical festivity within Jonson's work, so Marcus regards as "problematic" the Bakhtinian notion that "festival forms are completely separate from the official culture" (7). On the contrary, she continues, popular festivity "can constitute a process of adjustment within a perpetuation of order" (7). Thus festival can include "both normative and revisionary impulses," and "the precise balancing of the functions depends on local and particular factors and creates different effects at different places and times" (Marcus 7). Likewise, Stallybrass and White incline toward a relatively disillusioned view of the liberating potential of carnival, wondering "whether the 'licensed release' of carnival is not simply a form of social control of the low by the high" (13). Their conclusion is to view carnival as an instance of symbolic transgression—that is, as one of the many discursive sites upon which high culture "attempts to reject and eliminate the 'bottom' for reasons of prestige and status, only to discover, not only that it is in some way frequently dependent upon that low-Other . . . , but also that the top *includes* that low symbolically, as a primary eroticized constituent of its own fantasy life" (5).

Such reassessments embody revisions in leftist political thought like those inspired by Foucault and Althusser. Just as the Euro-American political experience of 1968 and thereafter has made it increasingly difficult to conceive of an unadulterated moment of popular liberation, so recent Bakhtinian readings of Jonson have become markedly cautious and nuanced in their discussions of the carnivalesque as a vehicle of social emancipation. The versions of Jonson promoted by Marcus and Stallybrass and White thus improve on Bakhtin by replacing Bakhtin's broad and celebratory analysis of popular festivity with something more complex and narrower in its scope for personal empowerment. As a general rule, this procedure is both sound and carefully executed. However, the binarism of the Bakhtinian model sometimes obtrudes through even the most skillful efforts to reshape it, and Jonson provides a case in point. Both Marcus and Stallybrass and White incline toward a tragic, or at least an agonistic, view of the poet's work—a view that gains force from the poverty, illness, and neglect of his last years. Thus Stallybrass and White conclude that "in *Bartholomew Fair*, Jonson was 'subdued' not only by the Hope audience but also, from the perspective of the classical aesthetic, by his own choice of subject-matter" (71). In fact, they continue, Jonson's work in general remains "subdued to the elements he worked in, but these appear as negated or denied elements, taking on a new and different form under the sign of their negation" (76). Likewise, Marcus views the masque *For the Honor of Wales* (1618) as "a capitulation on Jonson's part to prevailing taste and opinion" (127); *The Devil Is an Ass*, in turn, emerges as "the expression of a Jonsonian stalemate: the moralist fatally and fundamentally at odds with the milieu within which he was required to function as court poet" (104).

In short, whereas psychoanalytic studies of Jonson have been largely fixated on the issue of personal neurosis, neo-Bakhtinian studies have been increasingly consumed by the issue of social neurosis. Stallybrass and White's book on Bakhtin starts with Jonson and ends with Freud, arguably because the work's modified Bakhtinian theoretical model leads inescapably to a conception of neurosis as generated by the opposition of "normative and revisionary" social impulses within the individual subject. Still more recently, this tendency has invested political studies of Jonson even when those studies have not been primarily concerned with Bakhtin. Richard Burt's recent and thoughtful work on Jonsonian censorship, for example, invokes the term *neurosis* not as a marker of individual psychopathology, but rather as a social metaphor—a way "to suggest that Jonson's decentered subjectivity marks a compromise formation between different censoring spaces and agencies" (50). Although very much in sympathy with this view of matters, I hope in the present book to recover a little of Bakhtin's original optimism, both for Jonson's sake and for my own, while nonetheless moving even farther away from the binarism that invests Bakhtin's opposition between grotesque and classical bodily canons. Proceeding from the position that Jonson's work is indeed the product of a "decentered subjectivity," and that it may indeed display the coexistence of "normative and revisionary impulses," I would like to conceive of those impulses as occupying the relative position not of antitheses, but of two among many mutually necessary and mutually enabling conceptual possibilities. These possibilities, moreover, are capable of changing their own sociopolitical character in accordance with shifts in the context within which they function. The durability of Jonson's achievements (particularly in areas such as the establishment of modern notions of literary professionalism) would suggest that the agonistic approach to the poet's career might have trouble recognizing the ways in which he succeeds. After all, in the battle between subject and structure the outcome is always weighted in favor of the collectivity.

Moreover, to read Jonson's work as an instance of conflict between "artist" and "milieu," or between "normative and revisionary impulses," may fit it too neatly into the subversion/containment debate that has characterized much political criticism since 1980, and may thus make one's understanding of Jonson's work subject to the governing binarism of that debate. One object of the present study is to retain recent criticism's emphasis on the social agency of literary work while conceiving of this agency through metaphors of accommodation or flight rather than of confrontation. As Theodore Leinwand has recently observed, social change need not be metaphorized as guerrilla warfare: "A negotiation-based model of social relations that can account for change or for resistance to change has the significant advantage of recognizing that the lower orders are not limited to a choice between quietism and insurrection. . . . Talk of subversion and containment may in fact melodramatize the historical record" (480–481). It may seem odd to invoke nonconfrontational metaphors in connection with so truculent a figure as Jonson, but even Jonson's own famed belligerence cannot be wholly characterized as the attitude of an ex-soldier spoiling for a fight. On the contrary, one of the remarkable things about the poet's career is the readiness with which stable relations distill into serious arguments and then redistill back into friendship. There is the strange tale of Jonson and Marston, for instance, or the relationship between Jonson and Campion (which Robert Evans understatedly calls "a bit ambivalent" [*Contexts* 116]), not to mention the various fallings-in and fallings-out with Inigo Jones, George Chapman, and others—all of which parallel the poet's complex and vacillating relationship to Catholicism. To modify the Clausewitzian adage, Jonson's many quarrels would seem to be personal diplomacy conducted by other means. The present study seeks to understand the nature of that diplomacy—the methods whereby Jonson sought to make a unique literary identity for himself out of the common and often inconsistent self-presentational materials of his generation—and to understand why the poet's diplomatic efforts sometimes metamorphose into acrimony. But just as important, this book aims to appreciate Jonson's enduring literary and personal successes—successes rendered all the more striking by the air of controversy with which the poet was so frequently surrounded.

Anthropology

In addition to Freud and Bakhtin, certain anthropological authors have influenced recent writing on the early modern drama in general, and on Jonson in particular. In a sense it is arbitrary to try to separate the influence of these authors from that of Bakhtin, for in recent studies the Bakhtinian and anthropological approaches tend to fuse together, abetting and underscoring each other in various ways. Thus, although pursuing an avowedly Bakhtinian line of argument, Stallybrass and White use anthropological material throughout their work; nor is Marcus any stranger to anthropological ideas; and Gail Paster's important recent study of bodily embarrassment in Renaissance drama, although largely anthropological and sociohistorical in focus, also bears the mark of Bakhtin. As a result, it may be helpful to consider recent anthropologically based scholarship as another aspect of the political criticism to which Bakhtin's theories have proven so amenable.

For immediate purposes, the two most influential anthropological authors are probably Pierre Bourdieu and Mary Douglas, whose theories of bodily culture and pollution avoidance, respectively, have opened up productive avenues of scholarship in early modern drama. Bourdieu's work is especially helpful in explaining the complicity between anthropological and Bakhtinian theory. As Paster has observed, Bakhtin's notion of the grotesque body treats the body itself more as a social metaphor than as a concrete assemblage of tissues, functions, and behaviors: "the grotesque body is a thematizing image of the popular body which by definition cannot belong to or be identified with selfhood, with the discrete, pathetically finite boundaries of the individual in life and time" (15). As a result, Bakhtin's work is not always well equipped to explain the specific historical activities of specific individuals; it is more concerned with theorizing a broad and abstract tradition of popular festivity than with investigating the minutiae of human interaction as constrained by the variables of time and place. Bourdieu, on the other hand, is preeminently interested in the latter subject, and his work takes as its province "the countless acts of diffuse inculcation through which the body and the world tend to be set in order" (92), and which Bourdieu collectively describes by the term *habitus*.

For Bourdieu, one of the central elements in the ordering of bodily experience (and hence in the construction of the habitus) is ritualized behavior. Sacred and secular ritual, because of its repetitive nature, tends to place an organizational frame around the events of the world—to structure events into categories and thus to render them intellectually assimilable. As a result, "the mind born of the world of objects does not arise as a subjectivity confronting an objectivity: the objective universe is made up of objects which are the product of objectifying operations structured according to the very structures which the mind applies to it" (Bourdieu 91). Those structures, in turn, are provided by a wide array of preexisting social practices (educational, hygienic, religious, ceremonious, etc.) that inculcate behavior "beyond the grasp of consciousness, . . . instilling a whole cosmology, an ethic, a metaphysic, a political philosophy through injunctions as insignificant as 'stand up straight' or 'don't hold your knife with your left hand'" (94).

This perspective on bodily culture complements Bakhtin's stress on the political character of the popular bodily canon while also compensating for Bakhtin's relative fuzziness as to particular sociohistorical practice. Bourdieu's arguments clearly enhance any effort to understand the forms and principles of alimentary behavior, for the microorganization of table manners arguably instantiates a given society's "cosmology," "ethic," or "metaphysic." In similar spirit, Mary Douglas's classic study *Purity and Danger* surveys the Mosaic dietary prohibitions, concluding that they constitute a set of categorical distinctions through which "holiness was given a physical expression in every encounter with the animal kingdom and at every meal" (57). For Douglas, as for Bourdieu, social rituals (including those of table and outhouse) work to inculcate a sense of order in individual subjects; to that extent, studying a given culture's alimentary habits is tantamount to studying its view of the world. For Douglas, the distinctive thing about such habits is their consistent division of the world into the bidden and the forbidden, the pure and the polluted. Categorization of this sort aims to reduce the ambiguities of experience to a system of reliable and predictable terms, and to this end, Douglas argues, anomalous events are neutralized in various ways by social practice. They can be "reduced," assimilated in some way to the preexisting categories they threaten to violate (39); they can be physically eliminated (39); they can be "labelled dangerous" and thus used to "strengthen the definitions [of things] to which they do not conform" (39); or they can be "used in ritual for the same ends as they are used in poetry and mythology, to enrich meaning or to call attention to other levels of existence" (40).

This conflation of "poetry and mythology" with "social ritual" has proven particularly inspiring to literary scholars. Using Douglas's arguments, Frank Whigham has studied the alimentary motifs in a series of non-Jonsonian Renaissance plays, concluding that the digestive concerns of these plays uniformly express a fear of sociosexual contamination. Works like *The Merchant of Venice* and *The Changeling* employ "figures of ingestion, retention, and evacuation" to "mirror relations between parts of the social body" ("Conflict" 334). These alimentary images give voice to the anxieties of a "thoroughly penetrated ruling elite" ("Conflict" 339) whose efforts to "refuse assimilative intercourse in intermarriage" are gradually being broken down ("Conflict" 337). Thus the Renaissance drama seeks to reaffirm on the symbolic level an "established notion of genealogical purity and authority" ("Conflict" 344) that has come under increasing pressure at the material level, and to this extent, the drama functions as a kind of secular ritual.

In a more recent book-length study of embarrassment in Renaissance drama, Gail Paster has valuably extended this line of argument. Noting the growth of emphasis on various forms of bodily propriety in early modern England, Paster contrasts this emphasis with the theory and practice of humoral medicine, which view the body as largely out of control and therefore not reducible to canons of strict behavioral regulation. Paster thus identifies "a contradiction between a popular medical practice authorizing experiences of somatic uncontrol in the form of humoral evacuation and an emergent ideology of bodily refinement and exquisite self-mastery" (14). This contradiction—rather like Whigham's opposition between notions of "genealogical purity" and a "thoroughly penetrated ruling elite"—then becomes available for imaginative exploration via the early modern English drama. Paster's work focuses particularly on the way in which oppositions between "bodily uncontrol" and "exquisite self-mastery" can be translated onstage into distinctions of gender—distinctions that associate femininity with incontinence, menstruation, lactation, and so on. Yet in the process, Paster takes time to develop an extended reading of Jonson's *Alchemist* (1610) in which individual characters' "self-mastery" is signaled by their virtuoso control of excretory functions. Subtle asserts his superiority over Face through the ability to fart at will (1.1.1); Face responds with a demeaning recollection of Subtle as "piteously costive" (1.1.28); and both figures combine to project their aggression onto the play's various gulls through such expedients as locking Dapper in an outhouse.

This application of anthropological scholarship—an attempt to investigate "the social formation of the internal habitus" (Paster 5) in early modern England—returns us to Freud's concern with anality, while helping to suggest ways in which that concern might be regarded as a generalized cultural phenomenon. By focusing not on the anal morbidity of the individual but rather on the social institutions that make anal morbidity conceivable in the first place, Paster valuably interconnects two largely disparate wings of the alimentary theory to be employed in this study. In the following pages, I attempt to develop a view of Jonson's work that in many ways parallels those offered by Paster, Stallybrass and White, and others. But in the process I seek to complicate matters by moving still farther away from the tropes of contrastive binarism that have characterized such studies. One function of the habitus may be to reduce ambiguity to distinct oppositions of this sort. However, as Mary Douglas herself has pointed out,

It is not always an unpleasant experience to confront ambiguity. . . . The richness of poetry depends on the use of ambiguity, as Empson has shown. . . . Ehrenzweig has even argued that we enjoy works of art because they enable us to go behind the explicit structures of our normal experience. Aesthetic pleasure arises from the perceiving of inarticulate forms. (37)

This insight provides the basis for much of my own effort to add to the foregoing bodies of theory.

Deterritorializing Bucklersbury

At the risk of travestying the richness and particularity of the materials I have just surveyed: Freudian readings of Jonson's work have valuably identified that work as a field for the representation of anal drives, but have generally tended to elide the poet's anality with patterns of oedipal aggression and to ignore its wider social grounding. Bakhtinian and anthropological readings, on the contrary, have defined Jonson's use of alimentary motifs through various kinds of more- or less-nuanced binaristic struggle— between popular and classical traditions, artist and milieu, social theory and social reality, bodily uncontrol and bodily self-mastery. Although it may seem unfortunate to add to this already considerable methodological tangle, I would like to introduce a slightly different perspective to the discussion of Jonson's alimentary imagery, a perspective drawn from the work of Deleuze and Guattari.

Deleuze and Guattari are most famous for their early critique of traditional psychoanalysis, *Anti-Oedipus*. In this and their later work, they develop an elaborate response to what they call the "metaphysics" of psychoanalytic thought (*Anti-Oedipus* 75): the structures of oedipal relation that work to "crush and repress" the polyvocality of the unconscious (*Anti-Oedipus* 52). For Deleuze and Guattari, the truth of the unconscious resides precisely in its multiplicity, and Deleuzian theory thus aims "to schizophrenize the domain of the unconscious as well as the sociohistorical domain" (*Anti-Oedipus* 53). This procedure involves a vigorous effort at rethinking the categorical relations to be found within the body, between the body and other bodies, and between the social and extrasocial spheres; in sum, Deleuze and Guattari seek to reconceive space so as to do away with the static and unitary self. In contradistinction to modes of psychoanalysis (either Freudian or Lacanian) dominated by a universalized and universalizing structure of oedipal desire, and in contrast to Foucauldian cultural analysis, in which all social practice is subsumed within the totalizing category of power, Deleuzian theory seeks to articulate a "positive figure of opposition to power" (Patton 66) that is characterized by notions of nomadism, exteriority, becoming-other, deterritorialization, and flight. Deleuze and Guattari promote such concepts in order to move beyond the "objectifying . . . structures" (Bourdieu 91) central to Western thought and the Western habitus. For present purposes, the interrelated notions of "deterritorialization" and the "line of flight" hold particular interest.

In their late work, Deleuze and Guattari define these terms by mutual reference. Deterritorialization is a "movement by which one leaves the territory," a movement effected by "the operation of the line of flight" (*Plateaus* 508). The Deleuzian notion of "territory," in turn, operates on multiple levels. From one perspective, it denotes specific geographical and social spaces to which particular qualities of property and value have been assigned. From another point of view, it characterizes the individual body and subjectivity, assigned a restricted identity within concomitantly restricted chronological, spatial, biological, and cultural coordinates. From yet another standpoint, as William Kelly has noted, it functions "in a linguistic stratum in which the fixing of values as meaning is performed":

> If language is taken as a social construct in which are inscribed the values and even the possibilities for action and thought afforded by the dominant ideology within any specific culture, then an author immersed in, and yet foreign to, the culture predominantly represented by that language must seek some linguistic construct that allows an alternative to the predetermined values and meanings of the major language. (23)

This flight from—and through—the signifying structures of the dominant social order constitutes the motive behind a certain kind of deterritorialization: a deterritorialization of language that Deleuze and Guattari identify with what they call "minor literature" (*Kafka* 16). It is also—as I argue at length in subsequent chapters—typical of Jonson's life and work. For the moment, it may be enough to observe two related manners in which Jonson's career may be characterized by the operation of linguistic lines of flight. First, there is the poet's retroactive erasure of his humble origins. In a social structure that affords relatively great opportunities for personal transformation via aristocratic patronage, but that offers the meaner sort of individuals only very limited access to potential patrons, it becomes imperative for Jonson to fashion himself into a proper object of courtly attention. He does this in a readily available way, often employed, *mutatis mutandis*, by successful aristocrats themselves: by revising his past so as to ignore his own former status as a bricklayer's apprentice and to identify instead with his gentle grandfather. To this extent, using self-presentational possibilities encoded into the structure of early modern English social practice, Jonson engages in what Deleuze and Guattari might call a "becoming-courtly."

But of course becoming courtly—as any reader of Castiglione knows—is a project that far transcends the issues of lineage and personal history. Likewise, the negotiation for patronage relations requires one to bring to the table skills and services in proportion to the benefits requested. Jonson's response to these challenges involves another act of deterritorialization: one made possible by the historiographical and imitative doctrines of Renaissance humanism. As Richard Peterson has argued, "Perhaps no other poet of the period shows such an uncontrived sense of the immediacy of the Roman past" as Jonson (57), nor is this fact coincidental to his success as a courtly poet. Indeed, Jonson insists with particular ferocity on the immediacy of the past *in him and his work*. The constant paraphrase and translation of Greek and Roman authors, the self-assumed identity of the English Horace, and the insistence that "*Poets*, as *Homer, Virgil, Lucan, &c.*" are "the substantiall supporters of *Fame*" (*Masque of Queens* 684–88): such gestures take us beyond the pale of metaphor and imitation and toward a literal insistence upon Jonson's own status as a living monument. To this extent, the poet fashions another line of flight—a way out of the limited constraints of his individual subjectivity—through what one might call a becoming-classical. This deterritorialization—enabled by the paradoxical humanist claims that classical imitation both "speaks for us" and "enables us to speak for ourselves" (Lloyd-Jones 35)—offers Jonson an additional index of courtliness as well as a unique claim to employability. More than any other writer of his day, he becomes the classical world incarnate.

Nor does this emphasis on flight contradict Jonson's repeated tendency to stake claims—of authorship, ownership, originality, literary status, and more. Indeed, Deleuze and Guattari posit a reciprocity between non-absolute processes of de- and reterritorialization such that the very lines of flight one may employ to escape a particular set of semiotic, social, or physical relations may lead to the marking of new boundaries, the establishment of new rituals or hierarchies of meaning. The reciprocal work of de- and reterritorialization has been described by Ronald Bogue in an example of some interest for the present study:

[André] Leroi-Gourhan argues that one can trace in human evolution a complementary modification of the function of the hand and the mouth that makes possible the development and use of both tools and language. When men [*sic*] assume an upright posture, their hands are set free from the task of locomotion (deterritorialization) and made available for fashioning . . . tools . . . (reterritorialization, or technological recoding). With hands and tools for seizing prey, men no longer need muzzle-shaped jaws and mouths suited for grabbing and tearing prey; hence the mouth is set free from its primary hunting/eating function (deterritorialization) and made available for speech (reterritorialization and linguistic recoding). (128)

In like fashion, Jonson's appropriation of the classics frees him from a position of cultural belatedness and social inferiority (deterritorialization) by repositioning himself within the canon of classical authors (reterritorialization). In Thomas Greene's words, "'Ben Jonson' can translate himself by hosting a Roman guest" (*Troy* 283). This is one of Jonson's greatest achievements.

For their part, Deleuze and Guattari are interested in achieving a state of "absolute" deterritorialization which "relates 'a' body considered as multiple to a smooth space that it occupies in the manner of a vortex" (*Plateaus* 509). To this end, they seek lines of flight not severed by concomitant blockages or reterritorialization. If "the classical image of thought . . . is that of conceptual systems whose relationship with the outside is always mediated by some form of interiority, whether this be the soul, consciousness, or concepts themselves" (Patton 61), such lines of flight offer a way "towards thinking a new body and a new spatiality—a body and a spatiality which are, among other things, . . . smooth and sleek; a body and spatiality whose 'archetypal model is the sea'" (Jardine 51). Thus, as Alice Jardine summarizes the Deleuzian project, "to be caught up in a 'becoming animal' means that one will resemble neither Man nor the Animal, but, rather, that each will 'deterritorialize' the other. The final stage of 'becoming' is to become 'imperceptible'—beyond any *percipio* as historically required for Man to master the world" (Jardine 52).

However, one need not regard Deleuze and Guattari's larger project as feasible—or even desirable—in order to apply their terminology usefully to the study of literary history; Deleuze and Guattari themselves develop their theory through the study of cultural phenomena incommensurate with their final aims. Thus, while this book can scarcely contribute to Deleuzian theory in the broadest sense of the term, it can—and does—seek to demonstrate how the notions of flight and deterritorialization may help us appreciate Jonson's repeated investment in alimentary, digestive, and convivial subject matter. The ensuing pages show how pervasive Jonson's interest in this material was. But Deleuzian theory becomes a useful instrument for the analysis of this subject matter because Deleuze and Guattari themselves regard language as a reterritorialization of the alimentary functions. Indeed, they locate a "high level of deterritorialization" within the "signifying regime" (*Plateaus* 508) via the analysis of Leroi-Gourhan rehearsed above:

Only humans have lips, in other words, an outward curling of the interior mucous membranes; only human females have breasts, in other words deterritorialized mammary glands: the extended nursing period advantageous for language learning is accompanied by a complementary reterritorialization of the lips on the breasts, and the breasts on the lips. (*Plateaus* 61–62)

Whether one accepts the claim that only human beings have lips and breasts, one may recognize in this passage certain tendencies that are helpful for understanding Jonson's alimentary and convivial discourse. First, this passage views language as a function that, by virtue of its origin, remains irreducible to the "terms of a literary analysis" (Stivale 29); it is equally implicated in a whole series of biological, semiotic, and social becomings. Second, these becomings—the redistribution of anatomy, the formation of the mother-child bond through an extended period of nursing, the development of language out of the eating function—are all multiply interrelated; not only do they entail each other on the developmental level, but they remain available within one another on a continuing basis, as mutually enabling possibilities. And third, this ready interavailability results in a circulation of energy from one field of deterritorialization to the others and back again.

Just such a circulation of energy distinguishes Sir Epicure Mammon's plan to dine on "the swelling vnctuous paps / Of a fat pregnant sow, newly cut off" (*The Alchemist* 2.2.83–84). On one hand, this image echoes the epigrams of Martial (e.g., 13.44), constituting a small move in Jonson's program of classical imitation. At the same time, it speaks to Mammon's logarithmically expanding ambitions, for sow's udder remained a popular delicacy at the tables of early modern aristocrats (see, e.g., Licht 17). But Katharine Maus, sensitive to the anatomical peculiarities of the image, has called it "positively matricidal" ("Economies" 72),[8] and she is right to do so. Mammon's fantasies are disturbing—this one more than most—because they so relentlessly transgress territorial boundaries. Mammon's mouth, for instance, trembles among the equally tempting pleasures of literary enumeration, of suckling at an abundant breast, and of rending an animal's boiled flesh; the sow's paps, for their part, metamorphose into a dish at table, yet in Mammon's imagination they retain their anatomical status ("*paps* . . . , newly cut off") and even their maternal signification ("of a fat *pregnant* sow"). The adjectives "swelling" and "vnctuous" are a descriptive masterstroke, simultaneously recalling both the richness of the sow's milk and that of her flesh, leaving no space whatever between the customarily disparate functions of nursing and dining. Such play of imagination lends itself well to Deleuzian analysis.

Indeed, if Jonson conflates the literary and the culinary processes, it is arguably because they play themselves out on the same bodily terrain—because the literary process constitutes a destructuration and concomitant restructuration of the space of eating. Similar gestures of deterritorialization, operating on virtually every level of Jonson's discourse, comprise one of the most distinctive features of the poet's work. On the axis of spatial reference, Jonson's verse repeatedly develops geometrical, architectural, and sculptural metaphors in ways that escape confinement within their original conceptual categories. Richard Peterson has pointed to Jonson's "combination of human and geometric forms" both in the epistle "To Elizabeth Countess of Rutland" (*The Forest* 12) and in *The Masque of Queens* (Peterson 99); he has also remarked on the poet's use of figures of "combined roundness and straightness" to express an ethical ideal in the "Epistle to Master John Selden" (*Underwood* 16; Peterson 90). A. W. Johnson has more recently noted "the tension between a circular conceit and the necessary linearity of language . . . in the epigrams to William and Thomas Roe (*Epigrammes* 128, 98), where moral squareness is extended into trapezoid and pillar forms" (97), and so forth. Such images, organic and acquisitive, develop into something rich and strange as they escape the limiting conditions of their initial conceptualization. A formalist sensibility might dismiss these images as mixed metaphors, of which there is no shortage in early English writing, but as Peterson has shown, the energy with which Jonson employs such tropes comprises one of the distinctive features of his epideictic verse. His poems of praise are monuments that aspire beyond a purely marmoreal fixity.

More widely, in the ethical sphere, this search for an escape from intellectual confinement stands as one of the signature characteristics of Jonson's work. Thomas Greene seizes upon the poet's use of circle imagery as representative of his commitment to the "metaphysical, political, and moral ideal" of "harmony and completeness . . . stability, repose, fixation, duration" ("Self" 326). This ideal, in turn, involves a complex interplay between notions of a personal moral center (implied by, but absent from, the figure of the circle itself) and a circuitous periphery. In other words, the circle becomes a "dual image of circle and center" (325): simultaneously a two-dimensional geometrical form and the unidimensional point whose absence subtends that form. Such *coincidentiae oppositorum* aptly represent the ethical paradoxes informing Jonson's work as a whole: "Jonson seems to see his centered figures moving perpetually through [the] purgatory of the Protean, still at rest when active, just as the vicious are unstable when torpid" (332). As Jonson himself observes in his first epigram to Sir Thomas Roe (*Epigrams* 45), "He that is round within himselfe, and streight, / Need seeke no other strength, no other height" (3–4); roundness superimposed upon straightness metamorphoses into height, and the poet's geometrical representations of virtue reterritorialize themselves in an entirely new spatial dimension. If, as Michael McCanles has claimed, "Jonson distrusts metaphor and conducts an unrelenting campaign to demystify it by deliberately violating its rules" (41), the result can hardly be called a Raymond Carveresque minimalism, still less an ethical positivism. On the contrary, Jonson's startling and unthinkable figures of speech develop as an effort to revise the "objectifying structures" whereby language renders the world intelligible. To this extent, Jonsonian rhetoric comprises an extended deterritorialization of the signifying regime in service of the ethical.

As Stanley Fish has characterized Jonson's epideictic procedure, his poems "continually proclaim their inability to describe or 'catch' their objects" (33). This inability, in turn, effectively reconstitutes the object of a given poem beyond the customary range of linguistic signification—in a new territory, as it were. Moreover, this same tendency invests the poet's various uses of alimentary imagery, too. To return to the first of the examples with which this chapter began, the epigram "To My Booke-Seller" develops initially through a reconceptualization of London business space, superimposing Paul's churchyard upon Bucklersbury, the booksellers' district upon the grocers':

> Thou, that mak'st gaine thy end, and wisely well,
>   Call'st a booke good, or bad, as it doth sell,
> Vse mine so, too: I giue thee leaue. But craue
>   For the lucks sake, it thus much fauour haue,
> To lye upon thy stall, till it be sought;
>   Not offer'd, as it made sute to be bought;

> Nor haue my title-leafe on posts, or walls,
>   Or in cleft-sticks, aduanced to make calls
> For termers, or some clarke-like seruing-man,
>   Who scarse can spell th'hard names: whose knight less can.
> If, without these vile arts, it will not sell,
>   Send it to *Bucklers-bury*, there 'twill, well.
>   (*Epigrams* 3.1)

Opening in the mode of descriptive address, the poem sizes up its bookseller so as to render his identification with London's greengrocers inevitable: "Thou, that mak'st gaine thy end, and wisely well, / Call'st a booke good, or bad, as it doth sell, / Vse mine so, too" (1–3). The closing couplet, with its advice to send the book to Bucklersbury for guaranteed sales, stands as the logical corollary of the business attitudes specified in the poem's first two lines; also, the sense of formal balance in the poem's conclusion is underscored by a chiasmic repetition of the opening couplet's rhyme words. As a result, Jonson's poem rearranges the system of mercantile and conceptual enclosures it originally invokes, turning apparent opposites, bookseller and greengrocer, into specular counterparts.

In effect, the initial principle—the conceit—of Epigram 3 thus involves the erasure of distinctions between different sorts of merchants, their respective merchandise, and the geographical enclaves that imprint these distinctions upon the terrain of seventeenth-century London. But however surprising and delightful this deterritorialization may be from the rhetorical standpoint, it challenges the poet's own ability to differ from other laborers via the authority he exercises over the products of his work. As Elizabeth Eisenstein has pointed out, the rise of printing encouraged a massive increase in the distribution of literary material under the rubric not of the author but of the publisher: "As self-serving publicists, early printers issued book lists, circulars and broadsides. They put their firm's name, emblem and shop address on the front page of their books. Indeed, their use of title pages entailed a significant reversal of scribal procedures; they put themselves first" (1:59). Likewise, the later lines of Epigram 3 express uneasiness about the forms of distribution to which an author's work might be submitted by its enclosure within a system of literary commodification that privileges middlemen. By equating verse with cabbages, Jonson's bookseller accords the poet himself a severely restricted, subordinate position within the city's economic order; the poet, ploughing a pregnant row of versified rutabagas, becomes virtually indistinguishable from his garden-planting, grocery-raising stepfather.

The epigram then responds to this dilemma with a gesture of ironic acquiescence. Jonson superficially defers to the standard business practices of his bookseller with the remark "vse [my book] so, too," but what at first appears to be a sign of authorial submission at once translates into an implicit assertion of authorial control: "Vse mine so, too: I giue thee leaue" (3). As Joseph Loewenstein has recalled—and as Mark Rose has noted more recently in detail—"a Renaissance author never quite *owned* a literary work, or at least not a literary work as we now somewhat abstractly conceive it" (Loewenstein, "Script" 102).⁹ Indeed, there is something irrelevant and even cheeky about an author who grants his bookseller "leaue" to dispose of a book that is not, strictly speaking, his (the author's) in the first place, and whose very existence confirms the author's lack of absolute control over his work. The next lines of the poem complicate matters still further, for they imply the author's right not only to claim his writing as his own, but also to control the manner of its distribution:

> But craue
> For the lucks sake, it thus much fauour haue,
> To lye vpon thy stall, till it be sought;
> Not offer'd, as it made sute to be bought;
> Nor haue my title-leafe on posts, or walls,
> Or in cleft-sticks, aduanced to make calls
> For termers.
>
> (3–9)

The result is that an apparent act of deference to the bookseller rematerializes as an assertion of superiority over him; an acknowledgment of the claims of the literary marketplace turns into a refusal to engage in standard forms of literary marketing; and an apparent equation of authorial labor with agricultural labor turns into a calculated act of distinction between the two.

But if a bookseller is not a grocer, and if a poet is not a kitchen gardener, what makes them different? Epigram 3 can be read as a reaction to the enclosing conditions of the early seventeenth-century literary marketplace, conditions that tended to commodify texts in much the same way as they commodified other goods. Such commodification inclines, as Jonson clearly understood, toward what Peter Womack has called "the incipient proletarianizing of the writer" (19). The poet's response to this threat, in turn, is to seek an avenue of escape from the socioeconomic circumstances that surround him. The escape route he chooses is a classic one, proffered in a gesture that Jonson repeats ever more ingeniously as his career progresses: he insists on the poet's fundamental difference from others ("Solus rex, aut poeta, non quotannis nascitur"), and then, refusing to define the precise character of the difference, he claims the resulting indefinition as proof that the difference itself exists. The poet is distinct from the gardener, in other words, precisely because of one's inability to articulate the qualities that make him special—because he escapes linguistic categorization. As Fish has remarked, "Although the question of record in a Jonson poem will often be, 'What is friendship?' [or, just as often, 'What is poetry?'] the answer can only be, 'If you have to ask, you couldn't possibly know'" (48). That, I believe, is why Loewenstein describes the poet of Epigram 3 "as a man ambiguously engaged with the literary marketplace, giving the bookseller leave to esteem the volume according to its sales, but refusing to condone any active appeal to a consuming public" ("Script" 109). As Robert Evans has observed, the poem advertises itself by refusing to engage in advertising ("Epigrammes I–III," 9). Jonson stands both within and outside the marketplace at the same time, apparently by virtue of the poet's simultaneous existence in separate but parallel universes.

I introduce the reference to parallel universes not—at least not wholly—out of whimsy. For Jonson is interested in realignments of the temporal, as well as the spatial, axis of things; he is an inveterate distorter of the space-time continuum. Again, Epigram 3 is a fine case in point. Just as it folds space so as to make Bucklersbury impinge on Paul's, so too does it fold time, superimposing the Silver Latin past on the Jacobean present. Scholars have long recognized that Jonson employs the classical practice of *imitatio* in order to cultivate a sense of the "simultaneity of newness and oldness" (Peterson 54). Likewise, it is well known that Jonson's Epigram 3 reworks Martial 14.194: "Some there are that say I am no poet: but the bookseller that sells me thinks I am" [Sunt quidam qui me dicant non esse poetam: / sed qui me vendit bibliopola putat].[10] To this extent, Epigram 3 arguably participates in the mode of Jonsonian laureate self-definition extensively described by Richard Helgerson. Helgerson emphasizes Jonson's identification with Horace, a transtemporal association that aims to legitimize the later poet's undertakings as satirist (109–116), but Martial exerts an influence on Jonson scarcely inferior to that of Horace. As an urban satirist, a more or less self-made man, a court poet of the emperors Titus and Domitian, and Rome's preeminent epigrammatist, Martial seems a highly appropriate precursor to invoke against the proletarianizing influence of the seventeenth-century literary marketplace. Jonson's allusion to him in Epigram 3 would thus appear to offer a neat escape from the professional dilemma the epigram itself sets out: escape through temporal redefinition, consolidating one's identity with an earlier poet for whom the proletarianizing of the author is already a dead issue.

Yet here too, as with the poem's spatial and mercantile references, the situation is more complicated. For one thing, the act of identification with Martial is not precisely what it seems; Martial's epigram 14.194 is itself a commentary of sorts on the work of the Roman poet's erstwhile friend and mentor, Lucan, and it occurs within a run of thirteen literary epigrams in the midst of Martial's fourteenth book, the *Apophoreta*. The conceit of this book is that the poems themselves are to be inscribed upon "praemia convivae" (Martial 14.1.6)—presents of the sort given by Roman hosts to their banquet guests during the Saturnalia (Sullivan 12). Each epigram describes the gift it accompanies, using the tones of admiration or contempt that the object itself merits. The literary epigrams (183–196) were supposed to accompany books, and the poems themselves therefore comment on those books in a wide range of ways. Sallust is praised as the "first of Roman historians" [primus Romana . . . in historia (14.191)], and great Verona is said to owe as much to Catullus as little Mantua owes to Virgil [Tantum magna suo debet Verona Catullo, / quantum parva suo Mantua Vergilio (14.195)]. On the other hand, Martial proposes that Licinius Calvus's lost poem on the uses of cold water be thrown into a river (14.196), and the *Culex* attributed to Virgil gets an insult that cuts ambivalently against its author, its reader, and the taste of the gift giver who selected it: "Receive, studious reader, the Gnat of eloquent Maro; you need not then lay aside your nuts to read 'Arms and the Man'" [Accipe facundi Culicem, studiose, Maronis, / ne nucibus positis "arma virumque" legas (14.185)].

Amidst this wide range of judgments, the epigram on Lucan emerges as precisely what, for Jonson's aims as an extracommercial author, it should not be: affirmation of the literary market's ability to esteem texts properly on the basis of sales. As J. P. Sullivan has recalled, Martial deliberately followed Lucan in developing an unpretentious poetic with little use for the machinery of gods and goddesses (102; 73 n.32), and Martial defends such writing against the censure of traditionalists by invoking the authority of the marketplace (Sullivan 14). Moreover, as Jonas Barish has shown, Jonson could easily adopt a similar attitude when travestying the Elizabethan rage for classical mythology (232–233). Yet as we have seen, the enclosure threatened by the authority of the marketplace prompts Jonson's third epigram, which may be taken to echo Martial ironically. Jonson's poem may thus be read as an attempt to escape a literary tradition—represented by Martial 14.194—that parallels and lends precedent to the encroachments upon authorial integrity threatened by the seventeenth-century English literary market. Insofar as that market elides books with cabbages, after all, it would seem to follow the example of Martial.

But there is more to add to our analysis of the identifications, elisions, and avoidances of Epigram 3. In echoing Martial 14.194, Jonson was not simply recalling a specific poem; he was also invoking an entire body of work with which he was famously familiar, and whose overall attitudes to literary commerce deserve review in light of Jonson's achievement. In fact, Martial's epigrams are well known for the attention they pay to the poet's booksellers. Here, for instance, is Martial 1.113:

> All the light verse I penned once as youth and boy, and my worthless efforts which not even I myself now recognise—these, if you want to spend good hours badly, and have a grudge against your leisure time, reader, you can get from Pollius Quintus Valerianus. It is through him my trifles are not allowed to perish.
>
> [Quaecumque lusi iuventis et puer quondam
> apinasque nostras, quas nec ipse iam novi,
> male conlocare si bonas voles horas
> et invidebis otio tuo, lector,
> a Valeriano Pollio petes Quinto,
> per quem perire non licet meis nugis.]

This sort of thing is typical of Martial. Apparently, certain booksellers paid him for first access to his manuscripts, and he, in turn, used his verse to recommend those booksellers to his readers. Epigram 2 of Book 1 thus counsels bibliophiles to "Seek out Secundus, the freedman of learned Lucensis" [libertum docti Lucensis quaere Secundum] for copies of the poet's work; Epigram 117 of Book 1 mentions a certain Atrectus; and the bookseller Tryphon receives similar notice elsewhere (4.72). Such moments are sufficiently numerous—and Jonson was sufficiently enthusiastic about Martial[11]—for them to deserve review in light of Jonson's own epigram "To My Booke-Seller."

The result is that Martial, whose poem on Lucan seems to endorse literary attitudes Jonson finds objectionable, elsewhere exemplifies a way out of the authorial dilemma set forth in Jonson's verse. Martial's numerous epigrams upon his booksellers point to a literary world in which the author, rather than the merchant, would seem to be the empowered figure—a world in which writers advertise booksellers rather than vice versa. This aspect of the Roman epigrammatist's work is only magnified by the considerable variety of booksellers he in fact advertises. As classicists have noted at least since the time of Theodor Birt, the proliferation of Secundi and Valeriani in Martial's poems tends to place the booksellers in a confusing, disadvantageous light vis-à-vis the author, whose own superior status as originator of the work in question is forcefully implied by his singularity.[12] I believe this idealized view of classical literary relations lies behind Jonson's pointed insistence in Epigram 3 that his verse should remain the vehicle, rather than becoming the object, of advertisement. Of course, it would be misleading to assume that authors were idyllically empowered figures in Martial's Rome, but the present argument does not depend on that assumption. It is enough that certain of Martial's epigrams could be read by later poets as indicative of such empowerment, and that Jonson would have been inclined to entertain such a reading. If that is the case, then we must grant that the classical source of the epigram "To My Booke-Seller" offers a whole range of attitudes toward Jonson's subject matter: Martial can become the classical *auctor* with whom Jonson identifies for the purposes of his poem; the exponent of literary attitudes that Jonson's poem sets out to escape; and the exemplar of a mode of literary commerce to which Jonson aspires but which, by the testimony of his own poem, does not exist in Jacobean London. Moreover, these historical positions parallel the positions offered by the poem's spatial and mercantile contexts as well, contexts that initially elide literary and gastronomic commerce, then ironically reinstate the distinctions between these modes of market activity, and then reach toward a moment at which—for the poet at least—such distinctions both do and do not exist.

I would resist suggesting that any one of these attitudes toward literary commerce ultimately negates or refutes the others, as if Jonson's poem progressed to a moment of Hegelian conceptual synthesis. On the contrary, I would emphasize the simultaneity and interdependence of these various notions of authorship, each of which arises as a solution to a problem generated by one of the others, while in the process generating difficulties of its own, which render the previous attitudes indispensable in their turn. In this way Epigram 3 recalls Kenneth Burke's description of literature as "equipment for living."[13] It rehearses a series of "strategies," neither entirely "conscious" nor perfectly "methodical" (*Forms* 297), for dealing with the curtailments of literary authority that may be imposed on a writer at any moment, from any direction. In his recent discussion of Jonson's attitudes toward censorship, Richard Burt argues that "it was impossible for [Renaissance] authors to know in advance what one could or could not say, how to evade regulations, how to decode, and so on" (53). For Burt, thus, writers like Jonson were always subject to a wide range of potential pressures, which necessitated the development of an extremely flexible system of responses. Something of the sort may be gleaned from Jonson's third epigram as well, with its elaborate negotiations between apparently incompatible perspectives on the literary marketplace. From the theoretical standpoint, Epigram 3 offers us not a Hegelian synthesis but a Deleuzian "assemblage": a "territorial" aggregate of "organism and . . . milieu, and the relation between the two" (*Plateaus* 504) that "is constituted by *lines of deterritorialization* that cut across it and carry it away" (*Plateaus* 504) and that, being "immersed in the changing state of things" (Massumi xii), is not confined to a rigid logic of representation. From the social standpoint, Epigram 3 exemplifies Mary Douglas's claim that "aesthetic pleasure arises from the perceiving of inarticulate forms" (37). Certainly one may say of Jonson's poems, as of the rituals Douglas discusses, that "they confront ambiguity in an extreme and concentrated form" (170), and that such confrontation is essential to their success.

The frame of alimentary reference of Epigram 3 is thus multivalent and unstable. The mention of Bucklersbury both conjoins the poet with and seeks to distinguish him from the commercial milieu of the London greengrocer; likewise, the poem's invocation of classical precedent retroactively discovers a similar ambivalence to commerce in the Roman literary tradition. In fact, the governing concept of Martial's *Apophoreta* suggests a mutable, hybrid approach to convivial matters—an approach that informs Jonson's work as well. To compose a book of verse as an adjunct to supper gifts, after all, is to place the act of versifying in very tricky conjunction to the act of dining. How, in fact, does one make sense of the *Apophoreta*? They are occasioned by the custom of saturnalian convivial gift giving, and hence one may view the epigrams as prompted by, but materially distinct from, the custom. But at the same time the epigrams are at least nominally committed to interpreting specific gifts, and one may, with little stretch of the imagination, view the laudatory poems as literally to be inscribed upon the artifacts they interpret—mediating, as it were, between the territory of the dinner gift and the space of poetic composition. Moreover, the book of verse composed by the epigrams (as Epigrams 183–196 clearly attest) could itself have constituted such a gift as the individual poems describe, in which case the poems are both conceptually and materially a subset of the festive occasion. Jonson's Epigram 3—at once a versified contract with the poet's bookseller, a nervous admission that no such contract is viable, an advertisement for the book of which it is a part, a part of the book that it advertises, and a refusal to engage in advertising at all—expands Martial's ambiguities well beyond the breaking point.

Finally, the literary instability that Jonson's epigram exploits is linked to that of the convivial and alimentary materials the poem also employs. If Paul's churchyard was home to a volatile and expanding trade, so was Bucklersbury. As Alan Everitt has pointed out, "the art of 'gardening for profit' spread rapidly in the latter half of the period [from 1500 to 1640]":

> its success was crowned in 1605 by the incorporation of the London Gardeners' Company.... By the mid-seventeenth century a labour force of some 1,500 persons was employed. An aldermanic report of 1635 speaks of 24,000 loads of roots—no doubt carrots, parsnips, and turnips—being sold annually in London and Westminster. (Thirsk 4:510)

Such increases in the volume and variety of the market produce supply also fueled expansion in other sectors of the economy:

> Quite apart from the fact that dozens of new London market places were formed [from 1500 to 1640], while the older ones became "unmeasurably pestered with the unimaginable increase and multiplicity of market folks," a whole community of factors and drovers came into being to serve the London market. (Thirsk 4:512)

The result, in short, was a dramatic commercialization and concomitant depersonalization of the market trade.

This commercialization seems to have effected a shift in the significance of food itself for early modern English society. Joyce Appleby has noted that "the Tudor codification of laws against forestalling, regrating, and engrossing" explicitly denied "the food producers' freedom to manipulate the market for personal gain," while reaffirming the conviction "that the growing and marketing of corn, the milling of flour, and the baking of bread were principally social rather than economic activities" (27–28). By the 1650s, on the other hand, after abundant midcentury harvests, "there emerged the possibility of treating food like any other commodity. Once liberated from the restrictions justified by scarcity, food could assume its place in a rational economic scheme as an interchangeable commodity equalized by a price tag" (85). Jonson's Epigram 3, composed within a decade of the end of Tudor rule and the creation of the London Gardeners' Company, is situated at the virtual midpoint of the economic trends cataloged by Everitt, Appleby, and others.[14]

Coincidentally or not, Mark Rose and Natalie Zemon Davis have argued that books and the book trade were undergoing a similar shift of socioeconomic significance at roughly the same time. According to Rose, "the medieval conception of learning as a gift from God" entailed a view of books as "transmitters of a divine gift . . . , indeed as objects in which God himself might be understood to have some rights" (13). Davis, for her part, recalls Joyce Appleby when describing a residual medieval tendency to view the book as a "privileged object which resisted permanent appropriation and which it was especially wrong to view only as a source of profit" ("Market" 87). In their capacity as objects of community rights and community investment, the book and the cabbage were both in a basic way exempted from the process of getting and spending, until introduced into that process by sixteenth- and seventeenth-century developments in agricultural and bibliographical production.

To this fact we may perhaps ascribe the nervousness of Epigram 3 about the influence of impersonal contacts upon the author's and work's integrity. Jonson's poem worries about being clapper-clawed by unfit readers: "some clarke-like seruing-man / Who scarse can spell th'hard names" (9–10), or the servant's knight, who is even less literate than his footman. Likewise, the poem's title, "To My Booke-Seller," imposes a certain impersonality on the author's relations with John Stepneth, the merchant in question (Herford, Simpson, and Simpson 11:1). The distance and anonymity preserved in such lines, intrinsic to the determination of value by market demand, has arguably begun to invest both the bookseller's and the greengrocer's trades at roughly the time of Jonson's writing. In response, Jonson's epigram seeks to move through and beyond the circumstances of the early modern marketplace and to establish with individual readers a rapport unmediated by the processes of bookstall commodification; as Epigram 1 entreats its reader, "Pray thee, take care, that tak'st my booke in hand, / To reade it well: that is, to vnderstand." Likewise, Jonson's work repeatedly gestures toward an idealized space in which literature and dining acquire an ideal character as interlinked elements of a community that transcends considerations of profit and loss. For Jonson's purposes, the *fons et origo* of this community was the classical symposium, whose practices are partly exemplified by the Martialic epigrams we have already considered. But Jonson's use of that tradition and its ambiguities makes another story that demands its own chapter.

Becoming Alimentary

To summarize so far: this book seeks to examine Jonson's fondness for interrelated tropes of alimentary and literary behavior. The scholarship on this material is already rich and varied; the present study aims not to supersede such earlier work but rather to assimilate it, with necessary modifications, to a Deleuzian theoretical model that provides space for inconsistency, fluidity, and difference. The resultant reading of Jonson's strategies for alimentary representation should emphasize their involvement in an organic socioliterary process not governed by the rules of linearity and homogeneity: a process of community development that also helps shape the modern literary sensibility. This sensibility emerges for Jonson out of the convivial setting, and it does so at roughly the same time that the terms of early modern English convivial activity themselves undergo an unprecedented series of changes. Hence Jonson's interest in the digestive tract may perhaps be described as an effort to influence—or at least to keep up with—the poet's own shifting status among various audiences and markets.

One valuable mode of recent Jonson scholarship—exemplified by the work of Maus, Peterson, and others—has sought to elucidate the poet's work via a variously interpreted classical or humanist tradition. Another important line of commentary—represented by the work of Paster, Burt, and Marcus—has sought instead to relate Jonson's career to notions of contemporary politics or popular culture. One possible strength of the present study is that it offers a means of combining these disparate scholarly approaches. Matters of the digestive tract offer perhaps the best instance in the entire Jonson canon of a self-conscious conjunction between modes of classical and popular reference. Jonson the humanist invokes notions of classical sympotic order when pondering issues of food and drink, arguably because the classical sympotic tradition marks a historical identification of the literary and culinary arts as vehicles for promoting social harmony. But as he thus invokes the classical tradition of dining, Jonson necessarily brings it to bear upon specific contemporary issues, including the protocols of court banqueting, the incipient commodification of English markets for food and poetry, and even the disposition of sewage within the city of London.

Hence the chapters of this work are organized both to touch on the classical grounding of Jonson's conviviality and to apply Jonson's alimentary discourse to the developing social situation of Jacobean England. Chapter 1 examines the tradition of the Greco-Roman symposium in light of the English poet's efforts to appropriate that tradition; this first chapter may be viewed, in effect, as an essay on the classical origin and character of Jonsonian table manners. Chapter 2, which focuses on tropes of banqueting, sets the theory of classical sympotic behavior against the dining-practices of Jonson's own day. Chapter 3 explores the poet's use of digestive metaphors (often drawn from the work of classical authors) to characterize the process of literary composition as the relation between tradition and the individual talent. Chapter 4 looks closely at the end products of alimentary activity: the sewage that occurs and recurs throughout the Jonson canon and that was arguably becoming more and more difficult to miss in Jacobean London, too. Finally, Chapter 5 deals with some of the indigestions, emetics, and purges—for example, the famous vomitting scene from *Poetaster*—that populate Jonson's plays and poems.

This procedure, which divides Jonson's alimentary discourse into distinct categories of mutually exclusive inquiry—manners, dining, digesting, excreting, vomiting—offers the reader a sequential overview of some of the poet's most characteristic alimentary concerns. For that very reason, however, it has an accompanying disadvantage: it threatens to present these different concerns far more tidily and hermetically than does Jonson himself. One of the main points of Jonson's interest in digestive tropes lies in the organic, shifting character of the alimentary processes. The digestive tract offers Jonson a good metaphorical equivalent for the situation of authorship exactly because both are subject to flux and contingency: the multiple media and markets within which Jonson worked find their parallel within the interrelated processes of consumption, ingestion, excretion, and indigestion, as well as in the shifting social and material ground upon which those processes play themselves out. Hence one characteristic Jonsonian alimentary trope—some examples of which begin this introduction—intermingles the very alimentary categories that this work uses as its organizational armature. Just as for Justice Overdo alligator piss mingles with tobacco and newt bodies with ale, so for Jonson different ways of conceiving the organic social function of authorship tend to sediment themselves atop one another in layer after layer. The result, as in the case of Epigram 3, is an uncannily complex and ramifying series of gastroliterary equivalences. The present study is committed, for organizational purposes, to systematizing Jonson's multivalent alimentary language; however, one point of the study itself is that Jonson's work evades the stasis of analytical categories. If this book sacrifices the fluidity of Jonson's language for the stability of easy critical distinctions, it should be discarded at once.

I

The Genealogy of Manners

> Quod tam grande sophos clamat tibi turba togata,
>   non tu, Pomponi, cena diserta tua est.
>   Martial 6.48

THERE IS A STRANGELY NEGLECTED EPISODE of *Gilligan's Island* in which the castaways discover they are sharing their island with an inarticulate, loincloth-clad stranger. The interloper's identity is naturally of interest, so Thurston Howell III devises a test to determine his educational background. Placing a coconut pie before the man, Howell explains the test to his wife: if the stranger holds the fork with his right hand, he must come from Harvard; if he holds it with his left hand, then he must be a Princetonian. At this point, the action assumes the austere inevitability of Greek tragedy; neglecting utensils altogether, the stranger grasps the pie in both hands, leaving Howell to exclaim in distress, "Good heavens, Lovie, he's a Yale man!"

The joke here, such as it is, works on various levels, using Howell consistently as the butt of the humor. First there is the premise of the scene: Howell's inability to imagine an education beyond Harvard and Princeton plays good-naturedly with the limitations of vision imposed on the wealthy snob by his own circumstances. Then there is the methodology of Howell's little experiment: to equate one's manner of holding a fork with one's overall educational attainment is a suspect maneuver, and it says much about Howell's own view of the purpose of education. And finally, there is the wrenching outcome of things, as Howell plunges into his own Lear-like vision of unaccommodated man.

But beneath the episode's ribbing of Thurston Howell, there is a larger instability at play—an instability of which the episode itself is only half aware. For in fact the stranger is no stranger at all. Although he has managed to convince all the castaways that he is an aboriginal Polynesian, his blond hair and blue eyes may suggest otherwise to the discerning spectator, and indeed, before the episode is over, the stranger reveals himself to be an American posing as an islander. The episode thus erects a whole series of divisions between the savage and the civilized, divisions coextensive with table manners, education, articulateness, and appearance, only to discard each of them in turn. What emerges is a sense that the distinction between savagery and civilization, good table manners and bad ones, is a mutable fiction, subject to open-ended vision and revision: more a site of individual improvisation than a repository of personal essence. The joke is ultimately not just on Howell but on us all, for behind the stranger's loincloth stands a man who may very well be just what Howell thinks he is: a Yalie in Polynesian drag.

If this situation seems hopelessly remote from Ben Jonson and Jacobean London, it nonetheless helps introduce a principal theme in Jonson's ongoing investigation of convivial behavior: the instability of the relation between manners and identity. For Jonson, as for Thurston Howell III, the attempt to read table behavior as indicative of personal character proceeds from relatively straightforward premises into a complex and unexpected series of negotiations. When, for instance, Augustus Caesar interrupts Ovid's blasphemous banquet in *Poetaster* (1601), he is infuriated by the diners' appropriation of divine personae to which their natural manners are incommensurate:

> Are they the Gods?
> Reuerence, amaze, and furie fight in me.
> What? doe they kneele? Nay, then I see 'tis true
> I thought impossible: o impious sight!
> Let me diuert mine eyes.
> (4.6.5–9)

Caesar's offense stems from the contrast between the banqueters' godly attire and their courtly self-abasement; the quivering obeisance of Ovid and his compatriots is Caesar's equivalent of the coconut pie test, distinguishing heaven from earth, rectitude from knavery, Harvard from Yale. Hence the emperor's fury, which seeks to reestablish a series of ontological and sacral categories that Ovid and his fellows have violated:

> Are you, that first the *deities* inspir'd
> With skill of their high natures, and their powers,
> the first abusers of their vse-full light;

> Prophaning thus their dignities, in their formes:
> And making them like you, but counterfeits?
> (4.6.34–38)

Such impostors must be banished from civilized society if society is to remain civilized at all: good heavens, Lovie, a Yale man.

To this extent, the banquet scene from *Poetaster* yields a view of social relations well summarized by George Rowe, a view in which Caesar's duty is "to preserve and protect the distinctions that provide the basis" for "a system of differences that constitutes the order of the Roman state" (83). Believing "blurred boundaries" to be "inimical to the existence of virtue and order" (Rowe 70), Jonson's Caesar—and arguably Jonson himself—is committed to maintaining those boundaries wherever possible, and to that extent the distinction between good and bad manners becomes an indispensable tool of public discipline. The dining room may be a space of recreation and communion for Ovid, a place where god meets humanity in an erasure of ontological oppositions, but this view of dining is intolerable to Caesar and the sociopolitical principle of "responsible hierarchy" (Parfitt 144) he represents. From this standpoint, Ovid takes his place in a long line of Jonsonian characters who embody the sinister conjunction of "good poetry" and "bad ethics" (Jackson 30).

But there is also another way to view Ovid's banquet, commensurate with Horace's description of it as "innocent mirth, / And harmelesse pleasures, bred, of noble wit" (4.7.41–42). From this perspective, the banquet itself does not constitute the signal offense of the day; on the contrary, the real problem for Horace would seem to lie in the malleability of the system of distinctions that Caesar himself seeks to maintain. It is this very system, as Horace observes, that enables the parasite Lupus to overthrow a more gifted character than himself, retailing Ovid's humiliation for his own putative courtly advancement:

> Was this the treason? this, the dangerous plot,
> Thy clamorous tongue so bellow'd through the court?
> . . . Such as thou,
> They are the moths, and scarabes of a state;
> The bane of empires; and the dregs of courts;
> Who (to endeare themselues to any'employment)
> Care not, whose fame they blast; whose life they endanger.
> (4.7.37–47)

From this standpoint, Lupus has committed a more genuine atrocity than anything Ovid has performed or intended. Moreover, by maintaining conditions wherein Lupus might profit by a betrayal of Ovid, Caesar is implicitly responsible for encouraging the more heinous fault—a responsibility that both Horace and Maecenas hint at when they implore the emperor's mercy on Ovid's behalf ("O, good my lord; forgiue: be like the Gods" [4.6.60]). Indeed, it can hardly be accidental that Ovid's banquet reiterates a historical event described by Suetonius and attributed to Augustus—a banquet, held during a food shortage, in which Augustus is said to have played the role of Apollo (Suetonius, Augustus 70; Herford, Simpson, and Simpson 9:567). As John Sweeney has put it, "Vice is not a problem in *Poetaster* until Augustus makes it one" (44).

Still further, there is a sense in which Jonson's text actually elides Ovid with Caesar via the latter's pet poet, Virgil. As Richard Helgerson has argued, Jonson's personal identification with the figure of Horace in *Poetaster* distances him equally from both Ovid and Virgil. Jonson/Horace may "detach . . . himself" from Ovid (Helgerson 112), but by the same token "Virgil's very perfection put[s] him out of reach" (113), similarly detached, albeit for different reasons. Moreover, from their parallel niches of abjection and elevation, Ovid and Virgil gesture toward one another in strange ways. When Virgil reads Caesar the famous passage from Book 4 of the *Aeneid* that describes Aeneas's union with Dido, he repeats a sexual rumor that has been applied earlier in the play to Ovid and Julia (Helgerson 115). Virgil's account of Dido and Aeneas advocates an "equivocal distribution of blame" (115) incommensurate with Caesar's extreme reaction to the banquet of the gods, and the account of Dido and Aeneas "may serve by its very subject to associate Ovid and Virgil as poets" (116). To this extent, if one were to engage in the futile task of binarizing *Poetaster*'s social vision, one would have to discard the distinctions Caesar/not Caesar, Ovid/not Ovid, and Virgil/not Virgil in favor of the coextensive opposition between Horace and not Horace—a binary function that challenges the integrity of the others with which it coexists.

In other words, this scene from *Poetaster* unsettles social distinctions in the very act of affirming them, and by doing so it places a primary instrument for the promulgation of such distinctions—the concept of manners—in a highly ambivalent light. The various character groupings in the play coalesce and disperse, form and re-form in ways that suggest the mannerly social elite to be less a category than a process. Like the figures in a complex anamorphic drawing, Jonson's characters take on different significance when viewed from different perspectives. Caesar may be the upholder of the stable distinctions from which social intercourse derives its form and meaning; the authority figure who allows the forms of social intercourse to be misappropriated and abused and is therefore responsible for their degradation; or a figure so inaccessible as to offer no practical pattern of social activity whatever. And a similar range of semiotic possibilities invests the other characters, too. In 1601 Jonson had not yet become the principal writer of entertainments for the court of James I. Still, it is tempting to read Ovid's banquet in *Poetaster* as anticipating ambiguities in the courtly context for which Jonson would produce his greatest masques, a context that frequently bred misbehavior comparable to that of Ovid and his companions.[1] To this extent, the masques may extend a process of exploration already begun in *Poetaster*—a process whereby Jonson investigates, in mobile and acquisitive fashion, the options for cultural and social self-construction that are available to him at a given moment.

The multivalence of this exploration—the astonishing agility with which Jonson adopts different alimentary and convivial personae in his work—may partly be explained by the ambiguities of the poet's own situation. Here it is worth recalling Norbert Elias's classic *History of Manners*, which, even as it traces general trends in the long-term development of a standard of Western civilized behavior, cautions readers against applying the developmental curve too crudely in individual cases:

> Consideration of the behavior of people in the sixteenth century, and of their code of behavior, casts the observer back and forth between the impressions "That's still utterly medieval" and "That's exactly the way we feel today." And precisely this apparent contradiction clearly corresponds to reality. . . .Behavior and the code of behavior are in motion, but the movement is quite slow. And above all, in observing a single stage, we lack a sure measure. What is accidental fluctuation? When and where is something advancing? . . . Are we really concerned with change in a definite direction? (83)

The strategic equivocations that dominate the banquet scene from *Poetaster* arguably derive from a social uncertainty much like that described by Elias. Indeed, if it is perilous for a scholar to assess the "accidental fluctuation" or definite "change" of a social standard from the safety of three hundred years' remove, one can imagine that the peril would have been nearly insurmountable for an author whose ability to interpret and forecast changes in a contemporary standard would spell the success or failure of his career. As Robert Evans has remarked, "Every poem [Jonson] wrote . . . was in some sense both an advertisement and a calculated risk" (*Patronage* 145).

Deleuze and Guattari observe, a propos of Freudian efforts to deal with collective psychology, that "Freud tried to approach crowd phenomena from the point of view of the unconscious, but he did not see . . . that the unconscious itself was fundamentally a crowd" (*Plateaus* 29). In what follows, I apply this proposition to the social unconscious manifest in Jonson's complex literary accommodations to the concept of mannerly table behavior. In this process, it first is useful to study the various and contradictory possibilities that constitute the crowd of the Jonsonian social unconscious and then to examine, in a limited space, the way in which the individual constituents of that unconscious interact. Following Elias's observation that the process of standardizing manners "has no beginning" (60), that "wherever we start, there is movement, something that went before" (60), I take as the starting point of the present analysis a set of sociohistorical circumstances that were manifestly important to Jonson himself: those of classical antiquity. Having examined the general fluidities that inform the literature of the classical symposium, we may then proceed, through a relatively dispersed reading of Jonsonian texts and historical materials, to a concentrated study of the one work in which Jonson self-consciously established a concrete, practical, and ostensibly unitary code of table behavior for himself and his companions: the *Leges Convivales* (1624) composed for the Apollo Room of the Devil and Saint Dunstan Tavern that served, in effect, as the club bylaws for the Tribe of Ben.

Jonson and the Classical Convivial Vocabulary

Douglas Duncan claims, with good reason, that "Jonson's scrutiny of festive behaviour and festive wit was based on a Roman ideal" (174). In particular, Duncan identifies the final lines of Martial 10.48 as crucial to Jonsonian conviviality:

> To crown [all] shall be jests without gall, and a freedom not to be dreaded the next morning, and no word you would wish unsaid; let my guests converse of the Green and the Blue [chariot-teams]; my cups do not make any man a defendant. (21–24)

[Accedent sine felle ioci nec mane timenda
    libertas et nil quod tacuisse velis:
de prasino conviva meus venetoque loquatur,
    nec faciunt quemquam pocula nostra reum.]

This promise, which finds its way into both Jonson's Epigram 101 ("Inviting a Friend to Supper") and his *Leges Convivales*, clearly engaged the poet's imagination. But it is interesting to consider the slight transformation that Martial's lines undergo at the later poet's hands.

Jonson paraphrases Martial's promise in Epigram 101 as follows:

> No simple word,
> That shall be vtter'd at our mirthfull boord,
> Shall make us sad next morning: or affright
> The libertie, that wee'll enioy to night.
>   (39–42)

But Martial's precise words are a shade different in sense. "Accedent sine felle ioci nec mane timenda / libertas et nil quod tacuisse velis" promises the reader that the guests will not say anything they might wish to have kept silent ("quod tacuisse velis"). The phrase "nil quod tacuisse velis" characterizes the evening's "libertas" through the double negation of emphatic litotes; the explicitly limiting "sine felle ioci" presents that same "libertas" as subject to the collective restraint of the participants in the banquet; and the phrase "nec mane timenda libertas"—literally "freedom not needing to be feared tomorrow"—introduces the gerundive as a self-consciously restrictive adjective. Given the exercise of collective discretion, the evening's liberty naturally need not be feared the next day. Jonson, on the other hand, promises that nothing said will sadden his guests the next day or disturb their convivial freedom that evening. Where Martial offers a gathering in which every guest is sensible enough to keep quiet on sensitive topics, Jonson seems to offer one in which the "libertie" to talk need not be restrained by fear of the morning after.[2] The perfect active infinitive "tacuisse" drops out of Jonson's rendering, as do the limiting adjective "timenda" and the causal relation of "sine felle ioci" to "nec mane timenda libertas." Where Martial draws attention to things unsaid, Jonson emphasizes words uttered.

This is not, to be sure, an earth-shattering realignment of sense. Martial's original meaning still remains available in Jonson's text to anyone who reads the latter with an awareness of its source. But Jonson's words nonetheless open a space for ambiguity in the convivial ideal he borrows from the Romans. How much, for instance, will the guests actually speak? In the *Leges Convivales*, Jonson requires his companions to be "nec muti, nec loquaces" (14); Martial's *convivae* seem to be distinguished by the certainty that they will remain *muti*, at least in respect of certain subjects; and in Epigram 101 the guests seem to have a preemptive "libertie" to speak their minds. All of these different positions jostle for advantage within the space of a single convivial ideal. Moreover, they are all additionally complicated by the various roles and prerogatives that Jonson's work and its precursors render available to the host. When Jonson again appropriates Martial 10.48, this time in the *Leges Convivales*, he once more alters the sense, although in this case he quotes Martial almost word for word: "Joci sine felle sunto" (19), and again, "Neminem reum pocula faciunto" (24). In the former of these two allusions, the only thing (other than word order) that Jonson has changed from line 21 of Martial's epigram is the main verb. But what a change it is. Where Martial operates in the indicative ("Accedent sine felle ioci"), Jonson works in the imperative, and in the legal imperative at that. The second reference proceeds in like vein, with somewhat more lexical substitution: "neminem" for "quemquam," deletion of the possessive "nostra," "faciunto" for "faciunt." In either case, what Martial offers as a promise, Jonson issues as a threat, or at least as an official command.

If these moments offer any indication of Jonson's general literary procedure, he cannot be called a mechanical imitator of the classics, but neither can he be viewed as deliberately undercutting the spirit of the classical texts with which he works. In a lengthy discussion of how to become an animal, Deleuze and Guattari offer a parallel situation in the case of "the local folk hero, Alexis the Trotter, who ran 'like' a horse at extraordinary speed, whipped himself with a short switch, whinnied, reared, kicked, knelt, lay down on the ground in the manner of a horse, competed against them in races, and against bicycles and trains" (*Plateaus* 305). In fact, as Deleuze and Guattari observe, "sources tell us that [Alexis] was never so much of a horse as when he played the harmonica: precisely because he no longer needed a regulating or secondary imitation"; he "became all the more horse when the horse's bit became a harmonica" (*Plateaus* 305) because the substitution of harmonica for bit signaled an organic coalescence of equine and human traits that moved Alexis beyond the pale of imitation. As Deleuze and Guattari summarize the case, "One does not imitate; one constitutes a block of becoming" (*Plateaus* 305). One might say the same about Jonson's appropriation of the classical convivial vocabulary; his absorption of classical precursors is most perfectly signaled by his departures from them, departures that indicate how fully Jonson has rendered classical precepts organic and integral to a nonclassical age and situation.

But what, precisely, was Jonson trying to absorb in the first place? Efforts to answer this question are complicated by the fact that Martial, too, was clearly playing the harmonica. Oswyn Murray has recently assembled much of the surviving evidence concerning the character of sympotic life and literature in classical Rome. This evidence suggests, among other things, that the cultural function of the Roman convivium was subject to flux; that the flux in question largely centered on issues of gender and social status; and that those issues were loosely keyed to the relative influence of Hellenistic customs on Roman life. To begin, Murray distinguishes between Greek and Roman sympotic practice on two main grounds. First, "the Greek *symposion* was essentially a male gathering, at which women were present only for the purposes of entertainment and sexual pleasures," whereas "in Italy from the Etruscan period women seem often to have been present as equals" (40). Second, "the Greek *symposion* was essentially a meeting of equals, in which social gradations were ignored. . . . In contrast, the Roman convivium was often arranged hierarchically, with the couches ranked in order of importance, the *clientes* stacked 'five to a couch' and served inferior food and drink" (40). Where the Greek *symposion* emphasized a homosocial *communitas*, the Roman model would seem to incline more toward the preservation of a heterosocial *nobilitas*.

This distinction, in turn, bred others. The role of poetry at the Roman convivium clearly would be affected by efforts to hierarchize the festivity, as would the behavior of the *convivae* themselves. "There is," in short,

> an important difference between what the Greek *cliens* may say and what is appropriate for a Roman poet. In Roman hands [one major sympotic] theme becomes the celebration of the *civilitas* of the great man who will honour an inferior. . . . Of course this is in overt opposition to the principle of equality embodied in the invitation to a Greek *symposion*; yet in a more subtle sense it enables the poet to suggest his acceptance by the great, and therefore his equality with them. (Murray 45)

Indeed, shifts in the character of Roman sympotic practice could entail further shifts not only in poetic discourse but in poetic identity itself. Thus Nevio Zorzetti has postulated the existence in archaic Rome of an indigenous sympotic literary tradition that was "anonymous, without being popular in nature" (300), that was committed to preserving "images of exemplary [civic] values" (301), and that came in time to view sympotic verse "written by professionals" as typical of a Hellenistic corruption of traditional customs (294). In sum, the sympotic practices of late republican and early imperial Rome—practices that affected both the work and the social status of poets like Horace and Martial—were set upon a cultural fault line.

In keeping with this analysis, it is reasonable to conjecture that a sympotic poetry based on unstable ideals of sympotic behavior might be unstable itself. Martial, the Roman poet with whom this study is most deeply concerned, provides a case in point. On one hand, he can describe a public banquet given by the emperor Domitian as a scene of "perfect harmony," with "emphasis, firstly, . . . upon large numbers, drawn . . . from all *ordines*, sharing equally in the feasting; secondly, upon lavish culinary bounty, equitably and theatrically distributed; thirdly, upon the emperor himself, a majestic presence and active participant in the communal meal" (D'Arms 309):

> Great as was the storied feast for triumph over the Giants, and great as was to all the High gods that night at which the good Sire reclined at table with the common crowd of gods, and Fauns had licence to call on Jove for wine; so great a banquet, Caesar, celebrates thy laurels won: our joys make glad the very gods themselves. Every knight feasts along with thee, the people too, and the Fathers, and Rome together with her chief partakes ambrosial fare. Large things didst thou promise: how much greater hast thou given! A dole was promised us, a banquet has been given. (Martial 8.50)
>
> [Quanta Gigantei memoratur mensa triumphi
>   quantaque nox superis omnibus illa fuit,
> qua bonus accubuit genitor cum plebe deorum
>   et licuit Faunis poscere vina Iovem,
> tanta tuas celebrant, Caesar, convivia laurus;
>   exhilirant ipsa gaudia nostra deos.
> vescitur omnis eques tecum populusque patresque
>   et capit ambrosias cum duce Roma dapes.
> grandia pollicitus quanto maiora dedisti!
>   promissa est nobis sportula, recta data est.]

As John D'Arms observes, this is clearly the poetry of political "mystification" (310); any reasonable effort to recreate the dining arrangements Martial describes here conclude that the poet's epigram exaggerates the social amalgamation in the festive scene it represents. (Indeed, Domitian's public banqueting is described in far more sober and less democratic terms by Suetonius.)[3] But one might add that the very improbability of the situation Martial rehearses is what lends it epideictic force. The fiction of Greek sympotic equality here actually ennobles the emperor, who descends, Jove-like, to bestow his bounty on the mortals and lesser gods. In fact, one could say that the Greek sympotic ideal is of literary value in Epigram 8.50 precisely because it is so out of place.

Conversely, as J. P. Sullivan observes, "when [Martial] is angry with an overbearing or unworthy patron, [he] invokes the insulting imagery of *rex* and *dominus*" (120). Thus he contrasts the duties of patronage with the ties of friendship when he lampoons his "vetus sodalis" Sextus for not having invited him to his (Sextus's) latest birthday dinner:

> But I know the reason. There came to you from me no pound of Spanish refined silver, nor smooth-napped toga, nor new mantles. Hospitality is not a matter of bargain; you are feeding presents, Sextus, not friends. (Martial 7.86.6–10; translation adjusted)

> [Sed causam scio. nulla venit a me
> Hispani tibi libra pustulati
> nec levis toga nec rudes lacernae.
> non est sportula quae negotiatur;
> pascis munera, Sexte, non amicos.]

At moments like this the Roman convivium seems to function mainly as a forum for the exercise of *clientela*: a social confidence game, in which the thin pretense of festive companionship both authorizes and is sustained by a pattern of coercive gift giving.

In fact, the pattern of coercion seems to have been a highly ambivalent one. Not only could patrons pressure their *clientes* into bringing them presents; the *clientes*, too, could pressure their superiors through the convivial setting. Here, for instance, Martial as *cliens* remonstrates with a nameless host who has failed to reward him for attending a dinner party:

> So not even six scruples of Septician silver plate have you sent me, nor a napkin given you by a peevish client, nor a jar ruddy with the blood of Antipolitan tunny, nor one containing small Syrian figs, nor a

stumpy basket of wrinkled Picenian olives, so that you could say you remembered me? You may deceive others with words and a benignant face, for to me in future you will be a detected pretender. (Martial 4.88.3–10)

[Ergo nec argenti sex scripula Septiciani
    missa nec a querulo mappa cliente fuit,
Antipolitani nec quae de sanguine thynni
    testa rubet, nec quae cottana parva gerit,
nec rugosarum vimen breve Picenarum,
    dicere te posses ut meminisse mei?
decipies alios verbis voltuque benigno;
    nam mihi iam notus dissimulator eris.]

As Sullivan has noted, such rebukes are predicated on the logic of exchange; they assume that Martial "was making a more than reasonable return for financial aid" through the exercise of his literary gifts in service of the host (122). Again, in an epigram that may have left its imprint on Jonson's *Alchemist*, Martial complains to a patron,

This man, whom your table, whom your dinner has made your friend—think you his heart one of loyal friendship? 'Tis boar he loves, and mullet, and sow's paps, and oysters, not you. Were I to dine so well, he will be my friend. (Martial 9.14)

[Hunc quem mensa tibi, quem cena paravit amicum
    esse putas fidae pectus amicitiae?
aprum amat et mullos et sumen et ostrea, non te.
    tam bene si cenem, noster amicus erit.]

In this latter poem, with its modulation from subjunctive to indicative in the final conditional construction, Martial accomplishes the considerable feat of denouncing the mercenary character of his patron's convivium at the same time that he angles for a better place at table.

Still further, the coercions implicit in the convivium inform literary practice not simply by providing poets with subject matter, but also by governing the critical reception of individual works and affecting the professional situation of individual authors. That is the point of Martial 6.48, which I have taken as the epigraph to the present chapter. Martial the successful poet, implicitly associating himself with the "Hellenistic professionalism" Nevio Zorzetti has identified as inimical to Roman table customs (295), attacks the patron Pomponius for using the convivium as a means to buy approval for his own verses:

> The full-dressed throng shout a loud "Bravo" to applaud you. 'Tis not you, Pomponius: it is your dinner that is eloquent. (Martial 6.48)
>
> [Quod tam grande sophos clamat tibi turba togata,
>   non tu, Pompone, cena diserta tua est.]

Here, at least, Martial would seem for professional reasons to be wholeheartedly opposed to the hierarchization of Roman sympotic practice, a hierarchization that not only places him in an attitude of social inferiority but also threatens to disrupt the critical standards intrinsic to his success as an author.

Finally, this brief survey of Martial's convivial discourse should end where it began, with Epigram 10.48, which, taken in the context of the poet's surrounding work, offers yet another perspective upon the nature of the convivium. Here the dinner is specifically not arranged with respect to the distinction between patron and *cliens*. The six invited guests will share the same couch ("Septem sigma capit, sex sumus, adde Lupum" [10.48.6]); the guests themselves are named in such a desultory manner ("Sex sumus, adde Lupum") as to suggest an extempore invitation rather than a carefully planned banquet; the poet himself, for once, is at least theoretically hosting the dinner; and the cumulative informality of the dinner arrangements pointedly accentuates the meal's intimacy. Even the dishes Martial offers his guests are carefully selected to be poor in quality, the products of an impromptu raid on a none-too-rich larder; there are cheap lizard fishes ("lacerti" [11]), a kid that has been mangled by a wolf ("haedus inhumani raptus ab ore lupi" [14]), a ham "that has already survived three dinners" [cenis . . . tribus iam perna superstes (17)], etc. The result is a kind of anticonvivium whose attractions lie in the act of nongovernance; Martial need not agonize about the food, the seating arrangements, the social distinctions that may separate individual guests, or the character of the dinner conversation, which will be regulated by the proven discretion of the guests themselves. Even the language of Martial's poem itself is loose, imitating what Thomas Greene has called "the unbuttoned chat of familiar conversation" (*Troy* 279). In short—here as in Epigram

10.48's sister poems, Epigrams 5.78 and 11.52—the poet doesn't have to worry about controlling anything; he is free to relax, without undergoing or devising any coconut pie tests. Yet if this poem represents an unconflicted celebration of convivial equality, it is a celebration that exists in counterpoint to the arrangements of Roman *clientela*—arrangements that lend the more modest surroundings of Epigram 10.48 their attractiveness, and that literally make the smaller, more intimate meal possible. After all, Martial's "rus . . . dulce sub urbe . . . parvaque in urbe domus" (9.97.7–8), like Horace's Sabine farm, were themselves the fruit of literary patronage relations.

My point is that Roman convivial literary practice, as represented by Martial (and Martial is as representative of such matters as anyone), cannot be said to serve or derive from a single ideal of proper behavior. On the contrary, Martial offers a wide-ranging repertory of convivial attitudes or postures, all existing in tension with one another, all generating difficulties of one sort or another while answering certain deficiencies of the others. His is less a convivial ideal than a convivial *vocabulary*, whose basic signifiers include (a) the celebration of a patron's *nobilitas* through the praise of his egalitarian behavior ("You're so much better than I am that you'll actually have me over for dinner"); (b) censure of those who use convivial fellowship to extract favors from others ("Dinner is about friendship, not a *quid pro quo*"); (c) expressions of willingness to perform favors in return for food ("I love you; when is dinner?"); and (d) a view of private festivity as an egalitarian space of personal relaxation, free of the protocols of *clientela* ("You're such a good friend that you won't mind if I serve you leftovers"). This vocabulary develops in a social space characterized by ambiguities. Moreover, as Jonathan Haynes has recently shown, Jacobean dinner parties experienced a similar kind of social slippage:

Jonson's organization of his plays around satirically observed parties [is] clearly related to socioeconomic developments. Such fashionable parties had a new character, were, within limits, a new phenomenon. These are *private* parties. . . . Unlike ceremonial occasions, where various ranks could sit together, but hierarchically . . . , in these parties all are potentially social partners and must talk together as provisional equals. (48–49)

Given social developments of this sort in Jacobean London, and given the precariousness with which ceremonial and private dining clearly intermingled, the classical convivial vocabulary would have been particularly useful to writers like Jonson. Thus all of Martial's convivial attitudes become available to Jonson's acquisitive classicism, and he makes use of every one of them sooner or later. Jonson invokes position (a) in "To Penshurst" when he praises the Sidneys for having him to supper and not seating him below the salt ("And I not faine to sit (as some, this day, / At great mens tables) and yet dine away" [65–66]); he assumes position (b) in Epigram 107 when castigating "Captayne Hvngry" for his practice of buying his way to table with promises of fabricated news reports ("Doe what you come for, Captayne, with your newes; / That's, sit, and eate: doe not my eares abuse" [1–2]); he has Bobadill employ position (c) in *Every Man in His Humour*, when he invites Matthew to take him to supper in return for companionship and fencing instruction ("Wee'll goe to some priuate place, where you are acquainted, some tauerne, or so—and haue a bit—Ile send for one of these Fencers, and hee shall breath you, by my direction" [1.5.152–155]); and position (d) surfaces, as we have already seen, in Jonson's self-conscious paraphrases of Martial 10.48. Nor is it possible to separate these often contradictory positions from one another, or to privilege one over the others. Just as the ghost of Greek social equality animates Martial's praise of Domitian, so Jonson's praise of the Sidneys' egalitarian hospitality can be viewed as a typical quid pro quo of the Jacobean patronage system. Each of the foregoing positions may be described apart from the others, but each of them inhabits the others as well.

All of this brings us back to Jonson, and should allow us both to appreciate the extreme flexibility of the sympotic traditions Jonson appropriates from classical antiquity and to recognize some of the ways in which Jonson adapts those traditions to answer the social exigencies of Jacobean England. Most of the sympotic improvisation we have considered so far is Martial's, but Jonson does a good bit of his own as well. To return briefly to the instance of Jonsonian classicism with which this excursus on Martial started, one thing that distinguishes Jonson's adaptations of Martial 10.48 from the original is the enhanced degree of authorial agency seized by the later poet within the convivial framework. As Sara van den Berg remarks, "Martial values the created play-world as a temporary refuge from the public world" (54), and thus Martial's poem may almost be read as one of undiluted self-reassurance. The distinctive thing about its dinner arrangements is their tendency to relieve the poet himself of the various responsibilities—for overseeing the menu, guest-list, accommodation, and conversation—that typically devolve upon the host at a convivium. (As a guest in Horace's Satire 2.8 exclaims sympathetically to his host, "To think that, in order that I may have lavish entertainment, you are to be racked and tortured with every anxiety!" ["Tene, ut ego accipiar laute, torquerier omni / sollicitudine districtum!" (2.8.67–68)]. In Jonson's case, however, the movement is toward greater and greater agency on the part of the host/poet. Epigram 101 (which I discuss more fully in the next chapter) issues expansive guarantees of convivial liberty based on the host's own vigilance; the *Leges Convivales* legislate table behavior according to the poet's self-imposed standard. Both of these postures are alien to Martial, and they arguably signal a reconstruction of authorship within the developing convivial setting of early modern England. In order to grasp this reconstruction more fully, we next need to consider the circumstances in which it took place.

"A Solemne Supper"

One of Jonson's recurring nightmares about dinner entertainment has to do with the inappropriate chatter of the guests. Such chatter, for him, epitomizes boorish table behavior. We get a distinctive taste of it in *Poetaster*, with the banquet scene discussed early in this chapter. Virtually the first sign that something is wrong with Ovid's party comes in the ground rules that initiate the celebration, and that specifically assign to all the guests

> free licence,
> To speake no wiser, then persons of baser titles;
> And to be nothing better, then common men, or women.
> (4.5.18–20)

This pronouncement leads to one of Jonson's patented scenes of belligerent festivity, comparable to the vapors game in *Bartholomew Fair* (1614), the various games of language and courtship in *Cynthia's Revels* (1601), and innumerable antimasques. Ovid insists that "He, that speakes the first wise word, shall be made cuckold" (4.5.42–43), the party immediately degenerates, and then Caesar makes his entrance to chastise enormities. The frequency of such moments in Jonson's plays has led Jonathan Haynes to describe the plays themselves as "almost entirely staged parties" (45).

More or less the same situation develops again in *Epicoene* (1609), this time minus Caesar. As soon as Morose has apparently completed the formalities of his wedding to the silent woman, she begins to talk, and this talk both initiates and helps to structure the charivari-like wedding reception with which Morose's downfall begins:

> Fye, master MOROSE, ... did you think you had married a statue? or a motion, onely? one of the *French* puppets, with the eyes turn'd with a wire? or some innocent out of the hospitall, that would stand with her hands thus, and a playse mouth, and looke vpon you.
>
> (3.4.25–41)

Within minutes, the babble of the arriving wedding guests has chased Morose to the roof of his own house; when he finally returns, with a rapier, he complains that the guests "haue rent my floore, walls, and all my windores asunder, with their brazen throats" (4.2.129–130). Of course, Morose is not Jonson, nor is he even a particularly sympathetic character. But, as Anne Barton has pointed out, his aversion to prattle nonetheless embodies "something like a voice of sense" because "the wise man eliminates the superfluous from his life; his sojourn on earth is short, and he tries to make good use of it, not waste his youth on trifles" (*Jonson* 131).

To this extent, at least, Morose and Jonson are comparable; they share the same idea of hell. For both of them, it is other people at a dinner party. In Epigram 107 ("To Captayne Hungry"), Jonson expresses this view of matters in *propria persona* (or something very close to it). As the cashiered soldier of the title sits down to eat, the poem's speaker requests only one thing of him: that he shut up. Indeed, the meal evolves as an elaborate means of purchasing the soldier's silence, and Hungry's conversation, in turn, is refigured as an excremental torrent that threatens to defile the food and drink:

> Giue your yong States-men, (that first make you drunke,
> And then lye with you, closer, then a punque,
> For news) your *Ville-royes*, and *Silleries*,
> *Ianin's*, your *Nuncio's*, and your *Tuilleries*,
> Your *Arch-Dukes* Agents, and your *Beringhams*,
> That are your words of credit. Keepe your Names
> Of *Hannow*, *Shieter-huissen*, *Popenheim*,
> *Hans-spiegle*, *Rotteinberg*, and *Boutersheim*,
> For your next meale: this you are sure of. Why
> Will you part with them, here, vnthriftely?
>
> (19–28)

The flood of foreign place-names in the soldier's conversation—all distinguished by italic type, juxtaposed more and more tightly as the polysyndeton of lines 21–23 gives way to the asyndeton of lines 25–26, and culminating in a series of encrypted nonsense-names like "Butter-home" and "Shit-house"—conveys an overpowering sense of strangulation *inter faeces et urinam*. As dinner gives way to conversation, so English gives way to the untreated sewage of macaronic name-dropping. It is a spectacle that Jonson seems to have found particularly loathsome.

That, it may be supposed, is one reason Jonson rewrites Martial 10.48 as he does. One consequence of that rewriting, as we have seen, is to give greater scope to the poet's own agency in determining what is done and said at dinner. To offer a rather crude formulation of the contrast here: Martial envisions the private dinner party of his epigram as a space of personal escape (from manipulation, responsibility, *officia*), in which *libertas* is the inevitable result of the particular friendly congregation; Jonson tends to view the dinner party more as a space of personal empowerment, and hence as a site to be defended actively against the Captayne Hungrys of the world. This distinction, in turn, may have something to do with developing patterns of bodily culture such as those traced by Norbert Elias and more recently by Gail Paster. If we accept, with Elias, that the history of Western manners involves an incremental "movement of segregation," a "'hiding behind the scenes' of what has become distasteful," and a concomitant steady expansion of the category of distasteful behavior itself (121), then we can see Jonson's increased sensitivity to dinner conversation as an index of his relative historical belatedness.

Indeed, Jonson's aversion to chatter in Epigram 107 can be directly related to the expansion of the concept of *delicatesse* in early modern Europe. As Elias observes in his lengthy survey of early modern *civilité* manuals, the sixteenth and seventeenth centuries witnessed a major codification and bourgeoisification of the rituals of courtly behavior, a process in which Erasmus's *De Civilitate Morum Puerilium* (1530) played a pivotal role. That treatise, like many others of its time, pays particular attention to the protocols of dinner-table hygiene, as well as to those of the privy; however, its injunctions are simple and general enough to suggest a relatively rudimentary system of behavioral distinctions. One is informed, for instance, that "to expose, save for natural reasons, the parts of the body which nature has invested with modesty ought to be far removed from the conduct of a gentleman" (*Manners* 277) [Membra quibus natura pudorem addidit retegere citra necessitatem procul abesse debet ab indole liberali (*De Civilitate* sig. A5v-A6r)]; that "if the conversation requires one to mention some private part of the body, it should be referred to by way of polite circumlocution" (*Manners* 287) [Si res exigat, vt aliq[uo]d membrum pudendum nominetur, circumitio[n]e verecunda rem notet (*De Civilitate* sig. B6r)]; and that "before sitting down [to supper] you should have urinated in private, defecated if need be" (*Manners* 281) [prius [cenam] clam reditto lotio, aut si res ita postulet, exonerata etia[m] aluo (*De Civilitate* sig. A8v)]. These principles, in turn, constitute a refinement upon still more rudimentary rules of late medieval behavior such as the reminder from a fifteenth-century treatise titled *S'ensuivent les contenances de la table*, "Before you sit down, make sure your seat has not been fouled" [Enfant, prens de regarder peine / Sur le siege ou tu te sierras / Se aucune chose y verra / Qui soit deshonnete ou vilaine (qtd. in Elias 129, 276)]. For Jonson's Captayne Hungry, moreover, this sociohistorical segregation of convivial matters from personal matters and table functions from privy functions takes on a still more refined character. Conversation takes the place of the original feculent matter, as Jonson envisions himself inundated by Hungry's *Shieter-huissen* logorrhea. In expanding on Erasmian precept, Jonson's epigram continues the process of distinguishing privy from dining room, but this time on the level of linguistic, rather than material, representation. Jean-Louis Flandrin has argued that one consequence of the development of table manners in seventeenth-century Europe was the placement of each diner within a kind of "invisible cage," separate from the others and allowed contact with the others only under tightly regulated circumstances (266); for Jonson, this invisible cage seems to exist on the discursive as well as the physical level. To this degree, at least, Jonson's concern with inappropriate table conversation may be viewed as an extension of late medieval and early modern systems of etiquette that operate concurrently with, but nonetheless remain sociogenetically distinct from, the poet's classicism.

In short, Jonson's concern with the regulation of talk at the dinner table signals his investment in a fastidiously maintained space of intellectual sanitation correlative to the space of bodily sanitation engineered by the sixteenth-century *civilité* manuals. This fact complicates efforts to read Jonson's work in light of the Bakhtinian opposition between classical and grotesque bodily canons, for if the classical body is defined, as we have already seen it to be, by its segregation from other bodies, we must simultaneously allow that very segregation to have been the historical product of a set of conduct manuals written increasingly in the vernacular, increasingly for bourgeois audiences, and—despite Erasmus's own impeccable and ubiquitous classicism—with only secondary concern for the Greco-

Roman cultural tradition. To this extent, the phrase "classical bodily canon" must itself be viewed as a misnomer of sorts. The classical and grotesque bodies exist for Jonson not so much as polar antitheses, but rather as layers of a cultural palimpsest, each visible within the other, each modifying the visibility of the other.

Much the same can also be said about the social distinctions that a notion of proper or courtly behavior must necessarily presuppose. As Frank Whigham has argued at length, the unprecedented popularity of conduct manuals in sixteenth-century Europe is in fact evidence not only of the ongoing maintenance of social distinctions, but also of their erosion.[4] In Jacques Revel's words, "'Rules [of behavior] created a space' within which a lengthy process unfolded, ultimately calling the rules themselves into question" (189–190); instructing the humbler sort of reader to conform his or her behavior to the better sort, the conduct manuals tended to render given social oppositions invisible and thus to encourage the institution of ever finer, ever more energetic efforts to discriminate between civility and savagery, Harvard and Yale. Such efforts could easily take on a bizarre, self-contradictory air. By 1663, for instance, in a notorious case of Restoration aristocratic misbehavior, Sir Charles Sedley deliberately violated Erasmus's rule against public self-exposure by appearing naked on a London tavern balcony, where he delivered a mock sermon on Genesis to an incensed, largely Puritan throng (Pinto 61–63). If, in fact, the Erasmian rule against revealing one's private parts was supposed in 1530 to embody a courtly standard of behavior, by 1663 that same rule would seem to have become so thoroughly bourgeois in character as to incur Sedley's aristocratic contempt. Sedley, for his part, embodies a literary tradition that can be traced back for two generations through the Sons of Ben directly to Jonson himself, and if standards of proper behavior seem to offer a dangerously unstable index of social station for Sedley, the same holds true of Jonson, too.

In fact, few people would have been better qualified to lecture Sedley on the social instability of manners than would Jonson himself. Even fairly early in his career, in *Every Man out of His Humour* (1599), Jonson presents the character of the social-climbing Fallace as pathetically impressed by the courtly table-manners of Fastidius Brisk:

> O, sweet FASTIDIVS! o, fine courtier! . . . How vpright hee sits
> at the table! how daintily hee carues! how sweetly he
> talkes, and tels newes of this lord, and of that lady! how
> cleanely he wipes his spoone, at euery spoonfull of any

whit-meat he eates, and what a neat case of pick-tooths he
carries about him, still!

(4.1.33–40)

A main point of Fallace's eulogy is to emphasize the disparity between the sophistication of Fastidius's manners and the utter vacuity of his mind; a second point is to emphasize Fallace's own corresponding vacuity, which prompts her to mistake manners for matter. Later, as unofficial court poet and masque writer for one of the most notoriously indecorous royal regimes of the seventeenth century, Jonson was even better situated to appreciate the ease with which the socially bidden could evaporate into the socially forbidden and vice versa.

Another of Erasmus's injunctions returns us to Jonson's concern with dinner conversation, and helps us to place that concern in the Jacobean courtly context. The rule in question is this: "Continuous eating should be interrupted now and again with stories. Some people eat or drink without stopping not because they are hungry or thirsty, but because . . . such habits . . . originate . . . in a sort of rustic shyness" (*Manners* 284) [Vicissitudo fabularum intervallis dirimat perpetuum esum. Quida[m] citra intermissione[m] edunt bibuntve, non q[uod] esuriant sitiantve, sed quod . . . ea res a rustico pudore profecta [est] (*De Civilitate* sig. B3v)]. Erasmus, in other words, shared Jonson's interest in the character of dinner-conversation, although in a somewhat broader and more rudimentary way. But in any case, the courtiers who performed Jonson's masques clearly cared little for such behavioral niceties. Orazio Busino's famous description of the void banquet following *Pleasure Reconciled to Virtue*, for instance, leaves little space for dinner conversation of any sort:

His majesty arose from his chair, and taking the ambassadors along with him, passed through a number of rooms and galleries and came to a hall where the usual supper was prepared for the performers. . . . He glanced round the table and departed, and at once like so many harpies the company fell on their prey. The table was almost entirely covered with sweetmeats, with all kinds of sugar confections. There were some large figures, but they were of painted cardboard, for decoration. The meal was served in large bowls of glass; the first assault threw the table to the ground, and the crash of glass platters reminded me exactly of the windows breaking in a great midsummer storm. (Orgel and Strong 1:253–254)

Jonson's Morose, as we have seen, complains that his chattering bourgeois wedding guests "haue rent . . . all my windores asunder, with their brazen throats." For Busino, a mute courtly "feeding frenzy" (Fumerton 161) produces much the same effect. Faced with such social instabilities, and with the apparent failure of established codes of behavior to reduce such instabilities to order, it is understandable that Jonson himself might have been increasingly tempted to take matters of comportment into his own hands. Once more, it is possible to see why the host of Martial 10.48, who views a private dinner party primarily as an opportunity for rest and relaxation, should assume a more active, interventionist character in Jonson's work.

In the next section of this chapter, we examine the *Leges Convivales* of the Tribe of Ben, which constitute Jonson's most deliberate effort to regulate the behavior of others at table. But before we proceed, one more observation needs to be made about the transformation of classical convivial discourse in Jonson's work. I have argued that Jonson appropriates a social vocabulary to be found in the verse of Martial and other Greco-Roman convivial poets; that in appropriating this vocabulary, Jonson realigns it in accordance with the demands of the courtly situation and traditions of civility within which he himself wrote; and that this realignment tends, among other things, to produce a convivial poet who is distinctively interested in exercising control over his surroundings, and who is particularly invested in exercising such control over and through the matter of conversation. I now add that even in diverging from his classical precursors Jonson finds one more important way to connect with them. Jonson's distinctive interest in table talk finds a secondary equivalent in the classical convivial tradition, an equivalent that once more is well represented by the epigrams of Martial.

On the whole, Martial is not much exercised by the inappropriate chatter of dinner guests; he has other things to complain about, foremost among them the stinginess and ostentation of hosts. (Horace, also, in his two convivial satires, 2.4 and 2.8, is clearly more concerned with the pretensions of hosts than with the crudeness of guests.) But one way for a host to impose on his dinner guests is through the recitation of his own verses at table, and Martial is highly sensitive to this particular faux pas. The silly Pomponius of Epigram 6.48, for instance, uses his hospitality as a way to buy approval of his poetry; the guests, Martial notes acidly, applaud him in Greek ("Tam grande sophos clamat tibi turba togata"), the word *sophos* signaling the host's pretensions and opening up a space between him and Martial that no number of Greek bravos could possibly bridge. In Epigram 5.78, Martial promises a prospective dinner guest that at his house no host (the word he uses, not accidentally, is "dominus") will "read a bulky volume" [Nec crassum dominus leget volumen (5.78.25)], and Epigram 11.52 ends with similar assurances. Then there is the unhappy Ligurinus, to whom Martial complains,

> Whether Phoebus fled from the table and banquet of Thyestes I don't know: we fly from yours, Ligurinus. It is undoubtedly choice, and laid out with rich viands, but nothing at all pleases us while you recite. I don't want you to serve me turbots, or a two-pound mullet, nor do I want mushrooms, oysters I do not want: hold your tongue! (3.45)

> [Fugerit an Phoebus mensas cenamque Thyestae
>   ignoro: fugimus nos, Ligurine, tuam.
> illa quidem lauta est dapibusque instructa superbis,
>   sed nihil omnino te recitante placet.
> nolo mihi ponas rhombos mullumve bilibrem
>   nec volo boletos, ostrea nolo: tace.]

Ligurinus is Martial's counterpart to Captayne Hungry: the dinner companion from hell whose silence would be worth worlds. Indeed, it is consistent with Jonson's relatively aggressive stand on the regulation of behavior that Martial's Ligurinus, a manipulative host whose influence the poet simply wants to escape, should be transformed by Jonson into a weaselly guest and thus made more fully subject to the poet's corrective ministrations. But such differences aside, Martial and Jonson clearly share an interest in censuring the literary pretensions of others within the convivial setting. As Stella Revard has noted, Jonson "frequently imitates [Martial] when he talks of poets, poetry, and poetasters" (144). Sara van den Berg agrees that Martial's emphasis on "plagiarists, poetasters, and readers of little or no taste" is a major thematic influence on Jonson's epigrams (90). Thus when Jonson promises in Epigram 101 not to repeat verses at the dinner table, he is, as Joseph Loewenstein has noted, repeating Martial's own verses in a highly multivalent and self-conscious gesture ("Corpulence" 496). Moreover, as Martial has observed in another epigram, the faulty recitation of others' verses can be as obnoxious as the recitation of one's own:

> That book you recite, O Fidentinus, is mine. But your vile recitation begins to make it your own. (1.38)

[Quem recitas meus est, o Fidentine, libellus:
 sed male cum recitas, incipit esse tuus.]

In short, Martial expresses interest in the regulation of dinner conversation precisely when such conversation impinges on—and, not coincidentally, threatens—his own chosen line of work. To this extent, Martial's concern to restrict the recitation of verse at dinner parties may be viewed as a counterpart to the literary attitudes also displayed by Horace in Satire 1.9, where the poet finds himself accosted in the street by a social climber who advertises himself as a scholar and prolific versifier (1.9.7, 23–24), and explored further by Lucian in the atrocious epithalamium recited by Histiaeus in the *Convivium* (41). In each of these cases, the classical source seems to have struck a resonant chord for Jonson; he repeats Martial's verses, uses Horace's satire as the situational basis for *Poetaster* 3.1, and alludes to Lucian's *Convivium* in the *Leges Convivales*. The most obvious reason for this sympathetic attraction is one of professional self-interest. Martial, Horace, and Lucian all have an obvious stake in policing the boundaries that separate good writing from bad, and Jonson shares their preoccupation with such matters. But irritation with poetastery is a fairly well delimited matter for Martial, Horace, and Lucian, all of whom tend to conceive their role as literary critic in ways that avoid a full-scale assault on the concept of *clientela* itself. Martial wants nothing more than to escape from the danger that his status as *cliens* might, in the case of convivial verse recitation, threaten his own vocational integrity. Although the nameless pest in Horace's Satire 1.9 obviously hopes that his literary pretensions will earn him an introduction to Maecenas, Horace himself simply wants to get away from his tormentor and does not present his predicament as a commentary on the Roman patronage system in general. (Indeed, part of the point of Horace's satire is arguably that Horace himself has become successful and prominent enough to attract aspiring *clientes*.) Lucian presents Histiaeus's idiotic poem as an object of detached fun, and not much more.

Jonson, on the other hand, develops his distaste for poetastery in conjunction with a larger investment in the overall regulation of dinner-table conversation. In the Jonsonian universe, the poet tends to expand until he encompasses—and thereby exceeds—everything else. Hence, as his "son" James Howell noted, Jonson can ironically end up producing the same kinds of inappropriate dinner conversation he reviles in others:

I was invited yesternight to a solemne supper by *B.J.* where . . . there was good company, excellent chear, choice wines, and joviall wellcome; one thing interven'd which almost spoyld the relish of the rest, that *B.* began to engrosse all the discourse, to vapour extremely of himselfe, and by vilifying others to magnifie his owne *muse*; *T. Ca.* busd me in the eare, that though *Ben* had barreld up a great deale of knowledge, yet it seems he had not read the *Ethiques*, which among other precepts of morality forbid self-commendation. (Herford, Simpson, and Simpson 11:419–420)

For Jonson, in effect, the boundaries of literary activity are elided with those of convivial discourse in general. Ben engrosses "all the discourse," magnifying his own muse in the process; everything said at a Jonsonian dinner party is always already a literary event, and thus subject to Jonson's censures as poet and as critic. If Jonson is indeed a distinctively aggressive legislator of table manners, this is perhaps one more reason why: his sense of the literary vocation forces him to establish a monopoly on language within the convivial setting as well as outside it. Howell's anecdote suggests that for Jonson the act of having others over for dinner could constitute something like an exercise in literary criticism. The conversations with William Drummond likewise suggest that even when Jonson was not technically hosting a given meal, his sense of literary self could nonetheless drive him into the same discursive position. In the very act of protecting one set of conceptual boundaries—separating poetry from poetastery, proper discourse from improper—he annihilates the parallel boundaries distinguishing guest from host and *cliens* from *patronus*.

Laws of the Table

In an important consideration of Jonson's debt to Martial, Joseph Loewenstein has argued that "the movement toward modernity in Jonson's imitation of Martial involves the recognition of middlemen" ("Corpulence" 498). Loewenstein, in other words, situates Jonson's work within the developing context of seventeenth-century market capitalism, a context also recently explored by Jean-Christophe Agnew, Peter Stallybrass and Allon White, and Patricia Fumerton.[5] As the preceding discussion of Jonson's classicism may already have suggested, I would like to extend Loewenstein's remark slightly further by taking the word *middlemen* in a sense other than the purely economic. I would suggest, rather, that Jonson himself emerges from his convivial negotiations as the middleman par excellence, his identity located at the junctures between a wide range of historical and literary and social subject positions. In terms of the Deleuzian theoretical model that informs this study, Jonson's literary self-construction thus comprises a pattern of "*experimentation* that is without interpretation or significance and rests only on tests of experience" (*Kafka* 7); it is more a mode of exploration than a sequence of preprogrammed interpretive correspondences. In what follows, I examine how such experimentation invests one of Jonson's more dictatorial and monumental works, the *Leges Convivales*, which are dictatorial in that they attempt to legislate the convivial behavior of others without appeal, and which are monumental in that they were actually carved on stone.[6]

The *Leges Convivales* have received relatively little scholarly attention, and on the rare occasions when they have been discussed and/or translated, it has usually been as an adjunct to the interpretation of Jonson's other works (e.g., Trimpi 185–190). But for this very reason, they retain an important marginal character that has been largely bled out of the Jonson canon as a whole by the great-books critical tradition. Even now the *Leges Convivales* stand out as a distinctively minor work in the Deleuzian sense of the phrase: a text characterized by "the deterritorialization of language, the connection of the individual to a political immediacy, and the collective assemblage of enunciation" (*Kafka* 18). The first of these criteria is admirably met by the Latin of Jonson's original text, a "paper language" (*Kafka* 19) like Kafka's German or Beckett's French, which through its determined artificiality defamiliarizes Jonson's laws themselves, estranging them from the surroundings in which they are formulated and function. The text's—and author's—"connection to a political immediacy" has been usefully demonstrated by David Shields in his recent derivation of early American private clubs from the "model of metropolitan sociability" projected by the Sons of Ben (295–96); Richard Burt has likewise recently emphasized the sociopolitical functionality of unofficial organizations like the seventeenth-century "play club or faction," and he, like Shields, takes the Sons of Ben as a primary case in point (40–41). The "collective assemblage of enunciation" that invests the *Leges* is perhaps one of the most important and least appreciated aspects of Jonson's work, and therefore it deserves more than a passing mention.

It may at first seem counterintuitive to credit Jonson, one of the most famous and determined literary self-promoters of his age (and a man whose emphasis on personal agency I have just been at pains to demonstrate), with a commitment to the collectivization of language. On the other hand, as I argue in Chapter 3 of this study, Jonson's self-promotion may be read as a reaction formation to the undeniably collective character of his linguistic assemblage. His work speaks as much from a dispersed self as from a centered one. To this extent, the marginality of the *Leges Convivales* is particularly useful; a set of club rules composed in Latin by a man with little formal education, cobbled out of odds and ends of classical and nonclassical learning, and created for the express purpose of regulating (or pretending to regulate) the behavior of drinking companions at an English tavern, they are at best an ambivalent expression of unitary authorial agency and unified authorial tradition. Their very quirkiness calls into question their status as literature. If, as Deleuze and Guattari have argued, Kafka's letters complicate any attempt to think of his work as a unified literary *oeuvre* (*Kafka* 29), the *Leges Convivales* perform the same function for Jonson. Not only are they quirky and idiosyncratic; in this respect they are typical of much that Jonson wrote. Plays (some collaborative) for the popular stage, masques and progress entertainments, a collection of prose *sententiae*, a textbook of English grammar, the occasional country-house poem and epistle mendicant: when considered piecemeal, much of Jonson's eleven-volume complete works assumes a quirky, marginal character. This aspect of the poet's productivity has been largely suppressed by his posthumous literary canonization, and it is perhaps well recovered via neglected texts like the *Leges Convivales*. In a sense, the aggressive monumentality of Jonson's authorial self has been urgently patched together out of the evidence of that self's collectivization and dispersal.

Moreover, the text of the *Leges* itself is really a collection of fragments: twenty-seven of them, twenty-four of which are numbered, three of which are distinguished from the others by italic or upper-case typography, and many of which act and react upon their predecessors and successors in ways that frustrate one's efforts to apprehend the whole as a whole. The standard (and, to my knowledge, the only) twentieth-century translation of the *Leges*, done elegantly in 1962 by Wesley Trimpi (186–187), suppresses all these characteristics of the work. Trimpi eliminates the numerals distinguishing law from law; removes all typographical peculiarities; elides separate laws (e.g., numbers 1, 2, and 3; 11 and 12; 13 and 14) in a single sentence, thus investing them with a continuity they do not unambiguously possess in the original text; and merges the entire work into a sustained plain-style paragraph. The result is a polished piece of prose, and a distinguished piece of scholarship, that manufactures the illusion of wholeness out of a linguistic hodgepodge. Since my primary focus is on the discontinuities that structure the work, I have replaced Trimpi's translation with a far more ungainly, and more literal, one of my own.

LAWS OF FEASTING

That it may be happy and auspicious in Apollo.

1. Let no one contributing nothing to the cost of the entertainment come hither, except for a shadow.
2. Let the tasteless, gloomy, base [ugly] ignorant man be absent.
3. Let the learned, urbane, cheerful, honorable be received.
4. Nor let selected women be rejected.
5. Let there be nothing in the provision that turns up the noses of the guests.
6. Let the dishes be prepared rather with respect to their distinction than to expense.
7. Let the caterer and cook be experienced with respect to the gullet of the guests.
8. Let there be no contention about [contrast in] the seating.
9. Let the servants of the feast be watchful [conspicuous] and silent; of the cups, attentive and swift.
10. Let the wines be supplied from pure sources; or let the host be flogged.
11. Let it be just for the companions to challenge each other in moderate cups.
12. But let there be more skirmishing in conversation than in wine.
13. Let the guests be neither silent nor talkative.
14. Let the drunken and sated not discuss serious or sacred matters.
15. Let no player on the harp [poet] come unless called.
16. Admitted: let our holy rites be celebrated with laughter, religious dances, choruses, song, witticisms, all festivity of the Graces.
17. Let the jests be without gall.
18. Let no tasteless poems be read.
19. Let no one be intended to write verses.
20. Let all rumbling of argument be absent.
21. Let there be a free corner for lovers' complaints and sighs.
22. Let it be unjust to fight with the goblets in the manner of the Lapiths, to smash the glassware together, to shake out the windows, to tear the household furniture to pieces.
23. Let him who carries forth either our words or our deeds be carried forth himself.
24. Let the cups make no one a defendant.

LET THE FIRE BE CONSTANT.

[LEGES CONVIVALES

Quod felix, faustumq, in Apolline sit.

1. Nemo asymbolus, nisi umbra, huc venito.
2. Idiota insulsus, tristis, turpis, abesto.

3. Eruditi, Urbani, hilares, honesti, adsciscuntor.
4. Nec lectae foeminae repudiantor.
5. In apparatu, quod convivis corruget nares, nil esto.
6. Epulae delectu potius, quam sumptu, parantor.
7. Opsonator & coquus, convivarum gulae periti sunto.
8. De Discubitu non contenditor.
9. Ministri a dapibus oculati & muti; a poculis auriti, & celeres, sunto.
10. Vina puris fontibus ministrantor; aut vapulet hospes.
11. Moderatis poculis provocare sodales, fas esto.
12. At fabulis magis, quam vino, velitatio fiat.
13. Convivae nec muti, nec loquaces sunto.
14. De seriis, aut sacris, poti & saturi ne disserunto.
15. Fidicen, nisi accersitus, non venito.
16. Admisso: risu, tripudiis, choreis, cantu, salibus, omni gratiarum festivitate, sacra celebrantor.
17. Joci sine felle sunto.
18. Insipida Poemata nulla recitantor.
19. Versus scribere, nullus cogitor.
20. Argumentationis totus strepitus abesto.
21. Amatoriis querelis, ac suspiriis, liber angulus esto.
22. Lapitharum more scyphis pugnare, vitrea collidere, fenestras excutere, supellectilem dilacerare, nefas esto.
23. Qui foras vel dicta, vel facta, eliminat, eliminator.
24. Neminem reum pocula faciunto.

FOCUS PERENNIS ESTO.]

(Herford, Simpson, and Simpson 8:656)

The first feature of this remarkable text that deserves note is the extreme ambiguity of the subject position from which it is written. To try to place the authorial voice with respect to the social arrangements it describes is to lose oneself in a hall of mirrors. There is, for instance, an immediate problem in the first-line allusion to the name of the inn room where the Sons of Ben met, the Apollo. As Herford and the Simpsons observe (11:295–296), this name is a self-conscious reference to an incident in Plutarch's *Life* of Lucullus. What needs to be added is that the incident in question deals directly with convivial ambiguities of the sort that regularly preoccupied and vexed Martial. In the story, as Plutarch relates it, Cicero and Pompey accost Lucullus in the forum and ask him one favor: that they might dine with him that evening just as he would have dined by himself (2:603–605). Lucullus, who has effectively granted the petition in advance, asks to defer the banquet to a later day, presumably so as to make it more sumptuous and appropriate for company, but Cicero and Pompey "refuse . . . to allow it, nor [will] they suffer him to confer with his servants, that he might not order any thing more provided than what [is] provided for himself" (2:603). Yet Lucullus outwits his companions by simply instructing a servant that he will eat that night in the Apollo Room, "for each of his dining-rooms, as it seems, had a fixed allowance for the dinner served there . . . , so that his slaves, on hearing where he wished to dine, knew just how much the dinner was to cost, and what were to be its decorations and arrangements" (2:605). As it happens, the allowance for the Apollo Room is fifty thousand drachmas, and thus Lucullus is able, without any special preparations or warning, to maintain his reputation for lavish dining.

But what could be the point of invoking such an anecdote in the *Leges Convivales*? Plutarch's life of Lucullus is not an unequivocally approving piece of biography. In fact, the anecdote in question occurs in a string of tales, all of which illustrate the thesis that "Lucullus took not only pleasure but pride" in his extraordinarily ostentatious way of life (2:601). Plutarch, for his part, does not share his subject's keen appreciation of fine dining; as he observes in his concluding comparison of Lucullus to Cimon, the Greek "seems to have been of ill repute and unrestrained in his youth, while Lucullus was disciplined and sober. Better, surely, is the man in whom the change is for the better" (2:613). Does Jonson's allusion to Plutarch also constitute an allusion to the historian's position of moral censure? Does it identify the society of the Sons of Ben with a latter-day mode of Lucullan self-indulgence? How does the reference to Plutarch position itself with respect to the ill-conceived subterfuge of Pompey and Cicero, which is in itself a bit hard to fathom as a gesture of wit? Are we to approve of Cicero and Pompey's effort to restrain their companion's extravagance? Are we to admire the cleverness with which Lucullus evades their devices?

I suspect the answer is yes, in all these cases. What the allusion offers us, in other words, is less a fixed position or convivial ideal than a series of possibilities, all held in coy suspension, all equally designating the space of the author. And when we move along to the first formal law of the text, matters grow only murkier. This opening rule at first seems straightforward enough; everybody is supposed to help pay for the entertainment. But there is an exception, of course, and that exception is coextensive with a second classical allusion. The "shadow" (or "ghost") that is not held responsible for entertainment expenses is another holdover from the Roman convivial vocabulary: an uninvited guest brought to one's dinner party by an invited *patronus*.[7] Again, even acknowledging Jonson's clear delight in gratuitous displays of classical learning, one has to adjust one's sense of the

Leges in order to make sense of the Latin reference. Does Jonson really mean that entertainment is to be offered in accordance with a classical protocol of convivial patronage that demands the uninvited companions of officials and benefactors be given free hospitality? Does he, on the other hand, endorse the obviously spiteful character of the nickname *umbra*, which was the imposed-upon host's revenge against generations of Roman party crashers? The shadow at Jonson's dinner party is the shadow of Roman *clientela*: clearly out of place, but nonetheless demanding accommodation.

Further, the *Leges* tend to structure themselves through point and counterpoint: to offer one injunction that is then qualified and re-formed (or reformed?) by the next one. Pairs of such rules include numbers 2 and 3, 11 and 12, 13 and 14; as already noted, Wesley Trimpi's standard way of translating these pairs is to amalgamate them in a single sentence, thereby supplying them with a syntactical and semantic cohesion they lack in the original text. Trimpi, of course, is interested in demonstrating that Jonson is an early and influential humanist advocate of the plain style, and thus Trimpi's approach to the *Leges* tends to present them as an unconflicted manifesto of the convivial *via media*: the Apollo Room's membership roster should be free of foolish and shameful individuals while favoring the learned and honest; moderate drinking is to be allowed so as to encourage the flow of conversation; and so on. But if taken in their original discontinuity, these rules offer something rather different. Numbers 2 and 3, for instance, may be read in such a way as to contradict one another almost entirely. Where the former only excludes tasteless, gloomy, base fools from the convivium, thereby implicitly admitting everyone else, the latter restricts explicit admission to the learned, urbane, cheerful, and honorable, thereby implicitly barring everyone else. Nor is it particularly clear how the adjectives in these lines are to be construed. Should they be taken in tandem, thus explicitly barring only individuals who are tasteless *and* gloomy *and* base *and* fools, while specifically admitting only those who (*mirabile dictu*) are learned *and* urbane *and* cheerful *and* honorable? Moreover, even if considered jointly, such rules comprise a disturbingly blunt social instrument; the binarisms that inform them have nothing at all to say about those of us who are Fortune's privates, the vast mass of humanity located in the ethical plenum between folly and learning, shame and honor. It is only an additional irony, therefore, that laws 2 and 3 exist in tension with the opening line of the verses "Over the Door at the Entrance into the Apollo," which "Welcome *all*, who lead or follow, / To the oracle of

Apollo" (1, my italics). This pair of rules, far from narrowing Jonson's convivial ideal to a single point of golden-mean certainty, arguably works to exclude, rather than to define, the *via media*. In the process, Jonson's rhetoric springs open a whole constellation of interpretive possibilities, all of which may be attached to—or detached from—the authorial subject position more or less at will.

Moreover, rules 2 and 3 are not really a pair. Their symmetry is retroactively disrupted by the *tertium quid* of rule 4: "Nec lectae foeminae repudiantor." This is Jonson's brief nod to the Roman (as opposed to the Greek) practice of allowing women as convivial guests. But it is, at best, a rather nervous nod. For one thing, it betrays uncertainty about the actual status of the *lectae foeminae* as people. The fact that a separate rule must be provided for them suggests that they have not been adequately described via the categories invoked for ordinary (i.e., masculine) human beings in rules 2 and 3; adjectives like *tristis*, *turpis*, *hilares*, and the undeniably masculine *honesti* do not seem to have taken women entirely into account. Furthermore, the precise terms in which rule 4 accommodates women are distinctly underwhelming. The construction "nec . . . repudiantor," "nor let [them] be rejected," stops conspicuously short of insisting that they actually be admitted. As Clough memorably observed, "Thou shalt not kill, but needst not strive / Officiously to keep alive." In a similar spirit, Jonson's fourth *lex convivalis*, with its uneasy negotiations around the category of the feminine, leaves his women dinner guests neither present nor absent, neither wholly alive nor completely dead. This effect of Jonson's prose is only intensified by the use of emphatic litotes in the phrase "nec . . . repudiantor." The Latin of the *Leges Convivales* is, after all, an artificial language, and its artificiality is foregrounded by the deployment of a phrase that swings in widely divergent semantic directions as one moves from Latin to English. Nor would this use of litotes be out of character for Jonson; as William Blissett has observed, litotes is the central trope in the *verbosa et grandis epistola* from Tiberius that constitutes the climactic moment of *Sejanus*. There Jonson clearly employed the trope to generate "a disorienting and spine-chilling mode of utterance" (Blissett 98). A measure of that same disorientation arguably pervades the *Leges Convivales* as well.

In certain cases, rather than allowing one *lex* to modify the reader's apprehension of another, Jonson composes single rules in a way that allows them to destabilize themselves. Two noteworthy instances of this gesture occur in laws number 6 and 8. The former insists that food should be prepared with an eye to distinction (or taste) rather than to cost, and this principle can be taken to support a kind of down-at-the-heels urbanity such as that embodied in Martial 10.48 or Catullus 13. The idea, from this standpoint, is that expense is a bad thing: better a cheap and tasty dinner than an extravagant one. But Jonson's ablatives of respect also favor an alternative construction, in which expense is neither good nor bad but simply irrelevant: a damn-the-price-let's-eat-the-whales epicurism like that advocated by Volpone when he promises Celia, "Could we get the phoenix, / (Though nature lost her kind) shee were our dish" (3.7.204–205). What matters, after all, is the taste and not the cost. Likewise, when Jonson insists in rule 8 that there be no contention over the seating arrangements, his use of the verb *contendere* enables two entirely different readings, correlative with the verb's discrete senses of "to contend in battle, fight" and "to bring into comparison, match, contrast" (*Oxford Latin Dictionary*, s.v. "contendere"). Either those who get seated below the salt are not to argue about the fact (as they do, to lamentable effect, in Lucian's *Convivium*), or there is to be no contrast in the seating at all (as, again, in Martial 10.48). In the case of this ambiguity, as of the others already mentioned, the principal beneficiary is the author, who holds in suspension a wide range of often mutually exclusive convivial arrangements.

But things become even more curious. Behind the various equivocations I have so far sought to chart, the *Leges Convivales* offer another level of uncertainty. They are, to take their title in its cognate sense, a set of convivial laws: an attempt to regulate behavior in a sociable and—one might reasonably hope—peaceable fashion. Yet the threat of violence in them is pervasive. On the one hand, we are warned in law 22 (a clear reference to Lucian's *Convivium*) that it is unjust to fight with goblets, smash windows, and trash furniture. On the other hand, we are informed in law 10 that if the wine is not pure, the host should be beaten. (Trimpi translates the verb *vapulare*, which usually denotes military flogging, with the generic "to be punished.") All rumblings of argument are supposed to be kept at a distance, but the drinking arrangements are clearly conceived as adversarial (Jonson uses the verb *provocare* to describe them). Moreover, so is the conversation, for which Jonson summons up the descriptive noun *velitatio* (another military term, this time meaning "skirmishing"). Nor is the threat of violence channeled in a single direction; the guests are to skirmish with one another in conversation, they may throw out anyone who publicizes their proceedings, and the host may be subject to a good whipping if he serves bad wine. The *Leges* assert themselves through a steady recuperation of the very convivial behavior that they are supposed to banish.

But to what spot is this behavior recuperated? The laws govern everyone, guest and host, *eruditi* and *insulsi*. To this extent, they issue from an authorial space that both encompasses and transcends the social space of the dining room itself. The site of the authorial voice, in other words, is *hic et ubique*; like the voice of Hamlet's father's ghost, it resonates from everywhere, encompassing everything, and not so much assuming concrete form as the illusion of concrete form. The *Leges* constitute an undeniable act of authorial self-assertion, but the self being asserted possesses a metamorphic capacity that renders it more collective than individual: an ability to shift forms, adopt multiple forms simultaneously, coalesce or disperse at will.

The *Leges* display one final distinctive quality, too: a tendency to activate the vocabularies not only of convivial and military experience, but of religious ritual as well. Law 16 describes the Apollo Room festivities as *sacra*—holy rites—to be celebrated with choral dance and song. The name of the Apollo Room itself, while clearly a reference to Plutarch, is also just as clearly an invocation of Apollo Musagetes, the god of song. This invocation, in turn, resonates in the verses composed by Jonson and inscribed over the entrance to the Apollo Room itself:

> Welcome all, who lead or follow,
> To the oracle of Apollo.
> Here he speaks out of his Pottle,
> Or the Tripos, his Tower Bottle:
> All his Answers are Divine,
> Truth itself doth flow in Wine.
> ("Over the Door at the Entrance into the Apollo" 1–6)

Even the command "Qui foras vel dicta, vel facta, eliminat, eliminator" can be read as pertaining to a religious, or quasi-religious, secret ceremony.

The wonderful thing about such language is its ability to transcend, even transfigure, material circumstances. Critical opinion has long maintained that Jonson dislikes metaphor (cf. Wayne 28–38; McCanles 39–45), and this opposition to the metaphorical use of language is one more characteristic that the poet's work shares with the literary preferences of Deleuze and Guattari (*Kafka* 18). But that being the case, the religious aspect of Jonson's dining-club vocabulary takes on a particularly equivocal quality. Not only are the meetings of the Sons of Ben "sacred rites"; the room in which the meetings occur is the "Oracle of Apollo"; and wine itself "is the Milk of Venus, / And the Poets' Horse accounted" ("Over the Door at the Entrance into the Apollo" 12–13). Such language works to deterritorialize the proceedings being described: to spirit them out of the world as we know it and into a socioliterary *ou-topos* rather like the one evoked for James I in Jonson's masques. And that is finally, one may suggest, because the Jonsonian convivial personality seeks a form of self-assertion that is not simultaneously a form of self-limitation.

This is not to deny that Jonson's rules of table behavior may be arranged, on the level of overt signification, into a traditional sequence of conservative humanist principles. To that extent, I have nothing but admiration for Trimpi's work. In fact, one can immediately understand why such an arrangement of principles would be important to Jonson. If his literary persona is indeed interested in self-assertion without self-limitation, then it is certainly necessary that he should at least be able to generate the appearance of method and sequence in his convivial thinking as a preemptive defense against the limiting charge that he has none. But to posit that method and sequence as the driving force behind the poet's various convivial negotiations is, I believe, to mistake an effect for a cause. As Don Wayne has observed of "To Penshurst," "while the poem ostensibly expresses admiration for rank, the essential qualities that ultimately distinguish good rulers from bad ones are qualities vested in an institution that threatens to transcend the distinction between lord and commoner" (26). Just as "To Penshurst" reworks traditional materials to provide a space for authorial self-empowerment, so too do the *Leges Convivales*. That space is marked out by the transcendent, quasi-religious, quasi-legal character of the authorial voice, which fills everything and comes from everywhere, touches everyone while being reducible to no one, and escapes rational concretization even as it commits itself to a stable code of traditional humanist behavior.

The Author's Eye

It is perhaps time now to pass from the subject of table behavior to that of dining itself. However, I do so with one final backward glance at the *Leges*, this time at law 21: "Let there be a free corner for lovers' complaints and sighs." Against the dense surrounding context of Jonson's allusive classicism, this command seems largely out of place. Catullus notwithstanding, the posture of the sighing, complaining lover would probably have struck Jonson as more Petrarchan than classical, and it is particularly strange in the work of a poet who has elsewhere advertised himself as writing not of love (*The Forest* 1). But perhaps more to the point is the idea of the free corner ("liber angulus"), also alien to the classical convivial tradition, which brings into focus a whole series of equivocations regarding the status of the Apollo Room proceedings as public display and as private retreat.

The Apollo Room, despite the trappings of Jonson's Latin, is not the scene of a Roman dinner party. It is the site of a private Jacobean literary society/dining club, whose membership is restricted, whose members are theoretically free from the threat of prosecution for their behavior *intra parietes*, and whose proceedings are to be kept secret on pain of expulsion. To this degree, the Apollo Room deserves a place among the various refuges of intimacy—"walled garden, bedroom, *ruelle*, study, . . . oratory"—described by Orest Ranum in his examination of the development of private space in early modern Europe (207). Yet the Apollo Room's elite hermeticism manifests itself again and again in public pronouncements: the *Leges Convivales*, the verses "Over the Door at the Entrance into the Apollo," the "Epistle . . . to One that Asked to be Sealed of the Tribe of Ben" (*Underwood* 47). It is as if the privacy of the club existed precisely so that it could be transformed into a kind of public literary spectacle. Moreover, this publication of the privacy of the Apollo Room leads, in the case of rule 21 of the *Leges*, to the establishment (and concomitant publication) of a further private space within the private club space already constructed: a "free corner" reserved for the moanings and wailings of frustrated lovers.

In her recent discussion of the architectural and dramatic space associated with the Jonsonian masque, Patricia Fumerton has emphasized the masque's relation to the increasing sequestration of private dining rooms in the great houses of seventeenth-century England. As Fumerton observes of these rooms, "By the fifteenth century, family and guests had withdrawn from [the medieval great] hall, leaving it to the servants, and moved upstairs to dine in a room called the 'great chamber'. . . . Almost immediately, however, a proliferation of rooms beyond the great chamber began, as well as a retreat within such rooms (which became subdivided) to ever more inward recesses of private dining" (113). One consequence of this development, Fumerton argues, is the construction, within private dining chambers and banqueting houses, of "a special place for subjectivity . . . a reverse *topos* or *un*commonplace increasingly displaced from the central places of living" (122). Another consequence is the installation of the Jonsonian masque within that uncommonplace, the banqueting house, as a public display of the monarch's otherwise invisible private self. In short, "there was something terrifyingly, mortally empty about the 'privacy' of James's entertainments. . . .While his entertainments seemed to project a world of intimate self-expression, they also intimated the characteristic unlocatability or insubstantiality of his, and his period's, subjectivity" (Fumerton 141).

That is the bad news: the courtly entertainments of seventeenth-century England commit their sponsors to a sense of personal identity that is annihilated by the very cultural displays that confirm it. But perhaps there is some good news here as well. If so, it would be for the literary sensibility whose capacity to place the privacy of others on display is so central to the fashioning of personal identity. The masques, that is to say, do not simply annihilate James's private subjectivity in the act of affirming it; they also manufacture Jonson's literary subjectivity in the same process. In fact, the breaching of private space—the transformation of the unseen and unheard into their opposites—is fundamental to Jonson's sense of writing. As he observes in *Discoveries*, "*Language* most shewes a man: speake that I may see thee" (8:625). The relation between private subjectivity and the Jonsonian literary sensibility thus assumes an almost symbiotic nature. Every locked door that the poet throws open, every dark corner that he illuminates, constitutes an act of literary self-expansion, propelling the poet into the *hic et ubique* that is to be his proper terrain. The universality of the poet's "I" is repeatedly demonstrated by the universality of his eye.

In his stimulating recent discussion of secrecy in Jonson's work, William Slights has described the poet in terms sympathetic to the present analysis: as a "libertarian in his own cause" (145), committed to preserving "the secrets of his trade or *mystere*" (172) while nonetheless taking "a fierce delight in invading every private space in London" (95). That is perhaps one reason why the twenty-first rule of the *Leges Convivales* offers the reader, within a secret and private club space already revealed by the text itself, a space of still further segmentation whose privacy exists to be laid open by the authorial voice. On this view, Jonsonian authorship is not coextensive with the poet's person; it is not to be pinned down in a private chamber, nor is it to be restricted to a univocal code of behavior. Unlike the wretched Pomponius in the epigraph to this chapter, a hopeless literary loser whose eloquence may be confined within the crust of a potpie ("non tu, Pomponi, cena diserta tua est"), Jonson devises his sense of authorship in terms that ever more ingeniously resist territorialization. Rather than taking on a local habitation and a name, Jonsonian authorship exists in the interstices between person and person, space and space; one may think of it, perhaps, as a highly mobile means of making connections. That is the sense in which I would suggest that Jonson is a convivial middleman par excellence, and this view of matters implies that for Jonson table manners are less a vehicle for the delimitation of personal essence than a conduit for its enlargement: a means of becoming other. They become, in effect, an extension of the foodstuffs whose manner of consumption they exist to regulate, and which provide the focus for the next chapter of this study.

2
Renaissance Overeating

WHEN JONSON THINKS ABOUT FOOD, which is often, these are the sorts of thing that come to his mind:

a. A water carrier named after a young herring (Cob), who complains that fast days "rauen up more butter, then all the dayes of the week, beside; . . . stinke of fish, and leeke-porridge miserably: . . . keepe a man deuoutly hungrie, all day"; and "would haue me turne HANNIBAL, and eate my own fish, and bloud" (*Every Man in His Humour* 3.4.43–54);
b. Zeal-of-the-Land Busy, "fast by the teeth, i' the cold Turkey-pye, i' the cupbord, with a great white loafe on his left hand, and a glass of *Malmesey* on his right" (*Bartholomew Fair* 1.6.34–36);
c. Sir Epicure Mammon, dreaming of "The tongues of carpes, dormise, and camels heeles, / Boil'd i' the spirit of SOL, and dissolu'd pearle, / . . . / The beards of barbels, seru'd, in stead of sallades" (*The Alchemist* 2.2.75–82);
d. A pig that, while being roasted, grows so "passionate" that it "has wept out an eye" (*Bartholomew Fair*, 2.4.58–59);
e. A grand supper in which the devil dines on "a *Puritan* poach't, / That vsed to turne vp the eggs of his eyes," "*Promoter in plum broth*," "Six picled Taylors sliced and Cutt, / Sempsters, tire-women fitt for his pallett, / Wth fethermen and Perfumers putt / Some twelve in a Charger, to make a *Grand sall[et]*" (*The Gypsies Metamorphosed* 1068–1081);
f. "A *Tun* . . . brought in to daunce, and so many *Bottles* about it" (*Pleasure Reconciled to Virtue* 68–69);
g. A watchman named Haggis, and a pig-woman who is rumored to have eaten herself to death on a meal of "cowes vdders" (*Bartholomew Fair* 2.3.16);

h. An "*Olla Podrida*" with "persons, to present the meates," as, for instance, "A brace of Dwarfes," "*Hogrel* the Butcher, and the Sow his wife" (*Neptune's Triumph for the Return of Albion* 240–331).

Obviously the meaning of these moments—and of others like them that recur in Jonson's work—depends in large part on their immediate literary context. But just as obviously, these passages comprise a general pattern of reference within the poet's work as a whole. Not only do they stake out a theme that repeatedly exercises Jonson's imagination; they also stake out a set of terms within which the poet's imagination consistently operates. To continue the argument of the preceding chapter, one could say these passages develop a culinary vocabulary that in many ways parallels the convivial vocabulary we have already examined.

For one thing, the passages listed above are all dominated by tropes of somatic exchange and convertibility. To my mind, this may be one of the most delightful features of Jonson's work, although it is perhaps more surreal than comical. Sir Epicure Mammon's vision of scarcely digestible delicacies calls in question the conceptual distinction between food and not food by conflating the eaten with the inedible (barbel beards for salads?). In a parallel gesture, the characters of Jonsonian drama tend to melt into anthropomorphic representations of food: walking, talking herrings, pigs, and bag puddings. Likewise, dramatic noncharacters such as the tailors and seamsters of *The Gypsies Metamorphosed* assume, within the fictions of which they are a part, the literal value of joints and chops. (I like to think of the "*Puritan* poach't," with eggs for eyes, as anticipating Joyce's famous description of Stephen Dedalus as "poached eyes on ghost.") Meanwhile, the weeping pig of *Bartholomew Fair* and the dancing tun and bottles of *Pleasure Reconciled to Virtue* acquire human qualities. The frontier that separates eater from eaten from inedible is traversed repeatedly in these passages, and in every possible direction. Not only does one of Ursula's Bartholomew pigs weep out an eye in the fire; Ursula also threatens her servant, Mooncalf, "In, you Rogue, and wipe the pigges, and mend the fire, that they fall not, or I'le both baste and roast you, till your eyes drop out, like 'hem" (*Bartholomew Fair* 2.5.68–71). Pig becomes man, and man becomes pig.

Such convertibility parallels the multivalence I have already remarked on within Jonson's discourse of manners. Moreover, it tends to characterize Jonson's culinary vocabulary not simply on the somatic, but on what we might call the ideological, level.[1] Not only is the distinction of eater, eaten, and uneatable multivalently unstable; so are the social, political, ethical, and religious distinctions that tend to overcode culinary activity. Not only is it unclear what constitutes food at any given moment; it is also uncertain what food means. Examples (a) and (b) above are interesting from this standpoint. On one hand, Cob's speech presents an early instance of the somatic convertibility I have already pointed out. The water carrier, named after a foodstuff, laments that fast days force him to eat his own kind—his "own fish, and bloud." Flesh becomes fish onstage in the person of Cob, simultaneously eater and eaten. But there is something else worth noting here as well. The fast day, after all, is a day of religious observance; it is also, to Cob's chagrin, a day of culinary dearth, stinking of fish and leek porridge, keeping a man devoutly hungry. Yet Cob's ambiguous status (rather like Caliban's) as man/fish hints at a transfiguration of fast into feast; to dine on one's own flesh and blood, particularly when the flesh in question has been represented as fish, is to participate in a wholly different religious observance from that of the fast. This second observance, the Eucharist, is also what emerges out of Zeal-of-the-Land Busy's foodfest in *Bartholomew Fair*. As the "rabbi" stuffs his face with turkey pie, the bread and wine on either side of him frame his gluttony with the ultimate Christian symbolism of self-abnegation.

So not only can we say that in the Jonsonian literary universe a pig is a man is a fish; we can also say that for Jonson a fast is a feast, and vice versa. Clearly the poet liked to disport himself with such ambiguities, not only in his work but in his life as well. To remain, for instance, within the eucharistic imagery we have just touched upon: Jonson told William Drummond that "after he was reconciled with the Church & left of to be a recusant at his first communion in token of true Reconciliation, he drank out all the full cup of wyne" (Drummond 314–316). Apparently this feat tickled the poet's fancy enough for him to make a point of recounting it. Likewise, it seems to have succeeded in capturing Drummond's attention. But the very thing that makes it memorable as a socioreligious gesture is also the quality that allies it to Busy's behavior in *Bartholomew Fair*: its extraordinary semiotic kinesis. In effect, Jonson signals his submission to the governance of the Church of England—his "true Reconciliation" with it—through an act that defies government, treating the Lord's Supper with the ceremony usually reserved for an all-you-can-eat breakfast buffet. The wit of the incident arises from the fact that it exists simultaneously as an act of respect and as a gesture of transgression, a ritual of personal submission and an affirmation of personal independence. Busy, whose exegetical gymnastics vis-à-vis the consumption of roast pig have been brilliantly analyzed by various scholars (Barish 201–203; Stallybrass and White 44–66), displays a similar discursive agility:

> Pigge, it is a meat, . . . and may be long'd for, and so consequently eaten . . . : but in the *Fayre*, and as a *Bartholmew*-pig, it cannot be eaten, for the very calling it a *Bartholmew*-pigge, and to eat it so, is a spice of *Idolatry*, . . . but it is subiect, to construction . . . ; there may be a good vse made of it, too, now I thinke on't: by the publike eating of Swines flesh, to professe our hate, and loathing of *Iudaisme*.
>
> (1.6.51–96)

Busy's pig, like Jonson's goblet of wine, exists simultaneously in a whole range of interpretive dimensions as food and as symbol. Indeed, the poet's ability to combine the different signifiers of his convivial and alimentary vocabulary, and in doing so to fashion the elements of dining into such complex and multifarious puns, lies at the heart of his literary practice.

Jonson's pervasive interest in the somatic and semiotic transformability of food takes on a further valence when considered in light of the poet's own changing body image. As David Riggs has observed, the dramatic expansion of the poet's waistline from 1601 to 1619 may be correlated loosely to increases both in age and in celebrity (82, 254). In any case, Jonson's late self-portrait in the epistle "To My Lady Covell" (*Underwood* 56) attests to the ravages of board and bottle; in unlovely detail, Jonson describes himself as "fat and old, / Laden with Bellie" (8–9). Continuing in this vein in the "Epistle to Mr. Arthur Squib" (*Underwood* 54), he self-consciously notes his weight as "twentie Stone; of which I lack two pound" (12). Similarly, "My Picture Left in Scotland" (*Underwood* 9) betrays the poet's embarrassment over his obesity; there Jonson laments that a prospective mistress has "read so much wast, as she cannot imbrace / My mountaine belly" (16–17) and has consequently rejected his advances. Yet in each of these verses the poet makes rhetorical capital out of his physical bulk. In "My Picture Left in Scotland," Alexander Leggatt suggests, "the delicacy of Jonson's art is somehow dependent on the grossness of his body" (219); in "To My Lady Covell," the poet turns his weight into an elaborate jest, remarking that he "doth hardly approach / His friends, but to breake Chairs, or cracke a Coach" (9–10). Jonson thus presses his own ill health and corpulence into the service of his literary reputation. In this sense, poems like "To My Lady Covell" and "My Picture Left in Scotland" seek to transform his fatness from an embarrassing disability into a virtue. His girth becomes both the vehicle and the emblem of his literary vocation.

By and large, this project seems to have succeeded. J. G. Nichols, for instance, opens a book-length study of Jonson by calling him "the heavy writer of a few light lyrics" (1). Gabriele Jackson begins another book with a despairing revision of the poet's epitaph: "O fat Ben Jonson" (5). And early biographers regularly associate Jonson's poetic achievements with his exploits as tippler and trencherman. Obesity and poetry become complementary functions of his personality; more interesting still, the personality they embody is officially dedicated to the ideals of formal balance, simplicity, and restraint. In this respect, the poet replicates his king and patron, James I, whom Leah Marcus aptly describes as "a curious and contradictory figure, combining a theoretical devotion to Stoic balance and moderation ... with a seemingly ungovernable appetite for excess" (10). Jonson's drama and poetry alike castigate vicious excess—including, in poems like "On Gut" (Epigram 118) and "To Captayne Hungry" (Epigram 107), immoderate dining—and critics of Jonson's verse regularly praise its "clarity and restraint" (Woods 84), virtues it ostensibly promotes on both the formal and thematic levels. The result is one of the more remarkable spectacles of English literary history: a famous fat man and legendary drunkard constructing a cult of personality around his own excessive girth while excoriating his contemporaries for eating and drinking too much.

This chapter aims to explore the peculiar, contradictory symbiosis between Jonson's weight and his work by invoking the fields of social practice within which his reputation develops. Thus, proceeding from Jack Goody's association of European culinary culture with "hierarchical man" (99), I begin by noting that Jonson's own addiction to the pleasures of the table parallels behavior that social historians like Lawrence Stone and Joan Thirsk document within the Stuart aristocracy as a whole. This age- and class-specific gluttony (which Stone relates to social display and conspicuous consumption) contrasts with the economic discomforts of the Jacobean peasant and merchant classes; according to one fairly recent estimate, for instance, between four-fifths and all of the average household income in early seventeenth-century England went to purchase food (Quaife 22). The conservative Stuart government, moreover, "feared the social tension bred by [economic] changes within a community of hard-pressed anxious peasants" (Thirsk 2:229), and Jonson's own transitional career propelled him from the ranks of city bricklayers to the chambers of Whitehall, where he abetted what Jonathan Goldberg calls King James's discursive "self-division" (165). It is therefore no surprise to find Jonson negotiating his own way through a similar process of literary self-division within the compass of his plays and poems.

In an earlier published version of this chapter, I suggested that gluttony is for Jonson what sex is for Foucault: both "an instrument and an effect of power" (Foucault, *History* 101). While still convinced that Foucauldian theory is correct to bring the bodily functions under scrutiny from the standpoint of political, ideological, and administrative pressures, I have come to regard post-Foucauldian analytical models of the sort proposed by Deleuze and Guattari as perhaps more sensitive to the transformational capacities of Jonson's alimentary language. The Deleuzian insistence on "linking desire to a fundamental *yes*" (*Anti-Oedipus* 244) may be particularly useful in developing our understanding of Jonson's alimentary and political rhetoric, for that rhetoric was clearly more than a defensive formation. At the very least, Deleuze and Guattari manage to replace Foucault's dark and carceral vision of western culture with something brighter, and to this extent their theories may be more responsive both to the comic element in Jonson's achievement and to the poet's capacity to refigure ideological coercion as personal emancipation. When, for instance, Deleuze and Guattari examine "transformations that blow apart semiotics systems or regimes of signs on the plane of consistency of a positive absolute deterritorialization" (*Plateaus* 136), it is clear that they are describing semiotic effects of the sort engineered by Jonson when guzzling his communion wine: "A transformational statement marks the way in which a semiotic translates for its own purposes a statement originating elsewhere. . . . The songs of black Americans, including, especially, the words would be a [good] example, since they show how the slaves 'translated' the English signifier and made presignifying or even countersignifying use of the language" (*Plateaus* 136–137). Jonson at his communion rail, like the African-American spiritual singer in the cotton fields, appropriates a religious vocabulary that has been thrust upon him through the coercive apparatus of the state, but he manages to make it into something that escapes submission to authority even in the act of manifesting that submission.

This view of Jonson's life and work carries with it certain consequences, both positive and negative, and indifferent. On the positive side, Jonson's nimble transformation of institutional doxa enables him to establish a space for personal development in terms other than those traditionally allotted by the institutions whose signifying practices he has transformed. Just as Don Wayne has argued that the resurgence of interest in perpendicular Gothic architecture in late sixteenth-century England "entailed the renormalizing of an old form to legitimize new content" (89), so Jonson's career appropriates traditional vocabularies of hospitality, manners, digestion, and so on in the service of a largely unprecedented and self-aggrandizing literary professionalism. On the negative side, this project requires intense energy, effort, and ingenuity; when it fails—as it increasingly does in the poet's more dogmatic and dependent later years—it tends to lapse into the contours of the old vocabulary the poet has sought to transform. On the indifferent side, the ethical component of Jonson's work is largely coincidental to the project of self-enabling discursive transformation that is the work's primary concern. As Jonathan Haynes has recently argued, "Emphasis on the moral and the formal in Jonson has been . . . worn out, if only by its own successes. Discussions of Jonson's historical situation are governed so entirely by these terms that the situation becomes inert and undialectical" (4). Still more recently, Robert Evans has expanded on this position, noting that "Jonson's ethical, aesthetic, and philosophical confidence seems somewhat old-fashioned today, and in any case it is hard to see how such certitude . . . can help us to a fuller, more complex, more neutral, and thus perhaps more nuanced understanding of this writer and his art" (*Contexts* 180). To a considerable extent the present argument must agree.

This is not to say that Jonson cannot use ethical distinctions and commonplaces to good effect; under the circumstances, he could hardly neglect to do so. But the ethical discourse in Jonson's work, when viewed properly, emerges as an adjunct to the more immediate and pragmatic task of expanding the poet's identity, celebrity, professional status, and waistline. In this latter capacity, Jonson's work embodies an unstable interplay between theoretically distinct notions of social order and ethical behavior. Committed on the one hand to celebrating the "civilized values" of the Stuart ruling class (Woods 84)—values that include conspicuous consumption and programmatic overindulgence in food and drink—Jonson's verse seeks on the other hand to assimilate those values to a discourse of restraint, balance, and classical severity. In the process, each of these notions of social value adopts the qualities and contours of the other, and Jonson's work thus anticipates the final scene of Orwell's *Animal Farm*, where the spectator looks "from pig to man, and from man to pig, and from pig to man again," unable to say which is which.

"Of this we shall sup free, but moderately"

Jonson has survived as the preeminent Jacobean poet of moderation. Again and again, critics have remarked on his work's simplicity, balance, and restraint. He has been credited with developing a "plain style" of writing that emphasizes "content . . . rather than expression" (Trimpi 95), and this rhetorical plainness, in turn, has been seen as serving analogous moral and aesthetic ideals. Thus, for instance, a poem like Jonson's "Inviting a Friend to Supper" (Epigram 101) can be, and consistently has been, regarded both as a "triumph of the plain style" (Loewenstein, "Corpulence" 491) and as a celebration of temperance. Douglas Duncan views it as an invitation to "true festivity"—that is, "freedom of behavior and liberty of wit, kept within the bounds of moderation and innocence" (173). Wesley Trimpi contrasts this poem to Petronius's Trimalchian feast, concluding that for both Jonson and Petronius "the richness of [a] banquet becomes a symbol for the moral poverty of the host," and argues that Jonson's ideal supper, like his epigram, avoids extravagance and vulgar ostentation (188). And Sara van den Berg, who discusses the poem at length, associates it with an Erasmian model of friendship governed by the qualities of "*humanitas, libertas,* [and] *simplicitas*"—or, as van den Berg translates these terms, "moral excellence," "free moderation," and "plainness" (60–61). In effect, these critics (and others)[2] agree that Epigram 101 constructs a utopian vision of restrained conviviality; hence Trimpi compares the poem with the *Leges Convivales* of the Apollo Room, finding within both texts an undisturbed insistence upon "moderate cups" and "refined taste rather than . . . expense" (187).

Here I intend not so much to contest these findings as to explore the conditions of their possibility. For if "Inviting a Friend to Supper" can be read as an invitation to temperate dining, the temperance the poem represents proves highly unstable. Richard Peterson rightly observes that Jonson's invitation mingles "ideas of physical and mental fullness" in a "hearty menu" that combines "morsels of Roman history" with "coneys and larks." The poem consequently emerges for Peterson as a celebration of temperance represented as satiety; and for this ideal satiety or fullness,

Peterson concludes, "Jonson's own bulk [can serve] as a fit emblem" (31). Likewise, Joseph Loewenstein regards Jonson's corpulence as a defense mechanism, "an attempt to shore up a fugitive being within a bulwark of flesh" ("Corpulence" 510).[3] Thus Epigram 101 navigates the distance from Jonson's austere classical ideals to his rotund Renaissance self—a distance that also separates the *doctus poeta* of Whitehall from Jonson the pub crawler, fat man, and rowdy.

If any single line from "Inviting a Friend to Supper" encompasses the instability of Jonson's rhetoric, it is the poet's assurance after reciting the menu: "Of this we will sup free, but moderately" (35). For a scholar like van den Berg, this assurance arrives at a welcome moment, tempering the "immoderate imagining of the menu" with a "final promise of restraint" (53). Yet the promise of restraint, in context, may call its own appropriateness into question; one may legitimately wonder, for instance, how it is possible to dine "free, but moderately" on a menu that includes eleven flesh or fowl courses, together with cheese, fruit, pastry, salad, eggs, and large quantities of wine:

> Yet shall you haue, to rectifie your palate,
>   An oliue, capers, or some better sallade
> Vshring the mutton; with a short-leg'd hen,
>   If we can get her, full of egs, and then,
> Limons, and wine for sauce: to these, a coney
>   Is not to be despair'd of, for our money;
> And, though fowle, now, be scarce, yet there are clarkes,
>   The skie not falling, thinke we may have larkes.
> Ile tell you of more, and lye, so you will come:
>   Of partrich, pheasant, wood-cock, of which some
> May yet be there; and godwit, if we can:
>   Knat, raile, and ruffe too.
>   (9–20)

The Rabelaisian expansiveness of Jonson's menu pulls against the self-announced restraint of the meal as the poet, unable to control himself, lies about the food. (Or *does* he lie? Some of the dishes, he insists, "may yet be there.") Hence the importance of Jonson's promise to "sup free, but moderately"; for if the circumstances of the meal were moderate to begin with, no such assurance would be necessary.

Yet it is precisely the moderation—indeed, even the poverty—of those circumstances that the poem begins by asserting:

> To night, graue sir, both my poore house, and I
>   Doe equally desire your companie:
> Not that we think vs worthy such a ghest,
>   But that your worth will dignifie our feast,
> With those that come; whose grace may make that seeme
>   Something, which, else, could hope for no esteeme.
> It is the fair acceptance, Sir, creates
>   The entertaynment perfect: not the cates.
>   (1–8)

The house is poor, the fare unworthy of esteem, the entertainment insufficient to attract the guest, whose presence would indeed dignify the feast. Still, having portrayed himself and his house as simple, unable to secure his guest's appearance by temptation or bribery, Jonson nonetheless immediately proceeds to attempt what he has just said he cannot possibly do: to lure the guest to supper with the promise of an extravagant meal. Hence the verse proceeds to the supper menu and the assurance that all shall "sup free, but moderately," seemingly the poet's attempt to reconcile the contradictory discursive spaces within which his poem has developed.

In this context the notion of supping free but moderately functions as an extended oxymoron, entirely typical of Jonson's wider alimentary and convivial behavior. "Inviting a Friend to Supper" seeks to create moderation out of juxtaposed and mutually exclusive extremes—both of rhetoric and of social practice. On one hand the poet assumes an air of hearty, good-natured poverty, asserting, in effect, that "we literati are simple folk." Yet as soon as this position becomes available, he snatches it back, replacing it with godwit, knat, raile, ruffe, Virgil, Tacitus, and Livy:

> My man
> Shall reade a piece of *VIRGIL, TACITVS,*
>   *LIVIE*, or of some better booke to vs,
> Of which wee'll speake our minds, amidst our meate;
>   And Ile professe no verses to repeate:
> To this, if aught appeare, which I know not of,
> That will the pastrie, not my paper, show of.
>   (20–26)

Here, in Jonson's promise not to subject his guests to his verse—a promise that, composed in verse itself, of course cannot be delivered without violating its own spirit—we may once more see the poet's typical method of producing moderate behavior. "Inviting a Friend to Supper" consistently describes expansive, even hypersophisticated pleasures (like listening to a manservant read aloud from Virgil) and then calls these offerings simple and poor. The poem immediately breaks its pledges, while cleverly ignoring the space thus generated between assertion and performance. As a result, Epigram 101 creates an interstitial space for the author: a space much like the one established in the *Leges Convivales*, which encompasses everyone and everything, and which transcends everyone and everything it encompasses.

I take the construction of this interstitial poetics to be one of Jonson's most revolutionary literary and social achievements, and in the next chapter I investigate at greater length its consequences for notions of literary professionalism. Here, however, one ought to pay some attention to the social character of Jonson's authorial voice. Stallybrass and White have observed that Jonson tends "to elide the position of poet with that of the monarch," which he unquestionably does (73). In the same vein, David Riggs has described Jonson's identification with "a self-contained aristocratic community that is answerable only to its own ancestral traditions" (180), and it may well be the case, as Riggs suggests, that it was to membership in this community that Jonson ultimately aspired.[4] But if so, the aspiration miscarried somewhat. The poet who boasted to Drummond that "he never esteemed a man for the name of a Lord" (Drummond 337), who judiciously avoided the honor of one of King James's inflated knighthoods, and who insisted that "*Poets* are far rarer births then kings" ("To Elizabeth Countesse of Rutland" [Epigram 79] 1), was clearly engaged in a complex sequence of social negotiations that includes, but cannot be limited to, an act of imaginative identification with the traditional gentry. I suspect, instead, that Jonson's interstitial poetics serves an ideal of social fluidity and not one of fixed identification, a fluidity that traditional Marxist thought has somewhat grumpily identified with inconsistencies within bourgeois subjectivity in general:

The *petit bourgeois*, by the necessity of his position, acts as part socialist and part economist, that is to say, he is dazzled by the magnificence of the big bourgeoisie and sympathizes with the sufferings of the people.... Such a petit bourgeois deifies *contradiction*, because contradiction is the basis of his existence. He himself is nothing but social contradiction, put in action.   (Marx 53)

Thus, at its most obvious, Epigram 101 invites the reader to have some homely, unpretentious brie and wash it down with a little humble Dom Perignon. One can only marvel at the superb self-assurance with which Jonson issues such an invitation, mediated as it is through the complex traditions of classical misrule and comic intemperance. Thomas Greene, describing Jonson's poetics of "the centered self" ("Self" 333), explains this peculiar behavior in typically paradoxical terms. For Greene, the morally centered Jonsonian character is "still at rest when active," rooted firmly to stable, internal values, "just as the vicious are unstable even when torpid" ("Self" 332). Yet while Greene argues that "the concept of an inner moral equilibrium . . . informs most of Jonson's verse" ("Self" 329), the contradictions of Epigram 101 support Stanley Fish's counterclaim that "the concept of an inner moral equilibrium escapes Jonson's verse which is always citing the concept as its cause, but never quite managing to display or define it" (30). That is, for Greene (and for Greene's Jonson) the notion of moral equilibrium ultimately reinscribes the scriptural adage "To the pure all things are pure" (Titus 1.15): "the married lecher is still in a sense adulterous" ("Self" 332); Jonson can eat and drink until he chokes and still remain temperate. "Captayne Hungry," by contrast, remains vile and gluttonous even when he refuses to eat ("Come, be not angrie, you are *HVNGRY*; eat; / Doe what you come for" [31–32]). Moderation becomes not something one does but something one is.

Hence the space of simple "libertie" that Epigram 101 constructs proves finally to be neither very simple nor uncomplicatedly free. Indeed, just as Jonson's menu can be both unworthy and sumptuous—and Jonson's guest can be both immune to seduction and infinitely seducible—Jonson's after-dinner conversation is both entirely free and thoroughly constrained: free because he says it is and constrained because of the complex ground rules he institutes to produce and maintain it. "[W]ee'll speake our minds, amidst our meate" (23), the poet tells his guest, but that assurance of conversational liberty, the opportunity to speak one's mind without fear, is immediately followed by a pledge to restrict speech: "Ile professe no verses to repeate" (25). Nor can this restriction apply to the host alone: "our cups [shall not] make any guiltie men" (37), the poet promises; "At our parting, we will be, as when / We innocently met" (38–39), he continues. However, these conditions cannot be fulfilled unless one can guarantee that none of the guests will repeat any verses, or conversation, either that night or the morning after. Only then can Jonson assert with total confidence, "No simple word, / That shall be vtter'd at our mirthfull boord, / Shall make us sad next morning: or affright / The libertie, that wee'll enioy to night" (39–42). As Robert Evans has remarked in a lengthy discussion of this epigram, "'Inviting a Friend to Supper' exalts a world—small, protected, and self-enclosed—in which the freedom to be oneself encourages rather than constrains the freedom of others" (*Patronage* 208); I would add that the poet emerges from his poem as the unique manufacturer and guarantor of that freedom. In contrast to its classical sources in Martial 5.78 and 10.48, Jonson's Epigram 101 imagines a convivial scene in which the security of the guests is a subset and affirmation of the author's omnipotence. The poem's closing vision of simple liberty and innocent friendship is thus fulfilled through and constituted as a series of policing gestures, whereby the party's host claims to keep his own—and his guests'—behavior within carefully defined limits.

As a result, it is thoroughly appropriate that Jonson's space of "libertie" should finally be produced and secured by the promise to police not merely the guests but the police themselves: "We will sup free, but moderately, / And we will haue no *Pooly*', or *Parrot* by; / Nor shall our cups make any guiltie men" (35–37). The freedom of the night's revelry is constructed through a process of rigorous surveillance instituted and controlled by the host. Jonson himself can guarantee safety and good cheer only by occupying an absolutist position within his poem—seeing all, controlling all, and defining all. From this position alone, totalizing and transcendent, can Jonson claim to embody the contradictions that structure his verse: humility and luxury, freedom and constraint, simplicity and sophistication, moderation and indulgence. It is only natural, then, that Jonson should describe his favorite drink, Canary wine, as a sort of ambrosial *elixir vitae*, "Of which had *HORACE*, or *ANACREON* tasted, / Their lives, as doe their lines, till now had lasted" (31–32). Tasting the cup of immortality, Jonson is no simple boozer; in a very real sense he is God, the deified, alogical self-assertions of Jonsonian authorship. For if anyone can eat and drink at will without harmful consequences, it is God.

The Politics of Overeating

In the early months of 1613, at the very time that Jonson was assembling his first and only book of epigrams, the policing of one's dining room might have struck any citizen of London as an immediate concern. That, at least, is how it struck Thomas Middleton, who in the same year satirized

Jacobean sumptuary regulations with his comedy *A Chaste Maid in Cheapside*. The preceding year had been one of "exceptional dearth" both within and outside the court (Marcus 99), the harvest of 1613 was expected to be poor, and there was widespread fear of food shortages. As a result, austerity measures were in force; a sort of Jacobean food police watched over the populace of London, enforcing the Lenten restrictions on meat with great severity. These police, or "promoters," find their way into Middleton's play as an emblem of governmental corruption,

> planted there
> To arrest the dead corpse of poor calves and sheep,
> Like ravenous creditors that will not suffer
> The bodies of their poor departed debtors
> To go to th'grave, but e'en in death to vex
> And stay the corpse, with bills of Middlesex.
> (2.2.62–67)

Prowling the streets and confiscating prohibited foodstuffs, these promoters assume the same powers of surveillance—and, by arresting corpses, the same ability to transcend life and death—that Jonson assumes for himself in Epigram 101. Moreover, they use those powers and abilities to much the same end Jonson does, creating a little private party for themselves and a few select friends, a party in which gluttony can reign under the sign of moderation: "This Lent will fat the whoresons up with sweetbreads / And lard their whores with lamb-stones; what their golls / Can clutch goes presently to their Molls and Dolls" (2.2.68–70). Thus when a client of theirs, having purchased protection for Lent, appears carrying "a rack of mutton . . . and half a lamb" (2.2.133), the promoters' vision cancels itself out at once, both working and refusing to work at the same time: "Go, go, we see thee not; away, keep close!" (2.2.135). Morality for these men, who are promoters both of the law and of themselves, takes tangible form in their ability to impose their will on others, and this ability requires not only that the promoters' prey be subject to the law but that the promoters themselves be above it.

The same self-cancellation of vision characterizes Jonson's life and achievement, allying the poet with the very spies, the Poleys and Parrats, that his verse seeks to exclude. For as Jonson promotes himself through his work, he increasingly asserts his independence from the ethical and aesthetic principles his work embodies. It is as if his qualifications as promoter of the moral law were a function of his superiority to it, a superiority to be displayed in every facet of his personal behavior. Noting "the obvious conflict between the real-life Jonson and some of his dignified artistic posturings," Arthur Marotti persuasively argues that Jonson is "an artistic schizophrenic, with a Dionysian and an Apollonian side" (210, 209). I would add that for Jonson this schizophrenia is necessary as well as convenient. That is, Jonson's literary success depends on his simultaneously playing a wide range of contradictory social and literary roles, including those described by Marx as intrinsic to "the *petit bourgeois*." Thus on the one hand, despite scholarly efforts to identify Jonson as an unabashed apologist for conservative and aristocratic values,[5] the poet cannot help but "sympathize . . . with the sufferings of the people." The most purely Roman of his plays, *Sejanus* and *Catiline*, present disturbing visions of royal and aristocratic corruption;[6] his personal life is marked by a whole series of fallings-out with various of the powers that be; and poems like "To Fine Lady Would-Be" (Epigram 62) and "To Courtling" (Epigram 72) bristle with resentment at the affectations and vices of courtiers.[7] On the other hand, however, Jonson is clearly "dazzled by the magnificence of the big bourgeoisie" and their precursors in the Stuart aristocracy. A mere glance at any of Jonson's masques will confirm the poet's capacity for flattery when under the spell of royal patronage. Hence it should be no surprise to find Jonson generating the same contradictions within his personal history, and his behavior at table supplies a crucial case in point.

"Jonson's social habits," one biographer remarks, are "legendary; whatever else, he established a lasting reputation for conviviality" (Miles 135). But Katharine Maus suggests that "something more complicated than an amiably extrovert personality . . . underlie[s] Jonson's commitment to social art" (*Roman Frame* 112)—a comment I would extend to the poet's general comportment as well. Drummond recounts an illustrative anecdote that Jonson himself reported: "At a supper wher a Gentlewoman had Given [Jonson] unsavory wild-foul & yrafter to wash sweet water, he commendet her that shee gave him sueet water, because her flesh stinked" (464–466). This self-promotion, of the Shavian "Madam, *you* smell; I stink" variety, betrays more self-assertive wit than amiable extroversion; Jonson emerges as a memorable bon vivant precisely because he refuses to restrain his behavior. David Riggs has argued that Ovid's banquet in *Poetaster* was conceived as an attack upon the social grossness of John Marston (74–75), and Riggs offers, as an example of that grossness, the following incident from the diary of John Manningham:

[Marston] daunct with Alderman Mores wives daughter, a Spaniard borne, fell into a strang commendacion of hir witt and beauty. When hee had done, shee thought to pay him home, and told him shee though[t] he was a poet. "'Tis true," said he, "for poets faine, and lie, and soe did I when I commended your beauty, for you are exceeding foule." (133)

But the truly remarkable thing about this anecdote, when viewed in conjunction with Jonson's remark about his hostess's stinking flesh, is how very little space separates it from the poet's own idea of a socially acceptable witticism. Marston addresses a woman, and so does Jonson; Marston offers his woman a "commendacion" of her beauty, while Jonson offers his a commendation of her "sueet water"; then each man reinflects the compliment so as to malign the foul appearance or stinking flesh of the woman in question. Not only does Jonson proudly engage in insulting behavior of a sort very similar to that which he satirizes in others; in doing so, he scorns the very kinds of social regulation that he promotes in "Inviting a Friend to Supper" and in his house rules for the Apollo Room, where "*Joci sine felle sunto.*" The result is certainly a monumental literary reputation, built in large part on dazzling and protean displays of comic resourcefulness (although, in my opinion, the stinking-flesh remark is not the most successful of these). But Jonson's career as a whole can hardly be called an unambiguous triumph of ethical vision or good-natured conviviality.

Other biographical sources record similar stories. For instance, Aubrey describes Jonson as entertaining King James with an impromptu grace that concludes by blessing "the Drawer at the Swanne Tavernne by Charing-Cross, who drew him good Canarie." "For this Drollery," Aubrey continues, "his Majestie gave him an hundred pounds" (179). Whether or not the report is reliable, Aubrey's remarks attest to the recognized connection between Jonson's reputation for drinking and his success as a writer. His Falstaffian behavior licenses him to cavort with the king of England and to be himself crowned king of poets; the more he overindulges in food and drink and audacity, the more he confirms his unique social and literary privilege. A display of wit described in Winstanley's *Lives of the Most Famous English Poets* (1687) shows this behavior at its obvious extreme and, if reliably reported, can easily have appalled its principal witnesses:

[Jonson] having been drinking in an upper room, at the *Feathers*-Tavern in *Cheap side*, as he was coming down stairs, his foot slipping, he caught a fall, and tumbling against a door, beat it open into a room where some Gentlemen were drinking *Canary*; recovering his feet, he said, *Gentlemen, since I am so luckily fallen into your company, I will drink with you before I go.* (124)

In Jonson's ideal monarchy of letters, not only can the poet drink until he is unable to stand, his sodden pratfalls become the stuff of nimble wit and are rewarded with—naturally—more wine.

Jonson's behavior in this last anecdote suggests the social grounding of his reputation, for it parallels one of Jacobean history's most famous moments of drunken immobility. The year is 1606, the place is Sir Robert Cecil's residence at Theobalds (soon to become crown property), the horrified spectator is Sir John Harington, and the inebriated principals are none other than King James I of England and King Christian IV of Denmark:

A great feast was held, and after dinner, the representation of Solomon his Temple and the coming of the Queen of Sheba was made, or (as I may better say) was meant to have been made, before their Majesties. . . . But, alass! . . . The Lady who did play the Queens part, did carry most precious gifts to both their Majesties; but, forgetting the steppes arising to the canopy, overset her caskets into his Danish majesties lap, and fell at his feet, tho I rather think it was in his face. . . . His Majesty then got up and would dance with the Queen of Sheba; but he fell down and humbled himself before her, and was carried to an inner chamber and laid on a bed of state; which was not a little defiled with the presents of the Queen which had been bestowed on his garments. . . .The entertainment and show went forward, and most of the presenters went backward, or fell down; wine did so occupy their upper chambers. (Harington 119)

While Harington's sardonic account proceeds famously to lament this spectacle, only an unsympathetic disposition finally separates his narrative from Winstanley's. Elsewhere King James could find sympathy aplenty, not least of all from Jonson himself. As Joseph Loewenstein notes, Jonson's masques display a fondness for matters of food and drink, fatness and revelry, and in *Pleasure Reconciled to Virtue* the Mount of Atlas, the "anthromountain," functions as a symbol of "roial education" ("Corpulence" 506). The relation between Jonson's authority and James's is oddly symbiotic: Jonson derives his privileged status from James's approval and returns that approval to James in part by representing "roial education" as a figure of indulgent corpulence.

In short, Jonson's work absorbs a popular Jacobean strategy for social aggrandizement: conspicuous consumption in the name of an all-powerful and all-virtuous monarch.[8] As Robert Evans has observed, "Jonson's comic catalogue of lavish food" in Epigram 101 "has the serious effect of reminding us of real, genuinely lavish banquets of the sort that were increasingly common in the Jacobean period" (*Patronage* 210). Indeed, so do some of

Jonson's surviving scribbles, including the marginalia in his personal copy of Peter Scriverius's 1619 edition of Martial's epigrams. This volume, now at the Folger Library, contains perhaps the most extensive interpretive notes to have survived from Jonson's hand, and they are most frequent, as David McPherson has observed (69), in Martial's thirteenth book. There the marginalia of Jonson's volume carefully record the gifts of food and drink that are the subject of Martial's verses; translate the Latin names for foodstuffs into their English equivalents; and produce, in the process, a truly Rabelaisian improvement on the bill of fare from Epigram 101. A very limited transcript of Jonson's notes (sigs. S1r-S7r) gives us, among other things,

Pepper. Beccafico. Frumenty. Metheglin. Meathe. Beane-*broth. Boyld-wheat* or *Barly. Lentels. wheat-floure....Dormise in the winter....*Godwits or *Knots. A crambd Hen. A fat capon....Partrich....Pidgeons....The ring-dove ... Peacock.* The purple-*Wing.* The *Pheasant.* The Turkey or *Guinea-hen.* The Goose. *Cranes. A woodcock or snipe.* The *Swan.... A Mullet. The Lamprey. The Turbot.* The *Hare.* The *Wild bore.* Fallow *deare.* The *Stag.*

Such sedulous annotation, concentrated as it is, attests to Jonson's scholarly industry, but it also suggests the particular attraction that such expansive lists of food could exert upon the poet's mind. It is as if here on the page Jonson could feel free to manufacture a machinic assemblage of culinary representation: a catalog of gastronomic delights to rival anything served on a courtly table. The dishes reserved for great men's feasts become Jonson's own conceptual and linguistic property through his study of earlier poets and their response to the circumstances of patronage.

At his best, thus, Jonson deploys his patronage vocabulary in such a novel and flexible way as to make the standard gestures of the court toady into a brilliant affirmation of personal independence. Nor is Jonson alone in seeking to revise the semiotics of conspicuous consumption; Robert Cecil's abortive attempt to rationalize taxation through the Great Contract of 1610 was at least partly driven by a desire to consolidate James's income after seven years of lavish court spending. Thus at least one major Jacobean legislative initiative sought to generate social reform out of courtly frivolity, and the implications of this project would have been clear to any of the socially mobile figures who, like Jonson, had built their fortunes on "important offices of state, professional careers, or success in business" (Thirsk 2:273, 286). On the other hand, the evasions and ambiguities through which Jonson manufactures his authorial persona are necessarily under constant pressure from various social and political institutions, not least of all the court at Whitehall. Jonson achieves his greatest prominence at court by composing masques (like the lost, anonymous *Solomon and Sheba* described in Harington's letter) to accompany royal feasting—works that complement the general caloric excess of the Jacobean table by mustering some of the most memorably exaggerated rhetoric of James's reign. Indeed, only when viewed through the glass of courtly behavior can Jonson's own eleven-course exercise in literary dyspepsia, "Inviting a Friend to Supper," assume the contours of moderation. For the inflationary tendencies of Jonson's verse find an even fuller expression in the banquets of the Stuart nobility. As André Simon, editor of *The Start Chamber Dinner Accounts*, observes, the worthy justices of the chamber were served "about 10 lb. of beef per Lord and per meal," a figure that, supplemented by a wide range of other flesh and fowl, "appears excessive, to say the least" (3). Likewise, one may recall Lawrence Stone's account of the great feast with which Lord Hay welcomed the French ambassador to Essex House in 1621: "There were 12 pheasants in one dish, 24 partridges in another, 144 larks in a third, a couple of swans in a fourth, a couple of pigs in a fifth. There were half a dozen enormous salmon from Russia, 6 feet long. The sweetmeats cost L500, the 6 lb. of ambergris used in the cooking cost another L300" (561). For Lord Hay, the food placed on the table is largely there to be wasted, and this waste confirms both his own status and that of his guests, whose "worth will dignifie [his] feast."

Thus Jonson is in constant and ambiguous touch with the kinds of gluttonous excess that disfigure characters like Volpone:

> A gem, but worth a priuate patrimony,
> Is nothing: we will eate such at a meale.
> The heads of parrats, tongues of nightingales,
> The braines of peacoks, and of estriches
> Shall be our food.
>   (3.7.200–204)

This observation squares with Don Wayne's argument that the "solidity and integrity" celebrated in Jonson's epideictic verse are "signified by . . . the same process that serves to designate the fantastic wealth imagined by Volpone and Sir Epicure Mammon and which Jonson represents in his plays as unnatural and excessive" (122). Indeed, Jonson as courtier finally cannot help participating in the same patterns of consumption and display that Jonson as moral critic denounces, for his own socioliterary transitionality requires that he live in at least two worlds at once. Maus identifies the problem succinctly: "Jonson praises his truest friendships by calling them 'free' . . . he deplores flattery as a corruption of the independence upon which real friendship is based" (*Roman Frame* 119). Still, Jonson's own formidable talents as a courtly flatterer are crucial in enabling him to promote his ideas of friendship, independence, and personal integrity. As a child of humble parents and as a former bricklayer and soldier, he insists that personal worth and moral value are independent of courtly display, that the true friend and worthy supper guest cannot be bought or coerced, yet it is precisely his participation in the discourse of display that validates his voice and leads to the material and professional success he enjoys. That success itself is a splendid thing, but it is not without its ironies, nor does it fail to exact a price from the poet who enjoys it. Hence the sad case of Ben Jonson: in order to assert his notion of moral value successfully, he transgresses it in the same gesture; he becomes the monarch of literary moderation by weighing 280 pounds.

Magic Kingdoms

For Jonson, ethical absolutism and royal absolutism end up occupying the same space, and it is through the latter that one affirms the former. This insight may help explain the "self-justification" that Goldberg has detected in Jonson's royalism (225). Jonson repeatedly signals the presence of an "inner moral equilibrium" by pointing to figures—the king, a particular nobleman or noblewoman, the poet himself in various guises—whose social status places them beyond the moral code and censure of others, situating them in another country entirely, as it were. Pig becomes man and man becomes pig, as in Orwell's metaphor, for the behavior of such figures is no longer an index of their moral stature. Thus an impulse to absolutist transcendence infiltrates Jonson's language at all levels. Even when the poet insists most adamantly that he is simple folk, celebrating simple values, he has always already seized a position of unique transsocial privilege.

In "To Penshurst" (*The Forest* 2), similar transformative patterns recur, now relatively uncomplicated by the classical resonances of Epigram 101. Jonson celebrates the family estate of the Sidneys in part by pretending it is a sort of agrarian Disney World: a magic kingdom replete with fauns, satyrs, and enchanted copses, maintained "with no mans ruine, no mans grone" (46), accessible to and beloved by all equally—"the farmer, and the clowne" (48) as well as King James and Prince Henry. This social utopianism culminates, predictably, in the poet's own promotion to king, for at Penshurst one's comforts are limitless and promiscuous: "All is there; / As if thou, then, wert mine, or I raign'd here" (73–74)—"Where the same beere, and bread, and self-same wine, / That is his Lordships, shall be also mine" (63–64). Yet to be king, as Don Wayne has pointed out (76–77), Jonson himself must be served, and he is ("A waiter . . . / giues me what I call, and lets me eate" [68–69]); to be an authoritative exponent of civilized leisure, the poet must be able to poke gentle fun at the clumsiness of those less refined than he, and he does ("Some bring a capon, some a rurall cake, / Some nuts, some apples; some that thinke they make / The better cheeses, bring 'hem; or else send / By their ripe daughters" [51–54]). Service continues, class distinctions remain, and in fact, as Raymond Williams has argued, Jonson's Penshurst is characterized by "a prolonged delight in an organised and corporative production and consumption . . . which is the basis of many early phases of intensive agriculture" (30). Still the poem manages, by sheer rhetorical determination, to consider such facts somehow inessential, as if, for instance, Penshurst could actually feed itself by Disney magic: "What can this . . . / Adde to thy free prouisions, farre aboue / The neede of such?" (57–59). The entertainment at Penshurst, like that of Epigram 101, is "free" to the point of "gluttony" (68) at the same time that the estate itself is modest, even relatively humble ("Not . . . built to enuious show, / Of touch, or marble," with no "row / Of polish'd pillars, or a roofe of gold: / . . . no lantherne, whereof tales are told; / Or stayre, or courts" [1–5]). In short, Penshurst becomes a perfect night spot for the author of "Inviting a Friend to Supper." Small wonder, then, that the poet enters his work in person only once: at the dinner table (65–75).

Similarly, Jonson reissues his supper invitation in 1629, and this time the results are not so gratifying:

> *You are welcome, welcome all, to the new* Inne;
> *Though the old house, we hope our cheare will win*
> *Your acceptation: we ha' the same Cooke,*
> *Still, and the fat, who sayes, you sha' not looke*
> *Long, for your bill of fare, but euery dish*
> *Be seru'd in, i'the time, and to your wish.*
>   (*The New Inn*, prologue 1–6)

Casting himself as a jolly, obliging cook, the poet promises to entertain his audience promptly and according to its "wish." As in Epigram 101, he prays for his guests' "acceptation"—their "fair acceptance"—but he immediately provides for the chance that it will be withheld, in effect remarking that disapproval is illness: "*If any thing be set to a wrong taste, / 'Tis not the meat there, but the mouth's displac'd, / Remoue but that sick palat, all is well*" (Prologue.9–11). Thus the geniality of "Inviting a Friend to Supper," repeated in the prologue to *The New Inn*, once more accommodates an absolutist dimension, too. Indeed, when *The New Inn* flops ignominiously, Jonson finds himself in the aftermath of a supper party like that of Epigram 101, with the guests irritated and his hospitality embarrassed. His response is to vilify the company at large.

Thus Jonson's second "Ode to Himself" replaces the swelling menu of Epigram 101 with a collection of sweepings, swill, and crusts:

> No doubt some mouldy tale,
> Like *Pericles*; and stale
> As the Shrieues crusts, and nasty as his fish-
> scraps, out [of] euery dish,
> Throwne forth, and rak't into the common tub,
> May keepe vp the *Play-club*:
> There, sweepings doe as well
> As the best order'd meale.
> For, who the relish of these ghests will fit,
> Needs set them, but, the almes-basket of wit.
> (21–30)

The fat, friendly cook of *The New Inn* unexpectedly metamorphoses into a disdainful nobleman who proposes to feed the common sort with sweepings from his table. As the posture of just-folks humility collapses, so too does Jonson's reputation for temperance and restraint. The poet's "Senecan ideal of perfect composure beneath Fortune's blows was beyond his capabilities" (Barton, "*The New Inn*" 398); the plain style and its vaunted moral equilibrium dissolve into a rage that, as the *Norton Anthology*'s notes suggest, "comes close to incoherence" (Abrams et al. 1:934 n. 2).

Yet, in Jonas Barish's words, "the presence of tension in Jonson reveals itself most obviously in his insistent claim to be without tension: the oftener he protests his imperturbability, the less we are inclined to believe it"

(87). Thus it is typical that the "Ode to Himself," one of Jonson's angriest and most violent poems, should ultimately transport the poet to the same serene space of literary nirvana marked out by the spirits of Horace and Anacreon in Epigram 101. Reviling the popular stage, Jonson exhorts himself to

> Leaue things so prostitute,
>   And take the *Alcaick* Lute;
> Or thine owne *Horace*, or *Anacreons* Lyre;
>   Warme thee, by *Pindares* fire:
> And though thy nerues be shrunke, and blood be cold,
>   Ere yeares haue made thee old;
>   Strike that disdaine-full heate
>   Throughout, to their defeate:
> As curious fooles, and enuious of thy straine,
> May, blushing, sweare no palsey's in thy braine.
>   (41–50)

Snubbed by his living supper guests, the poet seeks refuge with the dead ones; his rhetoric shrinks, as Greene would have it, "inward to a harder and isolated core" of independent selfhood ("Self" 347). There, divorced from "the immediate, heterogeneous crowd" (Womack 22), Jonson reemerges vigorous, successful, and unpalsied.

Yet even in its most concertedly isolated moments, the Jonsonian literary imagination manages somehow to connect with and even encompass the world in which it is situated. Even when withdrawn into his "beleaguered central self" (Greene, "Self" 329), Jonson nevertheless ends up referring the validity of that self and its values back to the social relation. He is talking, after all, not "to Himself" but (despite his refusal of direct address) to the very "curious fooles" whom his verse so elaborately scorns:

> But, when they hear thee sing
>   The glories of thy *King*,
> His zeale to *God*, and his iust awe o're men;
>   They may [be] blood-shaken, then.
>   (51–54)

In effect, Jonson signals his superiority to his detractors by excluding them from the special relation between sovereign and poet—by policing them out of the supper parties for which he had so long written the verses of entertainment. If, as John Sweeney comments, the theater "forced a choice between the approval of a select audience of judicious spectators and the approval of the 'beast multitude'" (208), Jonson's select audience has now disappeared entirely, only to be reconstituted within and by the poet himself, through a kind of literary *creatio ex nihilo*. Indeed, the "Ode to Himself" has no choice but to forget that Jonson is no longer writing masques for his monarch. *Love's Triumph through Callipolis* would not be commissioned for another year, nor would Jonson receive any noteworthy financial subsidy from King Charles until well after the failure of *The New Inn*. Thus the poet finds himself substantially fabricating a privileged relation to the king in order to compensate for the damaged relation to his theater audience. It is only a final irony that *The New Inn* seems to be "conscious critic[ism] of the court and the abuses prevalent within it" (Champion 102); if this assessment is valid, Jonson counters his popular critics by taking shelter within a court that he himself has just assailed in his latest play.

In responding to the unfortunate circumstances that generate the second "Ode to Himself," Jonson affirms the authority of his "centered self" by compromising its very centeredness and centrality. The Horace and Anacreon of Jonsonian classicism amalgamate with the politics of conspicuous consumption, and even when Jonson pretends to be talking to himself, he is mounting yet another literary spectacle for the benefit of others. As Harris Friedberg remarks, Jonson's verse seeks "a point of contact between the realms of poetic language and ordinary reality," aiming to affirm the poet's personal values and identity "in nature" (118), but what it discovers, instead of a point of contact, is a point of mutual absorption. The ideal of stoic restraint melts into the coercive, self-assertive rhetoric of dinner invitations and drunken tomfoolery: "Huskes, draffe to drinke, and swill." A failed supper party turns honored and noble guests into livestock from the common street. Pig becomes man, and man becomes pig.

A Private Patrimony

Instead of finding a point of contact between distinct symbolic orders, Jonson's second "Ode to Himself" discovers an avenue of deterritorialization. His discourse of moderation—assertions of stoic calm, gestures toward classical restraint and the plain style, and the pretense of cheerful humility—metamorphoses into the language of royal absolutism and autocratic display. Conversely, absolute monarchy, "The *unrestrained* presence of the sovereign" (Foucault, *Discipline* 49; my italics), repeatedly emerges in Jonson's work as the embodiment and origin of the golden mean. This absorption results naturally from the poet's complex attempts to modulate between conflicting social positions. As Don Wayne argues, personal circumstances require Jonson "to go beyond the existing hierarchical system for grounding social and psychological identity, to derive his truth and his being from a prior order, a natural order first codified in the texts of antiquity" (150). Yet Jonson's success in asserting the validity of this "prior order" depends very largely on his rendering it acceptable to "the existing hierarchical system." Without such acceptance, Jonson is at best doomed in his lifetime to genteel literary obscurity; at worst, he becomes a "poor crackbrain" whose critics suggest that he give up playwriting for innkeeping (Miles 241).

While agreeing with Wayne that Jonsonian classicism is "potentially if not intentionally egalitarian" (151), I would add that Jonson's egalitarianism necessarily remains potential. Deleuze and Guattari have argued that "What is proper to the minority is to assert a power of the nondenumerable, even if that minority is composed of a single member" (*Plateaus* 470). A clear advantage of Jonson's interstitial poetics is that they place the poet—an exemplary minority of one—beyond numeration, within and outside of everyone and everything. This characteristic of Jonson's verse displays distinct egalitarian potential; it propels the poet to a position that is equal to everything and everyone else in the universe, irrespective of distinctions in ascribed rank, class, or office. Yet this dynamic of self-promotion is by no means a reciprocal construct. Jonson opens the door to social self-advancement only far enough to accommodate his own mountain belly, and then he slams it shut. The poet functions as a synecdochic representation of a principle of universal social mobility, a principle that the poet, as the world in little, plays out within himself for the benefit of the world at large.

I began this chapter by citing various instances of Jonson's polymorphous culinary vocabulary, with its emphasis on somatic and ideological transformability. I then proceeded, through a reading of some limited texts, to identify this transformability as a general principle of Jonsonian authorial procedure and of Jonson's authorial self-construction. But, of course, the most celebrated instance of protean transformation in the Jonson canon is also the poet's most successful villain: Volpone. Volpone's efforts to woo Celia (3.7) arguably comprise the dramatic moment in which

Jonson allows the freest and most resonant play to the generative principle. As such, the seduction scene focuses the remarkable enumerative and transformative energies of the play as a whole.

Anne Barton has memorably described *Volpone*'s characters as "rummaging through the contents of some gothic lumber-room of the imagination, turning out tooth-picks and baboons, oranges, musk-melons, apricots, porpoises and lion-whelps, tinderboxes, onions, sprats, frayed stockings and Selsey cockles. There is a sense in which Mosca's inventory in the third scene of Act Five . . . is the single most representative act of the play" (*Jonson* 109). Indeed, it is no dramaturgical accident that the seduction scene concludes with an abortive rape; Volpone's language has been so expansive and mobile, his blandishments so resourceful and vigorous, that nothing less than an attempt at ravishment can reconfirm his status as villain. Moreover, the attempt at rape itself enacts a genitalized sexuality that seems not only appalling but somehow beside the point, decidedly anticlimactic, pedestrian and disappointing, after Volpone's remarkable language. As Richmond Barbour has noted, "Volpone does not woo only Celia in his dilation. . . . He reaches a state of overdetermined excitation, a multiply libidinous meantime" that "literalizes Gilles Deleuze and Felix Guattari's concept of the plateau: 'a continuous, self-vibrating region of intensities whose development avoids any orientation toward a culmination point'" (1010). Or, to revise Coleridge's famous remark about *Othello*, *Volpone*'s enumerations seem to enact the form seeking of a formless generativity.

This form seeking—an open-ended, fluid exploration of the possibilities of becoming—would seem more than anything else to epitomize Volpone's idea of a good time. It certainly invests the language with which he tempts Celia, language that returns us to the familiar Jonsonian tropes of alimentary transformation, this time with a vengeance:

> See, behold,
> What thou art queene of; not in expectation,
> As I feed others: but possess'd, and crown'd.
> See, here, a rope of pearle; and each, more orient
> Then that the braue *Aegyptian* queene carrous'd:
> Dissolue, and drinke 'hem . . .
> A gem, but worth a priuate patrimony,
> Is nothing: we will eate such at a meale.
> The heads of parrats, tongues of nightingales,

> The braines of peacoks, and of estriches
> Shall be our food: and, could we get the phoenix,
> (Though nature lost her kind) shee were our dish.
>   (3.7.188–205)

Volpone, like Sir Epicure Mammon with his barbels' beards for salads, is committed to traversing the boundaries between what can be eaten, what is eaten, what cannot be eaten, and who does the eating. The result is a world in which all activity seems to acquire a gustatory dimension. Volpone "feeds" the dupes Corvino, Corbaccio, and Voltore "in expectation"; they eat the air, promise-crammed. Yet Volpone contrasts this fake eating not to the literal ingestion of traditional meats, but to another sort of apparently fake eating entirely: "A gem, but worth a priuate patrimony, / Is nothing: we will eate such at a meale."

The distinctive character of this image derives from its ability to signify on at least three different planes at once. On the most obvious level, to eat a gem is not to eat at all, but rather to detach the practice of personal ornament from its customary position on the body's surface and to reterritorialize it within the alimentary tract. To this extent, to eat a "gem, but worth a priuate patrimony" is apparently to do the impossible, and that is a large part of the point of Volpone's seduction speech. But on a second level, the digestive reterritorialization of jewelry is available to Volpone not just as a contradiction in terms but also as a redefinition of terms; we arrive at the gem worth a private patrimony only via reference to "a rope of pearle; and each, more orient / Then that the braue *Aegyptian* queene carrous'd." The carousal in question, recorded in Pliny's *Natural History* (9.120–121), is made possible precisely by Cleopatra's ability to think in terms of the literal ingestion of jewelry—terms that, counter-intuitive as they are, elude Mark Antony:

> When Antony was gorging daily at recherche banquets, [Cleopatra] poured contempt on all his pomp and splendour, and when he asked what additional magnificence could be contrived, replied that she would spend 10,000,000 sesterces on a single banquet. . . . Consequently bets were made, and . . . in accordance with previous instructions the servants placed in front of her only a single vessel containing vinegar, the strong rough quality of which can melt pearls. She was at the moment wearing in her ears that remarkable and truly unique work of nature. Antony was full of curiosity to see what in the world she was going to do. She took one earring off and dropped the pearl in the vinegar, and when it was melted swallowed it. (3:245)

[Haec [Cleopatra], cum exquisitis cotidie Antonius saginaretur epulis, ... lautitiam eius apparatumque omnem obstrectans, quaerente eo quid adstrui magnificentiae posset respondit una se cena centiens HS absumpturam. . . . Ergo sponsionibus factis . . . , ex praecepto ministri unum tantum vas ante eam posuere aceti cuius asperitas visque in tabem margaritas resolvit. Gerebat auribus cum maxime singulare illud et vere unicum naturae opus. Itaque expectante Antonio quidnam esset actura detractum alterum mersit et liquefactum obsorbuit.]

So Volpone seems to be pointing Celia toward a world in which gems are both inedible and edible at the same time—in which the very implausibility of drinking a pearl freights the gesture with indescribable opulence and attraction. There is, further, a third level on which this image acquires additional resonance, for the inedible gem may be refigured into foodstuffs not simply by pulverizing it in vinegar, but via the process of economic conversion. In this latter sense, Volpone and Celia will eat the gem not by literally ingesting it, but by transforming it into an abstract metaphorical equivalent—an exchange value that represents its use value—and then re-solidifying this abstraction of the gem's value in a commodity of foodstuffs. In short, they will buy dinner with an amount of cash equivalent to the value of the gem. In the process, moreover, they will further complicate Volpone's alimentary conversions by subjecting the dining room to the "*principle* of exchange-value or liquidity" that according to Jean-Christophe Agnew transformed seventeenth-century English society by "translating the infinitely various contents of that society into a rich and readily transactionable stock" (53).

Given a commitment to this sort of liquidity, it is no wonder that Volpone should proceed with his seduction-speech by continuing to treat the bodily outside as the bodily inside, and vice versa:

Thy bathes shall be the iuyce of iuly-flowres,
Spirit of roses, and of violets,
The milke of vnicornes, and panthers breath
Gather'd in bagges, and mixt with *cretan* wines.
Our drinke shall be prepared gold, and amber;
Which we will take, vntill my roofe whirle round
With the *vertigo*.
(3.7.213–219)

In one sense, this passage simply foregrounds certain culinary tendencies Patricia Fumerton has described within Jacobean void dining as a whole;

to drinke "prepared gold, and amber" would not be entirely incongruous in a society whose comfit makers could on occasion add small quantities of gold leaf and pearl dust to their preparations.[9] But Volpone is clearly no pedestrian epicure. For him the gold and amber are not infused into the drink; they *are* the drink. Likewise, of course, "*cretan* wines" and "the milke of vnicornes" become substances to bathe in rather than to digest. Ingredient becomes whole, outside becomes inside, inside becomes outside, and, in a final grand gesture, Volpone's surroundings are invested with his own drunken dizziness: "*My roof* [shall] whirl round / With the vertigo" (my italics).

The sum of this fantasy—as Richmond Barbour has argued (1010)—comes close to embodying the Deleuzian "'plateau', a 'plane of consistency' or 'level of intensities' which traverses any number of traditional disciplinary domains and levels of analysis" (Bogue 125). If Deleuzian theory aspires to undo the philosophy of interiority, and therefore necessarily to "do away [with] any static concept of the body" (Jardine 49), then Volpone's somatic conversions and Deleuzian thought clearly aspire to similar ends. For Deleuze and Guattari a plane of consistency is, first and foremost, a way to dispense with static terms of individuation; a state of "pure intensities, free, prephysical and prevital singularities" (*Plateaus* 58), it develops through the heightened operation of desire as Deleuze and Guattari characterize that concept. Deleuzian desire, in turn, must be understood outside the western tradition, from Plato to Lacan, that identifies it as a consequence of lack or deficiency. For Deleuze and Guattari, on the contrary, desire is a preconscious, prephysical force similar to the Nietzschean will to power; it knows no negatives and it animates everything, creating an infinite series of possibilities for motion and flux. Such motion is effected through couplings of "heterogeneous, independent parts" (Bogue 92) into interconnected sequences that can be formed of anything and can channel desire polymorphously. The hand, for instance, can be viewed as part of an assemblage for crawling, signing, digging, fighting, writing, throwing, and more; stones may function alternatively within a piling assemblage, a hurling assemblage, a splitting assemblage, a collecting assemblage, and so on. The availability of such assemblages allows desire to flow in any number of different forms or directions. For Deleuze and Guattari, the heightened operation of these assemblages generates the "plane of consistency"—"a multiplicity that cannot be understood in terms of the traditional problems of the One and the Many, of origins and genesis, or of deep structures, in which any point can be connected with any other point, and any sequence of elements broken at any juncture" (Bogue 125).

Volpone's desire flows in just this way: multiply, on various levels, in headlong sequences of enumeration, without settling within a single function or organ. That, in part, is why his final decision to rape Celia affords such a glaring contrast to what has gone before. It is at just this moment that the flow ceases and the wooer's energies gather focus, congealed into a sadistic genitality that is both tawdry and all too familiar. During the preceding seduction speeches, on the other hand, multiplicity and kinesis are the rule, operating constantly and without culmination, and nicely embodied in the tension between numeration and infinitude of Volpone's song to Celia:

> We may, so, trans-fuse our wandring soules,
> Out at our lippes, and score vp summes of pleasures,
> *That the curious shall not know,*
> *How to tell them, as they flow;*
> *And the enuious, when they find*
> *What their number is, be pind.*
> (3.7.234–239)

This is not to claim that Jonson is of Volpone's party without knowing it. On the contrary, we might better understand Jonson's work and achievement if we dispensed entirely with static categories of the kind that make such wholesale ethical identifications possible in the first place. This is also not to say that we dispense with the categories themselves: for Jonson, the traditional ethical labels necessarily persist, and they may be applied nimbly to almost anyone at almost any moment. They are most advantageous from the standpoint of socioliterary practice insofar as they remain intrinsically meaningless; they form and re-form like iron filings in a magnetic field. This view of matters has the advantage of explaining why the poet should be obsessed with ethical distinctions and simultaneously committed to a mode of personal behavior and to an aesthetic that repeatedly bend such distinctions beyond practical recognition. In the next chapter, we consider the effect of Jonson's ethical distinctions on his theory of literary imitation and ownership, which George Rowe has nicely described as "a particularly militant form of comparison whose final goal is contrast" (21). In the meantime, however, we may note that Jonson's distinctive way of thinking about the body, as evidenced by his consistent fascination with patterns of alimentary convertibility, offers a model for his political, ethical, social, and aesthetic practices as well. In a series of formulations that could have come directly from Orwell's Ministry of Truth, Jonson claims that anger is calm, surveillance is liberty, nobility is humble, and drunken gourmandise is sober diet. This strategy rehabilitates the fat Jonson of courtly excess in the image of an almost revolutionary classical severity, much like the Roman republican virtue that later inspired revolutionary movements in England, France, and America. Thus Jonson's language leaves the poet vigorous, potent, unpalsied, and privileged—free to go on overeating forever.

This view of Jonson as a revolutionary poet, even as one whose revolutionary tendencies are limited or compromised, may strike some as peculiar, for modern criticism has typically regarded Jonson as an entrenched conservative. From Edmund Wilson's famous description of the poet as an anal-erotic preoccupied with hoarding goods (213–232) to Wayne's more recent remark that "Jonson is generally regarded as a traditionalist and a conservative" (152), this position has proved justly influential. It should be clear that I do not entirely reject this view of matters; instead, I aim to explain how Jonsonian virtue, with its unmistakably revolutionary tendencies, consistently transforms itself into a principle of royal conservatism, and vice versa. In this context it may be useful once more to recall Barish's remark that "tension in Jonson reveals itself most obviously in his insistent claim to be without tension." For where does Jonson make this claim more frenetically than in his celebrations of Jacobean absolutism? Marcus, for instance, has demonstrated how Jonson's masques, for all their extravagant commitment to the Stuart monarchy, laid the groundwork for Milton's *Comus*, a work that "writes Charles I and his policies [out of] the heavens" (182). And when Jonson—jailed for indirectly mocking King James in *Eastward Ho* (Chute 151–52)—asks of his monarch, "Who would not be thy subject, *James*, t'obay / A Prince, that rules by'example, more than sway?" ("To King James" [Epigram 35] 1–2), it is hard to view the question as entirely unconflicted. One may therefore legitimately ask under what conditions Jonson is able to succeed as James's chief metrical panegyrist.

The principal such condition may well have been one of political and ethical flux, a flux that in turn demanded the wholesale, ongoing transformability of Jonson's moral and aesthetic ideals. Thus, although I agree with Loewenstein's assertion that "for Jonson . . . an ethics of moderation was adaptive, part of the protection of an endangered liberty" ("Corpulence" 501), I would like to supplement that observation with another that is both immanent and contradictory to Loewenstein's view: that Jonson's liberty—his freedom to write and to eat and, most importantly of all, to succeed—depends on his ability to transform the ethics of moderation itself so as to adapt it to intersecting and contradictory pressures. At its best, this adaptation leaves the poet with something very like the space to which he aspires in Epigram 101: a space of liberty and unprecedented self-empowerment, maintained, like Volpone's schemes, by a constant, resourceful redefinition of linguistic categories. It is only one last irony of Jonson's situation—and one I think the poet himself would have appreciated—that his linguistic and ethical transformations eluded the capacities of the social order within which they developed. Jonson's verse may redeem the excesses of Jacobean courtly behavior on the page, but the unfortunate first Lord Coleraine choked to death in 1667 while "endeavouring to swallow the rump of a turkey" (Stone 561). He should not have tried Jonson's tricks at home.

3
A Well-Digested Work

THE IMMEDIATE SUBJECT OF THIS CHAPTER, Jonson's investment in the principle of digestion as an analogue for his ideas of literary production, has received important notice from various scholars. Richard Peterson, for one, has emphasized the poet's use of "digestive and apian metaphors" to characterize the process of selective absorption upon which Jonson based much of his poetic theory (9). For Peterson, "'Fullness' and good digestion are everything in [Jonsonian] imitation," distinguishing "the true imitator, who reads in many authors and in an assimilative spirit" from "bad imitators [who] have in common . . . a failure to turn or transform borrowed materials" (16–17). Richard Burt has likewise drawn attention to the way in which Jonson's "use of somatic metaphors for [literary] production and consumption enabled him to authorize an ideal, unified, self-identical critical community" (19). From the theoretical standpoint of the present study, Burt's remark leads back to the plane of consistency with which the previous chapter ended, for if the digestive process is important to Jonson, that is because it offers a model of what we might call somatic unity-in-difference. If—to quote Mary Douglas once more—"Aesthetic pleasure arises from the perceiving of inarticulate forms," the alimentary tract offers such pleasure in abundance; it is the biological *locus classicus* for the transformation, reduction, and reconfiguration of material difference. As James Riddell and Stanley Stewart have recently observed, "For Jonson, imitation . . . functions rather like the digestive system. Nourishment, individual vitality—*enargeia*—is [its] end-product" (37). Hence the idea of digestion offers Jonson not just a way to legitimize his use of other authors' work, but a means to reshape himself constantly in the process.

I want to start this chapter with a limited instance of such reshaping: an instance that, over the past four centuries, has allowed considerable scope for the play of critical unity-in-difference, and that is also a basic example of the selective assimilation that Peterson identifies with Jonson's use of the digestive metaphor. I am referring to the traditional distinction between Shakespeare, the poet of nature who never blotted a line, and Jonson, who blotted so many that he became famous for slow and laborious composition. For present ends, I rediscover this distinction in the briefest work that either poet ever produced: his name.

To put things simply, Shakespeare never bothered to regularize the spelling of his name, either in his personal practice or in the practice of others; Jonson did, in an aggressive and idiosyncratic way. The evidence on both sides is extensive. In Shakespeare's case, the surviving signatures point in various different orthographic directions; he is "William Shakspere," "William Shakspeare," "Willm Shaksp," and so on.[1] Quarto title-pages offer further variants, including "Shakespeare," "Shake-speare," and "Shakspeare,"[2] while the whimsy of the poet's contemporaries produces spellings as remarkable as "Shaxpere" and "Shakspeer" (G. Blakemore Evans et al. 1828). It would remain for later figures, arguably beginning with Edmond Malone, to try to impose some uniformity on this material.[3]

For Jonson, the case is largely altered. His name, as commonplace in the sixteenth century as in the twentieth, had already acquired de facto orthographic regularity, within a limited range of variation, and Jonson seems to have sought to personalize it by deleting the usual *h*. In David Riggs's words, Jonson "changed the spelling of his . . . name" to "proclaim his uniqueness" (114), yet Marchette Chute has noted that "It was a policy to which his contemporaries paid no attention. His friends and his enemies went on spelling his name with an *h*, and even the printers stopped cooperating as soon as Jonson was no longer there to watch them" (Chute 18–19 n.). Chute may slightly overstate the bibliographical record, but the general point holds. Quarto title pages call the poet "Iohnson" until 1605; then his mature Horatian persona asserts itself in *Sejanus*, *Volpone*, *Epicoene*, *The Alchemist*, and the 1616 folio;[4] thereafter, "Iohnson" creeps back into the printings of 1631 and 1640, resurfaces in advertisements for the folio of 1692, and reappears on the title pages of the 1710, 1716, 1729, 1732, and 1738 editions (Herford, Simpson, and Simpson 9:88, 129, 136, 152–153). Meanwhile, Jonson's contemporaries displayed a perverse consistency in the spelling of his name; among the sixteen legal documents that Herford and the Simpsons reprint in their edition of Jonson's work, the *h* is virtually everywhere—except in Jonson's own signatures on two depositions.[5] Moreover, the poet's surviving autographs tell much the same story; he drops the "h" from his name in 1605, apparently just after his imprisonment for *Eastward Ho* (cf. Herford, Simpson, and Simpson 11:3–4; 1:190–216; 7:147, 277–317; 8:371–372, 384, 402–408, 666).

This pattern is hard to ignore. It conveys the overall impression of an author finding himself (or, more properly, making himself) through literary revision of his own name—revision that he then seeks, with uneven success, to impose on printers and colleagues. This point may also be urged as a commonplace of Shakespeare/Jonson scholarship, distinguishing the poet of nature from his pedantic, obstreperous companion, and making Jonson the forebear of eighteenth- and nineteenth-century literary scholarship, with its rage for order. Where Shakespeare appears to have been genuinely indifferent to the alienating capacities of print, Jonson spent considerable time and energy trying to govern them. It is hardly surprising, therefore, that his efforts to do so should begin with the two most intimate—and most important—words in his vocabulary.

Of course, it is suspiciously easy to draw such distinctions between Shakespeare and Jonson. The present book, which is interested in Jonson's astonishing capacity to render difference fluid, would like to complicate the binary oppositions that have sometimes characterized thought about the poet, and the Shakespeare/Jonson opposition is no exception. In fact, matters are a good deal more complex than the preceding contrast implies, for a number of reasons. First of all, Jonson is not really a paragon of neoclassical regularity. He takes an important step toward the neoclassical ideal, but his practice is not always consistent with his theory, nor is his theory itself always committed to stylistic balance or symmetry. As Jonas Barish has observed, Jonson's Senecan prose style is characterized by "broken rhythms and perilous balances, rather than the stabler rhetorics of Euphuism and Ciceronianism" (89); hence "Jonson's 'Romanizing' tendency and his fascination with living speech unexpectedly reinforce each other," for the same rhetorical devices that "suggest pressure of thought and evoke memories of classical prose" also "create a sense of conversational *desinvolture*" (71). Moreover, the poet's irregularities are sometimes the most forward-looking things about him. Thus A. C. Partridge's old-style philological study of Jonson's accidence has noted how the poet's use of the possessive genitive introduces new forms while clinging to old ones at the same time.[6] In such cases, Jonson's tendency to rethink and resystematize the structures of grammar generates considerable initial confusion. Likewise, the vagaries of the grammar signal the tentative, intuitive character of the literary and social relations the grammar itself helps to instantiate, and the genitive of ownership provides a good case in point. Anne Barton has remarked that Jonson's revision of his own name "looks very like an effort to create a name that would stand out among the myriads of

Elizabethan 'Johnsons' as something, if not unique, at least personally his own" (*Jonson* 171); it is an effort to invest the name itself with a possessive genitive character. However, as the fate of Jonson's revised name demonstrates, the idea of regularizing literary markers of ownership cannot have been easy to advance in a social and literary dispensation committed to the dispersal of such markers. Finally, moreover, Jonson's rethinking of grammatical and literary relations is complicated by the fact that it is associated with various overtly reactionary goals, commensurate with a revival of Horatian classicism. To that extent, its progressive character is perhaps coincidental.

Still, Jonson's concern with his name remains. It is conventional in exploiting the literary valences of the author's subjectivity ("John Donne, Ann Donne, undone"). However, it also marks an attempt to restrict the scope of such exploitation by denying others the right to participate in it. In other words, Jonson's revised name comprises a basic instance of the literary imitation that Richard Peterson considers typical of Jonson's work as a whole. Proceeding with the literary material of another—the name "Johnson"—the poet subjects that material to "the dynamic process of judicious gathering in and transforming" (Peterson 21). The result is a name that has been digested so as both to resemble and to differ crucially from its antecedents. But just as important, it is a name that the poet then seeks to exempt from further processes of gathering and transformation. His imitation is to be the last of its kind, if he has anything to say about the matter. Jonson's name is to be Jonson's alone, not clapper-clawed by the multitude.

In short, Jonson's name reveals a complexly ambiguous attitude to the process of *imitatio*: both a commitment to participation in the process, as a means of self-assertion, and a desire to mark spaces within which the process ends with Jonson himself, once again as a means of self-assertion. By way of contrast, the paranomasial quality of Shakespeare's name play in Sonnets 135 and 136 (to take two obvious cases) tends to problematize the self, rather than to assert or define it; lines like "Think all but one, and me in that one Will" serve to elide the poet with the surrounding world—to make him individually unthinkable, or at least indistinct. Compare Jonson's warning in *Timber, or Discoveries* that "We must not play, or riot too much with [words], as in *Paranomasies*" (8:623). From this standpoint, words become first and foremost something one works with: a product of labor, and of individual labor at that. I believe this notion of authorial work develops in part to justify the poet's reflex to protect his own literary territory: to make the play of *imitatio* his own, and no one else's. As the product of authorial labor, words begin to acquire the legal character of other such products. They become, like the poet's name, personal property. And as unique property that serves to denominate its own owner, one's name also helps constitute one's identity in a distinctive and fundamental way.

There is also one further point to make about the name "Jonson." It may be disconcerting to think of the poet's nominal revisionism as presaging the late twentieth-century American tendency to personalize names that has born fruit in such figures as Gennifer Flowers, Thurgood Marshall, and Learned Hand. But I think the comparison may be useful. In postmodern America, such name play is often the province of limited demographic groups, among them rural southern whites, adolescent women, and the urban poor. These groups have arguably learned to exploit the literary resources of personal naming to compensate for the relative absence of other avenues for self-assertion. In the preceding chapter I likened Jonson's treatment of the Anglican communion ceremony to Deleuze and Guattari's analysis of African-American gospel singing. Perhaps the poet's concern with names offers another point of contact between the apparent antitheses of Jonsonian classicism and the culture of twentieth-century America. If so, the Jonson we are left with is rather different from the social-climbing conservative who has traditionally been portrayed—which is not to say that the social climbing and the conservatism are not there for the finding, but that they exist in a more complex and fluid suspension than has sometimes been thought. They exist in a state of constant and composite digestion.

This chapter, which focuses most immediately on Jonson's attitudes toward literary activity and his appropriation of digestive metaphors to image that activity, finds itself secondarily compelled to address a wide range of interrelated concepts, all of which intersect for Jonson in the writing process. The writer's study and mind are the figurative place within which authorial digestion takes place. As such they mark an area of constantly shifting interplay between imitation and originality, labor and leisure, art and nature, individual identity and cultural context, personal property and public domain, aristocracy and commonalty, and so on. What emerges from this interplay, I would suggest, is more a set of practical responses or reflexes than a codified body of literary theory, more a set of mobile amalgamations and contradictions than a system of orderly and consistent theoretical discriminations. This argument may at first seem counterintuitive; as Jonathan Haynes recently observed, "Jonson has usually been thought of as the great pedant of Elizabethan drama, or as combining seamlessly in ideal proportions classical art and English matter" (1). But as Haynes goes on to note, the poet's contemporaries (as represented in *The Second Part of the Return from Parnassus*) could censure him as a "meere Empyrick": "one who has not had theoretical training in his art" (1). From this latter perspective, there is less of the Whitehall Banqueting House in Jonson than there is of Hartshorn Lane, less of the figurative head of Jacobean society than of its anus.

The stomach is the place where head and anus meet, and thus it is wholly appropriate that Jonson should choose the operations of the stomach as an emblem for the dense relations of unity-in-difference that constitute his poetics. This chapter examines the relevance of the digestive metaphor to Jonson's literary practice, and then explores the ways whereby that literary practice simultaneously authorizes the consolidation and the dispersal of sociocultural distinctions such as those between literary property and literary source matter, tradition and the individual talent. This exploration will, I hope, shed light on the revolutionary social implications of Jonson's views on authorship, while also helping to explain some of the acrimony that surrounds the poet's career and cult of individual personality. Moreover, the very terms in which Jonson promotes himself and his work are rendered innocuous by virtue of their eventual acceptance, and this fact may help account for Jonson's perpetual status as second best in Renaissance English letters.

To pursue this agenda, I proceed through a brief discussion of certain passages from *Timber, or Discoveries*—the prose work in which Jonson states most clearly what he thinks an author should be and do, and in which his emphasis on notions of literary labor, property, and identity is directly linked to figures of digestion; to a survey of the general means whereby Jonson implements his attitudes toward authorship within his career at large; and then to a brief summary of contemporary reactions to the strategies for authorial self-promotion that the poet advances. Superficially, this procedure serves a traditional view of Jonson and Shakespeare as literary-historical antitheses: Jonson with his formidable learned sock, Shakespeare warbling his native woodnotes; Jonson working, Shakespeare playing; Jonson championing art, Shakespeare dallying with nature; and so forth. Such oppositional constructions were certainly available even in the seventeenth century. Jonson himself, when in the mood, could point to Shakespeare's lack of "art" (Drummond 133). For his part, Shakespeare seems to have sought (for instance, in the War of the Theaters) to distance himself from Jonson's pedantry. Heminges and Condell insisted that Shakespeare was "a happie imitator of Nature" and that "what he thought, he vttered with that easinesse, that we have scarse receiued from him a blot in his papers" (Hinman 7). Yet if Shakespeare has been designated the poet of nature, Jonson the "Empyrick" also makes his claim to the same distinction, repeatedly and with vigor. The problem for Jonson is that his vision of nature is so obviously and (given its novelty) so necessarily factitious. To use a resonant early modern medical term, Jonsonian nature is a *concocted* nature, always already subject to elaborate processes of authorial digestion. To this extent, Jonson's essays in literary essentialism are inevitably self-discrediting, whereas Shakespeare has little self left to discredit at all. The latter's work thus offers a more congenial vehicle for critical pronouncements on the nature of nature.

"A Stomacke to concoct"

Jonson dislikes Montaigne because the French essayist does not properly digest his reading. As a result, what he produces is not literature but linguistic vomit:

> All the *Essayists*, even their Master *Mountaigne* . . . , in all they write, confesse still what bookes they have read last; and therein their owne folly, so much, that they bring it to the *Stake* raw, and undigested: not that the place did need it neither; but that they thought themselves furnished, and would vent it.   (8:586)

Jonson contrasts this literary emesis with his own preferred method of composition, which he describes variously in two separate passages of *Discoveries*. The first of these passages counsels the aspiring writer to "reade the best Authors, observe the best Speakers," then "thinke, and excogitate his matter," then "choose his words," then "take care in placing, and ranking both matter, and words," and to "doe this with diligence, and often" (8:615). This painstaking, "labour'd, and accurate" process (8:615) is what Jonson refers to again when he counsels would-be authors to

> Convert the substance, or Riches of an other *Poet*, to [their] owne use. . . . Not, as a Creature, that swallowes, what it takes in, crude, raw, or indigested; but, that feedes with an Appetite, and hath a Stomacke to concoct, divide, and turne all into nourishment.   (8:638)

For Jonson, this is how one produces a well-digested work.

These two passages from *Discoveries* deserve juxtaposition because they offer differently nuanced perspectives on the same process of literary invention. On one hand, that process is presented as deliberate and painstaking, "labour'd, and accurate," involving a whole series of conscious decisions whereby the writer exercises control over the *materia in potentia* of others' work. From this standpoint, the author's study marks the spot where raw resources are transformed by artifice into a product of labor. On the other hand, Jonson's digestion metaphors tend to represent the same process of transformation as innate or autonomic, a metabolic sequence that kicks in automatically in the case of any "Creature, that . . . hath a Stomacke." On the crudest and most obvious level, these two passages seem to be in direct conflict with one another, the former describing literary invention as the operation of culture upon nature, the latter describing it as a faculty exercised by the poet's nature itself. But this stark and simplistic contrast is immediately complicated by instabilities internal to the two passages; if, for instance, the author is an artisan transforming raw resources, those raw resources are themselves not really raw, having been subjected to prior transformation by prior artisans. Hence the first passage does not really offer a contrast between nature (the raw material transformed by the author) and culture (the authorial labor that transforms such material). It would instead appear to offer a contrast between a cultural material that has by artistic fiat been assigned the preemptive status of natural matter and a cultural process that further refines that matter. That cultural process, in turn, is what Jonson then represents in the second passage quoted above as the automatic and reflexive (and to that extent, natural) process of digestion. The line between nature and culture, play and work, is drawn and redrawn, erased and reerased, both by the overt contrast between the wording of the two passages I have quoted and by the internal logic of the passages as taken separately. As James Shapiro has remarked, "we need to be cautious about accepting dichotomies like 'art' and 'nature'" in studying Jonson's work (153); such distinctions are important less for their intrinsic stability than for their status as "handy terms in the struggle for mimetic superiority" (153).

In fact, one arguable reason why Jonson likes to think of literary invention as a process of digestion is that digestion itself, in Renaissance popular and medical terminology, is a process that both collapses and reinscribes distinctions of the nature/culture variety. When early physicians try to make sense of what happens to food in the stomach, they repeatedly image digestion not as a metabolic process, but as a repetition of what has already happened to food before it enters the stomach. Nancy Siraisi, using Galen and Avicenna as her primary sources, summarizes the accepted wisdom thus: "Ingested food, having been transformed into chyle in the stomach, is subsequently transported to the liver and there concocted (literally, 'cooked') into blood, the two biles, and phlegm. Various stages of concoction purify the blood of superfluities which are excreted, and ultimately, part of the blood is refined into semen" (106). The term *concoction*, repeated above in Jonson's *Discoveries*, is of considerable importance here; in fact, although Siraisi locates concoction in the liver, Renaissance discussions of the subject view it as a multistage activity begun in the stomach. As Thomas Vicary, chief surgeon at Saint Bartholomew's Hospital during the reign of Elizabeth, explains, "The stomacke was ordeyned principally for two causes: The first, that it . . . shoulde desire sufficient meate for al the whole body: The seconde is, that the stomacke shoulde be a sacke or chest to al the bodie for ye meate, and as a Cooke to al the members of the body" (sig. K3r-v). Helkiah Crooke uses much the same language: "The Ventricle as it were a little Venter . . . is the common receptacle of meate and drinke, the Kitchin of the body . . . for the receyuing of the meat to be coqued of the whol body" (116, sig. L4v). In another passage, Crooke renders the element of artifice in the kitchen metaphor even more explicit by calling the stomach "the shop and forge of Chilification" (122, sig. M1v).

This idea—that the stomach is somehow a little cook, a little kitchen, or a little oven—is as much a province of Renaissance popular discourse as of early medicine. As Richard Curteys observed in a sermon preached before Queen Elizabeth within a year of Jonson's birth, "The teeth be called the grinders: for that, as the millstones doe grinde, bruse, and make small the corne that is to be baked: Even so the teeth doe grinde, chawe, and make small the meate that is to be baked or concocted in the stomacke" (sig. A5r). What goes on inside the stomach is identical to what goes on outside the stomach. Cooking and digesting, while intuitively distinct—functions of culture and nature, conscious artifice and somatic reflex, the bodily outside and the bodily inside, respectively—emerge from early modern somatic discourse as elements of an ongoing and graduated sequence of metabolic interrelations. Thus it should be no surprise to find that Jonson's own metaphorical process of literary digestion should eventuate in the production of—what else?—a banquet. As the Cook remarks in the antimasque to *Neptune's Triumph for the Return of Albion*, "A good *Poet* differs nothing at all from a *Master-Cooke*. Eithers Art is the wisedom of the Mind" (42–44). For Jonson, conceptual distinctions function like Russian dolls, nested within each other in an infinite regress. Peel away the body's skin and in the stomach you find a kitchen concocting a banquet; peel away the act of reading and you find the act of literary production within it. Strip the veneer from nature and art appears beneath it, and the two terms then combine into hybrid amalgamations of cultured nature, natural culture, cultured culture, and so on. The distinctions never go away, but neither do they stand still.

Brian Massumi has observed that classical Western representational thinking "reposes on a double identity: of the thinking subject, and of the concepts it creates and to which it lends its own presumed attributes of sameness and constancy. The subject, its concepts, and also the objects in the world to which the concepts are applied have a shared, internal essence: the self-resemblance at the basis of identity" (xi). Deleuzian efforts to think past bodily interiority are motivated in large part by a desire to do away with such self-resemblance, and thus to "replace . . . restrictive analogy with a conductivity that knows no bounds" (Massumi xii). The thick flux of Jonson's conceptual oppositions contributes to a similar end by constantly calling in question the integrity of perception as mediated through self-identity and negation. As a result, Jonson's *Discoveries* may largely be read as an attempt to mobilize representation against itself, or to move it beyond itself. If, as Nietzsche observed, language is inherently metaphorical,[7] the Deleuzian plane of consistency "is the abolition of all metaphor; all that consists is Real" (*Plateaus* 69). For its part, Jonson's use of metaphor, as in the case of the digestive tropes cited above, marks an effort to collapse distinctions between signifier and signified, vehicle and tenor, and enable free movement through the resulting space.

Hence Jonson's critical pronouncements manifest a steady interest in the muddying of critical, social, and ontological categories, and this interest grows most marked in connection with language's capacities for signifying interiority and essence. Jonson consistently regards words as an index of human nature. In a famous passage from *Timber* he thus declares that

Language most shewes a man: speake that I may see thee. It springs out of the most retired, and inmost parts of us, and is the Image of the Parent of it, the mind. No glasse renders a mans forme, or likenesse, so true as his speech.   (8:625)

For Jonson, one's words surpass one's external image insofar as they represent the inner person—the real thing, the mind, which otherwise passeth show. As Jonas Barish comments of this passage, "speech [for Jonson] provides the truest index to [one's] disposition and moral health" (90); indeed, it seems to be an index of one's mental health, too. Thus Jonson elsewhere observes that "Wheresoever, manners, and fashions are corrupted, Language is. . . . The excesse of Feasts, and apparell, are the notes of a sick State; and the wantonnesse of language, of a sick mind" (8:593).

And again, Jonson insists that literary study is

> in vaine, without a naturall wit, and a Poeticall nature in chiefe. For, no man, so soone as he knowes this, or reades it, shall be able to write the better; but as he is adapted to it by Nature, he shall grow the perfecter Writer. (8:640)

This argument tends to represent the articulate citizen as essentially superior to others; it supports what Arthur Ferguson has called an "emerging ideal" of Renaissance citizenship "founded upon a regard for the written—and published—word" (154–155). And the most superior of all superior citizens is apparently the poet. As Jonson explains, the poet "is the neerest Borderer upon the Orator, and expresseth all his vertues, though he be tyed more to numbers; is his equall in ornament, and above him in his strengths" (8:640). Given such excellence, poets transcend the law; they are not tied by external standards of linguistic usage, for they serve a higher internal authority:

> I am not of the opinion to conclude a *Poets* liberty within the narrowe limits of lawes, which either the *Grammarians*, or *Philosophers* prescribe. For, before they found out those Lawes, there were many excellent Poets, that fulfill'd them. . . . Which of the *Greekelings* durst ever give precepts to *Demosthenes*? or to *Pericles* . . . ? or to *Alcibiades*, who had rather Nature for his guide, then Art for his master? (8:641)

But in making such capacious claims for poetry, Jonson violates the categories of sense that he himself has established. Poets should not be bound to laws because, apparently, they "fulfill" those laws anyway and thus define the law for others. To this extent, the poetic freedom that Jonson advocates turns out to be servitude writ large. Moreover, not only is poetic freedom not free; poetry apparently is not poetry, either. Exploiting a philological slippage noted long ago by Burckhardt,[8] Jonson conflates the disciplines of verse and oratory (disciplines he had carefully distinguished only one page earlier) when he praises the poetic faculties of Demosthenes, Pericles, and Alcibiades. As a result, the passage's concluding distinction between "Nature" (the unfree freedom of the [un]poet) and "Art" (whatever that is) sketches out a continuum of malleabilities rather than a stable binary opposition.

Such confusion is not accidental. It arises because Jonson's poetics emphasize art as well as nature, and Jonson therefore needs a formula to relate the conflicting claims of these two terms. His standard way of making them agree is to inflect and qualify his distinctions until they no longer remain distinct at all. As Richard Peterson has shown, "Nature and Art are . . . so closely related [in Jonson's work] as to be almost indistinguishable in their effects" (183). Peterson rightly points out that this fact lends Jonson's work a distinctive balance and flexibility; indeed, one might argue that all of Jonson's linguistic, social, and ethical distinctions are rendered mutable in service of this flexibility. Immediately after his equivocal paean to Demosthenes and Alcibiades, for instance, Jonson pays tribute to Aristotle—who, we learn, has not really differed from the others at all in terms of practice:

Whatsoever Nature at any time dictated to the most happie, or long exercise to the most laborious; that the wisdome, and Learning of *Aristotle*, hath brought into an Art: because, . . . what other men did by chance or custome, he doth by reason. (8:641)

In other words, Aristotle's art is natural; Demosthenes' nature is artful; and the former differs from the latter only insofar as it evolves from reason rather than "chance or custome." (Indeed this distinction, too, could prove suspect if investigated, implying, as it does, that Demosthenes composed at random.) The means vary, but the end remains the same, and thus Jonson's discrimination between art and nature becomes virtually infinite in its capacity for practical application.

To "speake that I may see thee": if this is the end of language, then linguistic labor is important exactly because it transgresses the divide between outside and inside. The stomach may be a little kitchen, but language is a little stomach, concocting a banquet out of the "in here" of the author, and serving that banquet in the "out there" of the reader, where it acts as a necessary confirmation of the author's individual identity. There is a constant possibility, in other words, that one's identity will turn out to be inseparable from one's literary deeds—that, far from expressing "the most retired, and inmost parts of us," language will prove repeatedly and incontestably that those parts do not exist except on the page. Thus Jonson's remarks on the discipline of writing tend to unsettle the idea of personal nature in the very act of confirming it, turning the literary inside into the literary outside. For example, Jonson exhorts his readers to expand and revise and perfect their individuality through the medium of print: "To [the] perfection of Nature in our *Poet*, wee require Exercise of those parts, and frequent" (8:637). But the principal such exercise is imitation, and imitation aims to make the poet over in the image of others:

If his wit will not arrive soddainly at the dignitie of the Ancients, let him . . . come to it againe upon better cogitation; try an other time, with labour. If then it succeed not, cast not away the Quills, yet: nor scratch the Wainescott, beate not the poore Desk; but bring all to the forge, and file, againe; tourne it anew. (8:637–638)

It is interesting in itself to see Jonson, with his proverbial antagonism for the working classes (Gardiner and Epp 90–95), casting the writer in the Horatian role of blacksmith; more interesting still is the effect of such representation. For the manual labor of literary exercise ultimately encompasses the laborer him/herself. As Jonson explains in one of the passages with which this discussion began, "*Imitation*" allows the scholar

to convert the substance, or Riches of an other *Poet*, to his owne use. To make choice of one excellent man above the rest, and so to follow him, till he grow very *Hee*: or so like him, as the Copie may be mistaken for the Principall. (8:638)

This leaves the reader, and the writer, in a position at once both wellnigh impenetrable and replete with breathtaking possibilities. If one's literary work expresses one's inward nature, that nature itself becomes articulable through the internalization of another writer's sensibility. And despite Richard Peterson's insistence that this internalization is supposed to be partial and discriminating (8), passages like the foregoing suggest exactly the contrary. One is to act as a species of rhetorical bee, "turn[ing] *all* into Honey" (8:639, my italics), or one must become a kind of literary tapeworm, inhabiting the corpus of a classical author so as "to concoct, divide, and turne *all* into nourishment" (8:638; my italics). This process, pursued consciously over a prolonged period, will lead to the absolute assimilation of the host by the parasite—consummated in a triumphant and epiphanic moment when "the Copie may be mistaken for the Principall." Then, and only then, may one's "retired" and "inward" parts emerge fully and perfectly to view: when the author has effectively become someone else.

"A learned Plagiary"

If digestion and parasitism comprise possible metaphors for this process of literary assimilation, theft constitutes another. Just as the social parasitism of a Mosca or a Brainworm (whose names, of course, are carefully concocted to signal their natures) involves usurping the property of others, so the pursuit of Jonsonian imitation leads to what we could now call borderline plagiarism. This fact derives largely from Jonson's classicism, and thus Jonathan Bate has noted that "what we might condemn as plagiarism, classical culture would have praised as imitation" (27). But Bate's remark unfortunately implies that the opposition between plagiarism and imitation was a settled one for the seventeenth century. It clearly was not, either in theory or in practice,[9] and thus Jonson's use of the distinction generates yet another series of ambiguities and slippages. As John Dryden observed in the *Essay of Dramatick Poesy*—incidentally betraying the flimsiness of the distinction between imitation and theft—Jonson "was not onely a professed Imitator of *Horace*, but a learned Plagiary of all the other [classical poets]" (*Works* 17:21). Indeed, Jonson's tendency to lift whole passages from ancient sources was famous even in his own day, and given the cultural economy of late medieval textual transmission, such thefts would have been largely unremarkable. But Jonson deliberately makes them remarkable, for Jonson is unparalleled among Jacobean poets in the intense proprietary interest he exerts over the products of his own literary labor. He voraciously consumes others' texts in the process of producing his own; then he insists, as with his name, that what he has produced belongs to him and no one else.

This insistence develops in various ways. The gradually ripening dispute with Inigo Jones, for instance, presupposes a deep division between the two men on the question of who really creates and therefore owns their masques. In Joseph Loewenstein's words, the Jonson-Jones dispute "is a quarrel about the very ontology of the work of art" ("Script" 108). Furthermore, it is a quarrel in which Jonson seeks systematically to gobble up the accomplishments of his colleagues. As early as *The Masque of Blackness* Jonson asserts—despite passing credits to his colleagues—that the work's "inuention was deriued by me" (7:169). Eventually, his tendency to slight his collaborators culminates with the notorious second billing of Jones in the 1631 quarto of *Love's Triumph Through Callipolis*. Jonson establishes his authorship/ownership of the masques by displacing and disparaging his coauthors—by presenting their errors as theirs ("The Painters . . . lent small colour to any" [*The Masque of Beauty* 273–274]), while absorbing their successes into his own. Indeed, the 1631 text of *Love's Triumph* is itself an act of the purest Jonsonian imitation: a literary re-creation of a prior event (performance) that was itself an assimilation of still other prior events in the spheres of literary composition, musical composition, choreography, design, and so forth. The effect of such imitation is literally to urge that "the Copie" be (mis)taken—as far as questions of authorship go—"for the Principall," and that the masque thus be translated into a specifically literary genre. As Stephen Orgel has pointed out, "if it were not for Ben Jonson, the court masque would hardly find a place in the history of literature"

(*Masques* 2); the fact that it does so attests both to Jonson's determination and to his insecurity. Almost singlehandedly, he spirits the masque out of competing disciplinary circles and transforms it into his personal literary property.

Thus it is appropriate that *Neptune's Triumph for the Return of Albion* (1624)—which Orgel regards as one of the most "brilliant" of Jonson's masques (*Jonsonian Masque* 99)—should be saturated with questions of authorship and originality, nicely set forth in a lengthy antimasque conversation between King James's (supposed) poet and his (ostensible) master cook. From its opening moment, the masque confronts its spectators with patterns of doubling that seem both to demand and to resist discrimination between originator and imitator, "Principall" and "Copie." Even the opening set design consists of "two erected Pillars" (3), and these pillars, in turn, are decorated with twin inscriptions: "NEP. RED." and "SEC. IOV." (5). The former of these inscriptions, as Jonson's interpretive notes remark (n. a), derives from the Roman numismatic dedication "Neptuno Reduci"; in other words, the motto on the first of the twinned pillars itself constitutes a twinning of historical inscription. This twinning then generates further difference, for the phrase "Neptuno Reduci" can signify in at least two directions, concomitant with the active and passive senses of the adjective *redux*. First, there is the standard translation "To Neptune the restorer" (or as Herford and the Simpsons have it, "To Neptune that brings back home" [10:664]). This translation is obviously appropriate to the historical occasion of *Neptune's Triumph*—the return of Prince Charles and Buckingham from their unsuccessful marriage negotiations for the hand of the Spanish infanta. However, it should also be noted that this reading of the motto constitutes an appropriation, by Neptune, of an epithet customarily assigned to Jupiter.[10] To this extent, the inscription necessarily raises questions as to its own status as property (Jove's? Neptune's? Neptune's by grace of Jove?). Moreover, one can also read the phrase "Neptuno Reduci" in a different sense, as meaning "For the returned Neptune" (cf. the Virgilian phrase "reduces socii")—in effect, the Neptune who has come back home.

This alternate construction calls attention to the patterns of doubling whereby the masque presents Albion to Neptune (i.e., Prince Charles to King James) as his second self, "the most his owne" (134). Nor does this pattern of doubling end with the superimposition of Charles upon James. The image of Charles as James's alter ego bifurcates again into the paired images of Albion and Hippius, Neptune's "powerfull MANAGER of Horse" (137), whose name refers of course to Buckingham (James's master of horse), but which also, as another of Jonson's interpretive notes observes, points back to Neptune: "A power of NEPTVNES by which he is cald *Hippius* or *Damaeus*, [is] conferd on a person of speciall honour" (n. e). Within this dense web of couplings and doublings, it is perhaps inevitable that the second columnar inscription, "Secundo Iovi," should refer to the fact that "so *Neptune* [is] cald by Statiu[s] in Achil[l]eid. I. *Secundus* IVPITER" (n. b). Neptune copies James and Jupiter; Charles copies Neptune, Jupiter, and James; Buckingham copies Neptune and Jupiter, James, and Charles; the masque's inscriptions copy classical epithets; Jonson's redirection of those epithets away from their primary objects to secondary and tertiary referents copies classical usage yet again; and by instituting such redirection, Jonson also makes his historical audience—including James himself, the *fons et origo* of the masque—into a collective replica of classical myth. Before a single word has been uttered in *Neptune's Triumph*, the spectator is confronted with a hall of mirrors in which royal power divides logarithmically while reencountering itself infinitely.

Moreover, *ut pictura poesis*. The same relations of unity-in-difference that constitute royal authority in *Neptune's Triumph* also encompass poetic authority. The structural principle of twinning—columns, inscriptions, personages—extends to the overall design of the masque through the opposition between antimasque and revels, and within the antimasque through the colloquy between poet and cook. In this latter case, framed by the twin columns of which they are talking simulacra, James's poet (actually a copy of James's poet) and his master cook (again, of course, a copy) try to decide whether they are different people or fundamentally the same:

POET.
You are not his Maiesties *Confectioner*? Are you?
    COOKE.
No, but one that has as good title to the room, his *Master-Cooke*.
What are you, Sir?
    POET.
The most unprofitable of his seruants, I, Sir, the *Poet*.
. . . .
    COOKE.
Were you euer a *Cooke*?
    POET.
A *Cooke*? no surely.
    COOKE.

Then you can be no good *Poet*: for a good *Poet* differs nothing at all from a *Master-Cooke*.

(29–43)

The precise tone of this and the following banter is hard to gauge. On one hand, it is difficult not to agree with John Meagher that the cook serves as an object of ridicule (52–53), perhaps embodying Jonson's contempt for Inigo Jones. Certainly the cook's proposal to bring into the masque an artificial island, "floting . . . / In a braue broth, and of a sprightly greene, / . . . and then, / Some twentie *Syrens*, singing in the kettel" (185–188) must be read in light of Jones's experiments with stage presentation, experiments that the cook reduces to absurdity. Yet, as Orgel has noted, "it is the cook, not the poet, who begins to sound most like the Jonson who was King James's masque writer" (*Jonsonian Masque* 92). This fact is rendered particularly prominent when the cook announces himself as the author and apologist for the device of the antimasque, a device he defends against the poet's objections:

> COOKE.
> But where's your *Antimasque* now, all this while?
> I hearken after them.
> POET.
> Faith, we haue none.
> COOKE.
> None?
> POET.
> None, I assure you, neither doe I thinke them
> A worthy part of presentation,
> Being things so *heterogene*, to all deuise,
> Mere *By-workes*, and at best *Out-landish* nothings.
> COOKE.
> O, you are all the heauen awrie, Sir!
> For blood of *Poetry*, running in your veines,
> Make not your selfe so ignorantly simple.
>
> (213–228)

Contrary to the poet's complaint that antimasques are irrelevant to the main entertainment, the cook undertakes to defend the low part of the spectacle—the part most clearly stamped as Jonson's own contribution to the masque form. As a result, the cook himself assumes an ambiguous character as creator of the entertainment in question, and thus it is right that he should impinge upon the poet's work by producing an impromptu antimasque out of the ingredients of his kitchen. When the cook first declares to the poet that "A good *Poet* differs nothing at all from a *Master-Cooke*. Eithers Art is the wisedom of the Mind" (42–44), Jonson's marginal notes again deepen the ambiguities of his dialogue by citing Athenaeus's *Deipnosophists* as the source of the sentiment just uttered (n. c). In Athenaeus, in turn, this remark emerges as the moral of a complicated anecdote about culinary impersonation:

A. I was a pupil of Soterides, who, when Nicomedes was twelve days' journey from the sea and desired an anchovy in the middle of winter, served it to him . . . so that all cried out in wonder. —B. But how could that be? —A. He took a fresh turnip and cut it in slices thin and long, shaping it just like the anchovy. Then he parboiled it, poured oil upon it, sprinkled salt to taste, spread on the top exactly forty seeds of black poppy, and satisfied the king's desire in far-away Scythia. And when Nicomedes had tasted the turnip, he sang the praise of anchovy to his friends. The cook and the poet are just alike: the art of each lies in his brain. (1.7.d–f)

If taken out of context, Jonson's insistence that "a good *Poet* differs nothing at all from a *Master-Cooke*. Eithers Art is the wisedom of the Mind" may seem relatively benign, but in its original form this claim resides upon the principle that both poet and cook are fakers, equally involved in the project of unfixing identity. Just as for Athenaeus's cook a turnip can be an anchovy, so for Jonson a pig can be a man, a poet a cook, and the masque a (hence *his*) literary production. Given such implications, one may find the cook's later praise of his own art particularly enticing:

> A *Master-Cooke*—
> Thou do'st not know the man! nor canst thou know him!
> Til thou hast seru'd some yeares in that deep school,
> That's both the Nource, and Mother of the *Arts*,
> And hear'st him read, interpret, and demonstrate.
> . . . .
> He'has *Nature* in a pot! 'boue all the *Chemists*,
> Or bare-breeched brethren of the *Rosie-Crosse*!
> A *Souldier*, a *Physitian*, a *Philosopher*,
> A generall *Mathematician*!
> (83–106)

This passage could almost be a digest of Jonsonian attitudes toward literary creation. Beginning with art, it ends with nature, rendering the two inextricable in their forms and operations. Emphasizing the laborious process of study and apprenticeship, it ends with a vision of the cook as *übermensch*. In the process, it subsumes other professional categories—even mathematics and military science—under the rubric of gastronomy.

So Jonson's audiences are left with a curious and unresolved fluidity. On one hand, the poet seems to regard others' texts (and not just literary ones) as an open invitation to copy, imitate, and assimilate; on the other hand, he expends great effort to protect the boundaries of his own work—to render it inimitable and unassimilable. As Timothy Murray has remarked, "Jonson's plays, poems, and prose berate the gleanings and pickings of the Renaissance playwright—actions of which he too was guilty—for the degradation of poetry and authors" (650). One of the first authors to introduce the term *plagiarism* into the English language (Peterson 18), he clearly worries that others may redigest and repossess his writing. He thus heaps preemptive scorn upon figures like the "Poet-Ape" of Epigram 61, who "From brocage is become so bold a thiefe, / As we, the rob'd, leaue rage, and pittie it" (3–4); and "Proule the Plagiary" (Epigram 81), who claims the authorship of "all [he] hears" (5), and to whom Jonson therefore refuses to recite his verse; and "Play-Wright" (Epigram 100), of whom Jonson remarks that "Fiue of my iests, then stolne, past him a play" (4). Thus "Jonson's epigrams are full of those who have sullied the fair name of imitation by their thievery" (Peterson 18). What needs to be added is that the thefts in question seem almost always to be committed or threatened against the poet himself. Jonson practically never deploys the idea of plagiarism in a disinterested or universal way; it has specific self-aggrandizing applications, concomitant with the poet's own search for literary distinction.

In short, one moral of Jonson's poetics would seem to be "I write; more or less everybody else steals." Within Jonson's self-created realm of authorial property rights, this moral has a corollary: "My work is mine; everybody else's (insofar as they work at all, which is of course an equally slippery question) is more or less mine too." And finally, insofar as literary property is a product of labor, another corollary follows with reference to the concept of work: "I work; everybody else more or less plays." These attitudes—with their implicit, strategically fuzzy interrelations between authorial genius, property ownership, and labor—receive their primary monumentalization in 1616, with the appearance of Jonson's *Works*. As

David Riggs has noted, this volume "give[s] every appearance of having been written with labor" (238). The title speaks for itself in this regard, and the operative verb of the folio's Horatian epigraph is "laboro." The painstakingly produced 1616 *Works* are concocted, in Richard Dutton's words, to be "a deliberate and selective account of [Jonson's] career, emphasising those elements which the eminent man of letters wished to commemorate and quietly expunging those he did not" (11).[11] As W. H. Herendeen has shown, even the dedications and performance information supplied in the folio "proclaim [Jonson's] independence from any single company and present . . . him . . . as an employer of actors rather than as an employee" (53). Jonson is to become one of Europe's first professional writers; his main tool for creating this new socioprofessional identity, and for installing himself within it, is the 1616 folio.

As a result, Jonson's *Works* cut squarely against the residual tendency to disparage dramatic composition in the vulgar tongue. This point, although long recognized, is worth recalling in light of the epigrams that greeted Jonson's forays into folio publication. The poet's detractors insisted that his work was unworthy of being described as such—that "What others call a play, you call a work" (*Wits Recreations*, sig. F4r; qtd. in Bradley and Adams 271).[12] His proponents, on the other hand, strove vigorously to reaffirm Jonson's translation of dramatic writing into the realm of productive labor: "The Authors friend thus for the Author sayes, / Bens plays are works, when others works are plays" (*Wits Recreations* sig. F4r; qtd. in Bradley and Adams 271). The linkage between labor, property, and genius thus allows the poet considerable freedom for self-promotion. Jonson's writing is unlike anyone else's; it is unique because it is work; and because Jonson alone knows how to work, he is a better person than others and deserves canonization in folio. The book stands in for and proclaims the man, speaking that we may see him.

I take this complex of attitudes to be one of Jonson's most revolutionary contributions to Western literary history, leading as it does to the nineteenth- and early twentieth-century myth of elevated and autonomous authorial genius. Samuel Johnson's construction of Shakespeare as "the poet of nature"—whose "characters are not modified by the customs of particular places, unpracticed by the rest of the world" (301), and whose ability to create universal characters suggests his own essential universality—would be meaningless without some such underlying doctrine. Likewise, when Terence Hawkes refers to Shakespeare as a nineteenth-century "man of letters" (56)—and, more irreverently, as the "Phallus of the Golden Age" (60), whose individual "potency" can generate an entire cultural tradition—he is invoking notions of authorship that are self-consciously advanced, for perhaps the first time in English literary history, not by Shakespeare but by Jonson. In this way Jonson himself helps transform Shakspere into Shakespeare.

To put this argument differently: the Jonsonian idea of authorship—in which the author is a worker, producing distinct matter that serves to define his or her personal identity and over which s/he may exercise proprietary rights—helps change the entire landscape of early modern English literary practice. It constitutes a new mode of professional activity and enables a new sense of what is important and problematic about literature. Jonsonian authorship tends to focus on certain matters that earlier authors regularly ignore or mystify: the question, for instance, of how and when (and what) an author should publish, and the concomitant question of how to describe writing as a general pursuit—whether as productive or unproductive, as legitimate professional activity or trivial amusement, and so on. In addition, Jonson's idea of the author tends to assume a militant air vis-à-vis previous models of the writer's commitment, for its fluidities tend to violate settled views of literary behavior. As Richard Helgerson has shown, Jonson's "self-creation" threatens Renaissance traditions of avocational courtly authorship (101–184); as Joseph Loewenstein has observed, the Jonsonian notion of writing as labor requires a massive redefinition of the author's legal relations to the text ("Script" 102). By instigating such readjustment, Jonson's ideas pose a sustained threat to the livelihood of the preexistent authorial community, built as it is on assumptions incompatible with Jonsonian theory. As John Sweeney summarizes matters, the "real issue" at the heart of Jonson's career "is who 'owns' Jonson's play, who has the right to determine the value and meaning of his labour" (11). From this issue, a host of others follow.

Moreover, Jonson's own importance in redefining the idea of authorship condemns him to a subsidiary role in later literary history, for any model of literary progress grounded in nature must be embarrassed by evidence of its own factitiousness. The very digestive multivalence that makes Jonson's career so supremely flexible in the short run contributes, in the long run, to the poet's literary neglect. Insofar as literature is supposed to reflect and instantiate human nature—The Best That Has Been Thought and Said—it is imperative to represent that Best as a cumulative, continuously developing body of expression, not marked by rupture, acrimony, or self-repudiation. Hence the real irony of Jonson's attitude toward writing is that Shakespeare, not he, should be retroactively constructed as its representative par excellence: the Phallus of the Golden Age. This irony only becomes understandable in light of the very clearly artificial, labored, and concocted character of Jonsonian literary nature; such artifice speaks against the possibility of ever representing Jonsonian authorship itself as a natural, given, eternal, or enduring thing. The best way to accomplish this latter task is to discover an ideal instance of Jonsonian authorship not in Jonson's own writing, but in that of someone less openly committed to revolutionary notions of authorial digestion, concoction, property, identity, and labor.

Keeping Up with the Johnsons

The very radicalism of Jonson's literary theory forces him to the margins of the new literary history that he and it help to create. The most far-reaching and novel elements of his work also generate a kind of benign critical neglect—or, to use T. S. Eliot's famous phrase, a "perfect conspiracy of approval" (65)—once the novelty has been institutionalized. If, as I think, Jonson was aware of this problem, it must have come close to breaking his heart. In any event, the poet's detractors were more than happy to point out the inconsistencies between his cult of authorial essence on one hand and his assimilative tendencies on the other. Owen Felltham, in his "Answer" to Jonson's second "Ode to Himself," thus twits the poet,

> 'Tis known you can do well,
> And that you do excell
> As a Translator: But when things require
> A *genius* and fire,
> Not kindled heretofore by others' pains;
> As oft y'have wanted brains
> And art to strike the White,
> As you have levell'd right.
> (sig. C1r; qtd. in Bradley and Adams 151;
> Herford, Simpson, and Simpson 11:339)

Henry Parrot describes the massive Latin translations that flesh out Jonson's plays as "feathers . . . / Pluckt from a Swanne, and set vpon a Goose" (sig. G1v; qtd. in Bradley and Adams 85; Herford, Simpson, and Simpson

11:379). (Ironically, Parrot protests his own originality in another epigram, insisting that his verses "sauour not of stolne or borrowed taste" [sig. E5r]; once the door was opened to such claims, it could scarcely be shut.) And again, Inigo Jones charges Jonson with having

> writt
> of good and badd things, not with equall witt.
> The reason is, or may be quickly showne,
> the good's translation, butt the ill's thine owne.[13]

Indeed, a substantial body of contemporary opinion accuses Jonson of something very like the plagiarism that he ascribes to others. This opinion—concomitant with "the frequent charge that Jonson was imitative and uninspired" (Evans, *Contexts* 112)—is too widely held to be dismissed out of hand.[14]

This view of Jonson receives its classic statement in a work that also associates the poet's literary thievery with his reputation as a worker: Dekker's *Satiromastix*. Horace, the Jonson figure in *Satiromastix*, seeks to compensate for his own lack of natural wit by collecting bits of faux-classical verse and patching them laboriously into a poem:

> O me thy Priest inspire.
> For I to thee and thine immortall name,
> In—in—in golden tunes,
> For I to thee and thine immortall name—
> In—sacred raptures, flowing, flowing, swimming, swimming:
> In sacred raptures swimming,
> Immortal name, game, dame, tame, lame, lame, lame,
> Pux, ha it, shame, proclaime, oh—
> In Sacred raptures flowing, will proclaime, not—
> O me thy Priest inspyre!
> (*Works* 1.2.8–17)

Jonathan Haynes has called *Satiromastix* "an immeasurable help in understanding Jonson," and this passage is surely a case in point (88). It "demystifies" the "clouds of high-minded rhetoric" through which Jonson sought to expand his authorial persona (Haynes 86–87), and it derives a peculiarly corrosive satirical quality from the sharp contrast between its overt content and the poet's efforts at composition. Horace/Jonson emerges as a literary poseur intent on confusing the processes of labor with the "Sacred raptures" of the poet-priest. Likewise, Dekker's play aims to exploit the latent conflict between work and essential identity at the heart of Jonsonian literary theory. Insofar as the poet takes pains with his writing, he betrays his intrinsically unpoetical nature.

If, for Dekker, there is something fundamentally ridiculous about Jonson's characterization of literature as work, the ridiculousness is intensified when Jonson claims his works to be property. Insofar as he is not naturally a poet, his inspiration must come from others; insofar as this is so, his claims to ownership of literary material are vitiated from the outset; and hence Dekker's play ultimately forces Horace/Jonson to swear "not to bumbast out a new Play, with the olde lynings of Iestes, stolne from the Temples Reuels" (5.2.295–296). Thus, too, Dekker draws attention to the characteristic Jonsonian practice of disparaging one's associates while claiming authorial credit and glory for oneself:

You [Horace] shall not sit in a Gallery, when your Comedies and Enterludes haue entred their Actions, and there make vile and bad faces at euerie lyne, to make Sentlemen haue an eye to you, and to make Players afraide to take your part. . . . Besides, you must foresweare to venter on the stage, when your Play is ended, and to exchange curtezies, and complements with Gallants in the Lordes roomes, to make all the house rise vp in Armes, and to cry that's *Horace*, that's he, that's he. (5.2.298–307)

Here, as early as 1602, *Satiromastix* presents the entire constellation of opinions and rhetorical habits that typify Jonson's authorial practice. The individual constituents of this theory—the emphasis on labor and imitation, the problematic claims to originality, the concomitant tendency to charge others with plagiarism and incompetence, and the insistence that writing reflects one's inmost self—are not necessarily unique to Jonson; however, in large part by virtue of his emphasis on somatic and digestive figuration, Jonson integrates them into a cohesive whole. In the process, he becomes one of early modern England's first self-conscious representatives of literature as vocation.

One possible consequence of this fact may be Jonson's proverbial hostility to the lower social ranks. Critics habitually note the disdain that Jonson's plays express for the "vnderstanding Gentlemen o' th' ground" (*Bartholomew Fair* Induction.49–50).[15] However, Jonson's emphasis on literary labor tends to place the poet outside the residual social hierarchy which he celebrates and to which he does nominal obeisance. The moment he identifies work as a privileged vehicle for the construction of personal identity, the poet alienates himself from the very social superiors whom it is his task to please and to propitiate. An elaborately conceived antagonism to the lower social ranks may serve to compensate for this embarrassment, while the actual source of embarrassment itself—Jonson's covert sympathy with the idea of labor—survives unobtrusively at other levels of discourse. Surely Jonson's use of artisanal tropes deserves attention in this light— particularly because these metaphors themselves comprise a reworking, in new social and political circumstances, of an old Horatian commonplace.[16] Not only does *Discoveries* present the author as a laborer whose job it is to "forge, and file, [and] tourne" his lines; it also explicitly insists that "*A Poeme* . . . is the work of the Poet; the end, and fruit of his labour" (8:636). Jonson triumphantly resurrects his image of the blacksmith's forge in "To the Memory of my beloued, the Author Mr. William Shakespeare: And what he hath left us":

> That he,
> Who casts to write a living line, must sweat,
>   (Such as thine are) and strike the second heat
> Vpon the *Muses* anuile: turne the same,
>   (And himselfe with it) that he thinkes to frame;
> Or for the lawrell, he may gaine a scorne,
>   For a good *Poet's* made, as well as borne.
>   (58–64)

The upshot of such painstaking exertion is that "the race / Of *Shakespeares* minde, and manners brightly shines / In his well torned, and true-filed lines" (66–68); he has preserved his immutable essence, that is, by becoming a literary tool-and-die worker.

Elsewhere, too, Jonson's works articulate a modest sympathy for the meaner sort. In *A Tale of a Tub*, for instance, Dame Turfe curtly orders Hannibal Puppy to carry wood, and he retorts *sotto voce* with a promise to settle his score at the supper table:

> I wood to the vier? I shall piss it out first:
> You thinke to make me ene your oxe, or asse;
> Or any thing. Though I cannot right myselfe
> On you; Ile sure revenge me on your meat.
>   (3.3.52–55)

In this case, Dame Turfe's provender becomes a linguistic alter ego, a consumable substitute for her unassailable person. In another passage from the same play, when the servant Basket Hilts descants upon the arrogance of the propertied ranks, he degrades his social superiors by imagining them to be part of a giant fish stew:

> A good Dog
> Deserues, Sir, a good bone, of a free Master:
> But, 'an your turnes be serv'd, the divell a bit
> You care for a man after, ere a Lard of you.
> Like will to like, y-faith, quoth the scab'd Squire
> To th' mangy Knight, when both met in a dish
> Of butter'd vish.
> (2.4.10–16)

This is an almost Ibsenesque view of class politics, in which society functions like a sausage grinder. You put in boneheads, knuckleheads, and fatheads, grind them up, and get meatheads. The very worst qualities of social privilege rise to the top of Basket Hilts's bowl of buttered fish.

Again, there is the following passage from *The Case Is Altered*, in which the servant Onion addresses Count Ferneze with reverent formality, only to receive a rude rebuke:

> COUNT: Tut, tut, leaue pleasing of my honour *Diligence*,
>   You double with me, come.
> ONION: How: does he find fault with *Please his Honour*?
>   S'wounds it has begun a seruingmans speech, euer since
>   I belongd to the blew order . . .
> COUNT: Whats that, you mutter sir? will you proceed?
> ONION: Ant like your good Lordship.
> COUNT: Yet more, Gods precious.
> ONION: What, do not this like him neither?
> COUNT: What say you sir knaue?
> ONION: Mary I say your Lordship were best to set me to schoole
>   againe, to learne how to deliuer a message.
> (1.7.23–35)

All of the foregoing workers' protests are crafted largely as asides, and in my opinion they comprise a generally repressed corollary to Jonson's discourse of authorial labor. Onion, as his repeated attempts at formal speech are spurned by Count Ferneze, resorts to the same level of exasperation typical of Jonson himself when an audience rejects his plays. As one of the poet's representatives says in *The Magnetic Lady*, likening playwriting to textile work for the instruction of the throng, "A good *Play*, is like a skeene of silke: which, if you take by the right end, you may wind off at pleasure . . . : But if you light on the wrong end, you will pull all into a knot" (Induction.136–141). Apparently Count Ferneze and Jonson's hostile audiences have it in common that neither has ever actually worked a spool of cloth.

This muted sympathy with workers and servants may help to generate some of the ambiguities attendant upon the figure of the cook in *Neptune's Triumph*, too, who functions simultaneously as a salt-of-the-earth artisan and as *magister artium totarum*. Moreover, when the cook from *Neptune's Triumph* reappears as Lickfinger in *The Staple of News*, he again allows Jonson to expatiate upon the importance of productive labor:

> A *Master-Cooke*! Why, he's the *man* o' men,
> For a *Professor*! he designes, he drawes,
> He paints, he carues, he builds, he fortifies,
> Makes *Citadels* of curious fowle and fish,
> Some he *dri-ditches*, some *motes* round with *broths*.
> Mounts *marrowbones*, cuts *fifty-angled custards*,
> Reares *bulwark* pies, and for his *outer workes*
> He raiseth *Ramparts* of immortall *crust*;
> And teacheth all the *Tacticks*, at one dinner.
> (4.2.19–27)

Here Jonson digests and adapts his own work, just as he has done elsewhere to the work of others. However, the poet-cook's peculiar liminality survives the digestive process. Lickfinger is one of the more energetic and scabrous figures in *The Staple of News*, precisely because his identity is hard to fix in relation to the play's overall themes and character groupings. He prepares the grand banquet that constitutes the fourth act of the play, in which the prodigal son Penniboy Junior feasts a typical collection of Jonsonian gulls and sharpers and in which Penniboy Junior's father (Penniboy Canter), having feigned his own death in order to observe his son's behavior, confronts the assembled company and reclaims his estate. But when the elder Penniboy denounces his son's companions, he directs his satirical attacks on poetry and cookery at figures other than Lickfinger: the poetaster Madrigal (4.4.54–59) and the braggart warrior Shun-Field (4.4.94). In a single quip, Penniboy Canter caustically imagines Lickfinger reading "*Apicius de re culinaria*" to Penniboy Junior and his beloved Lady Pecunia (4.4.88–89), but this remark seems to be more of a slap at the prodigal son than at the cook. In any event, Lickfinger has had the sense to disappear (4.2.88) before the elder Penniboy reveals his true identity, reclaims his wealth, and excoriates the assembled company.

Elsewhere in the play, Lickfinger hovers at the margins of events as a sardonic commentator and provocateur, encouraging the other characters to display their worst tendencies and offering these to the audience as entertainment. In this respect he is akin to the various satirical observers—the Quarlouses and Winwifes, Well-Breds and Young Knowells, Dauphines and Truewits—that populate Jonson's other work. One of his most important tasks is to expose the meanness of Penniboy Junior's avaricious uncle, Penniboy Senior, and he does so by encouraging the old miser to treat him with the contempt born of privilege. Lickfinger accomplishes this first by agreeing to buy from Penniboy Senior the various gifts of food he has received of suitors, and then by arriving late for the appointment at which the transaction is to take place:

> P. SE. Pox vpon [you] kidney,
> Alwaies too late! . . . You stay'd of purpose,
> To haue my venison stinke, and my fowle mortify'd,
> That you might ha' 'hem—LIC. A shilling or two cheaper,
> That's your iealousie.
> (2.3.1–2, 20–23)

As in the cases of Hannibal Puppy and others quoted above, Lickfinger defends himself against the abuse of his social superior, and once again the defense plays itself out on the field of the dining table, for Penniboy Senior's greed manifests itself largely as a refusal to eat. He describes himself as "one that neuer made / Good meale in his sleep, but sells the acates are sent him, / Fish, Fowle, and venison, and preserues himselfe, / Like an old hoary Rat, with mouldy pye-crust" (2.1.15–18); he complains that "Grosse gluttony . . . / Eates up the poore" (2.3.31–34); and, at the same time that he sells good food to Lickfinger, he ironically ends up purchasing a bushel of rotten eggs, "For ammunition here to pelt the boyes, / That breake my windowes" (2.3.59–60). Simply by existing, the cook Lickfinger places such language and behavior in ugly relief.

Elsewhere, too, Lickfinger encourages the folly of others, dressing it with such art that it becomes entertaining in its repulsiveness. Having been commissioned by Penniboy Junior to prepare the banquet of Act 4, Lickfinger shops not simply for the evening's foodstuffs, but also for its conversation. This he finds at the news office from which Jonson's play derives its title:

> LIC. Ha' you no *Newes* o'the *Stage*?
> They'll aske me about *new Playes*, at dinner time.
> And I should be dumbe as a fish. THO. O! yes.
> There is a *Legacy* left to the *Kings Players*,
> Both for their various shifting of their *Scene*,
> And dext'rous change o' their persons to all shapes,
> And all disguises . . .
> LIC. What newes of *Gundomar*? THO. A second *Fistula*,
> Or an *excoriation* (at the least)
> For putting the poore *English-play*, was writ of him,
> To such a sordid vse, as (is said) he did,
> Of cleansing his *posterior's* . . .
> Since when, he liues condemn'd to his Chaire, at *Bruxels*.
> (3.2.198–212)

Lickfinger here bargains for exactly the kind of news that appears in Jonson's epigram on Captayne Hungry, and, just as in the case of Captayne Hungry, the news itself demonstrates a grotesque metamorphic quality that leads inevitably to the watercloset. The serial counterfeiting of the "*Kings Players*" is trumped by the counterfeiting of the news staple, which eventuates in a vision of Gondomar's confinement to a Flemish closestool. This latter confinement serves to fix the excremental quality of the newsmongers' imagination, just as Captayne Hungry's conversation declares his baseness. Yet at the same time, Lickfinger's questions impose a kind of aesthetic felicity on the news-rubbish being distributed. As the players "change . . . their persons to all shapes," they undergo a figurative progress through the body politic, from performance before the head of the kingdom to their unlikely reappearance as an arsewipe for the Spanish ambassador. At the heart of this progress lies the transformation of stage matter into page matter: the literary reconstitution that allows copy to be mistaken for principal. This reconstitution is Lickfinger's professional stock-in-trade, and it is Jonson's, too. The cook becomes something like a choric voice for the poet, commenting with satisfaction on the discomfiture of his play's various gulls and malefactors: Penniboy Senior, who, stark mad at the loss of his wealth, charges his dogs with disloyalty and imprisons them in "two old cases of close stools" (5.3.40); or the play's assembled rogues and jeerers, whom Lickfinger describes as a covey of quail scattering before the angry Penniboy Canter (5.3.56–57).

In the case of such figures, one may come away with the sense that Jonson's social identity is every bit as concocted as his literary identity. Just as his verse consists largely of other authors' work, consumed and redistributed, his personal voice seems to emanate from widely divergent social strata—to encompass a fond identification with the soldier's trade, for instance, as well as an extravagant esteem for King James and the Sidneys. Jonson redistributes himself within bits and pieces of the body politic, or he redistributes bits and pieces of the body politic within himself. Of course, the very same plays in which Jonson praises labor and offers at least indirectly sympathetic views of the lower social ranks also contain other passages, in which the poet reviles his humble contemporaries rather than sympathizing or identifying with them. They become a "rude barbarous crue, a people that haue no brains, and yet grounded iudgements," who "will hisse any thing that mounts aboue their grounded capacities" (*The Case Is Altered* 2.7.68–71). But such abuse does not obliterate the sympathy; it merely coexists with it, rather as a large and ill-tempered adolescent boy might coexist with his younger brother. For as it turns out, Jonson's model of authorship—and of himself—needs the sympathy as much as it does the vilification. Without strong views on the importance of labor, Jonson will lose his own best means of distinguishing himself and improving his lot. Without a means of distancing himself from other laborers, he will either (a) allow "the relationship of [literary] buyer and seller to harden into that of employer and wage-earner" (Womack 18) or (b) help improve everyone else's lot as well as his own, thereby making his personal attainments unremarkable. This is the essence of his professional dilemma: he must promote himself via the commonest of resources—hands, a mind, and a general willingness to work—yet he must avoid amalgamating with his countless namesakes who possess, or may possess, roughly the same faculties themselves. He must distinguish himself from the Johnsons.

Ben Jonson, Author of *Don Quixote*

This discussion has moved farther and farther away from its originating focus on Jonsonian metaphors of digestion. It has done so of necessity, because for Jonson digestion itself is never a self-contained, self-identical process; rather, the idea of digestion offers a convenient point of entry into an infinitely catenating series of literary distinctions and accommodations. I have already remarked on the tendency of Jonsonian digestive and culinary metaphors to overlap in the stomach, the anatomical site where consumption becomes production and inside becomes outside. It may be worthwhile to return now to this aspect of Jonsonian literary discourse, this time as it functions in the opening lines of *Pleasure Reconciled to Virtue*. There Comus, the belly god, is introduced, in a manner drawn from Rabelais (Herford, Simpson, and Simpson 10:587), as "*Prime master of arts*" and father of civilization:

> *He, he first inuented both hogshead & Tun,*
> *ye gimblet, & vice too; & taught 'em to run.*
> *And since, wth ye funnel, an hyppocras bag*
> *h'has made of himself, y^t now he cries swag.*
> *W^{ch} showes, though ye pleasure be but of fowre inches,*
> *yet he is a weesell, ye gullet that pinches,*
> *of any delight: & not spares from ye back*
> *what-ever, to make of ye belly a sack.*
>
> (21–28)

If digestion offers Jonson a prime trope for artistic transformation, it should be noted that the transformations in this passage work simultaneously in competing directions. On one hand, the belly god populates the external world with implements to serve his appetite: wine barrels, gimlets to pierce them, screw-stops and funnels, and more. But at the same time, these implements then imprint themselves reflexively on their own creator; Comus himself metamorphoses into "*an hyppocras bag*"—a sack for straining mulled wine. The belly digests the world, which simultaneously digests the belly.

One consequence of this ambivalence is that the boundaries separating subject from object in literal discourse are rendered permeable; they are overcoded by metaphor until it is no longer clear what constitutes tenor and what vehicle. Comus is simultaneously "ye god of *cheere*" and the belly incarnate; the belly, in turn, is simultaneously creator of the cultural order and an object for analysis and representation within the order it creates ("Some in derision call him the father of farts: But I say, he was ye first invento^r of great ordnance" [60–62]). Given such reciprocities, it is not really possible to ask whether Comus serves as the anthropomorphic representation of the belly or the belly as a metonymic representation of Comus, whether Comus is a body-without-organs or the belly is an organ embodied. Likewise, when Jonson repeatedly images literary consumption as digestion, while concurrently describing literary production as cooking, it becomes impossible to locate the literal referent of his overlapping metaphors. The metaphors effectively become the thing itself, or rather a thick soup of multivalent reference that occupies the space of the thing itself.

In *Pleasure Reconciled to Virtue*, a further consequence of this thick description is that Comus tends to grow like Topsy, with no recognition of limit. As "*deuourer of broild, bak'd, rosted, or sod*" (31), he becomes

> so wide i' ye waste
> as scarce wth no pudding thou art to be lac'd:
> but eating & drincking, untill thou dost nod
> thou break'st all thy girdles, & breakst forth a god.
> (33–36)

What Comus does, in other words, is to mimic the process of Jonsonian literary invention itself. If the stomach is like the writer's own inventive space because it serves "as a Cooke to al the members of the body," then when Jonson describes the poet as differing "nothing at all from a *Master-Cooke*," one is left with the unmistakable implication that *as* a cook, Jonson is subsuming the members of his audience within his own bodily space. Devouring the work of others and concocting it in his study, he prepares a new banquet of it, a banquet served to literary consumers who implicitly occupy the space of "al the members of the body." Jonson's authorial sensibility, like the belly god's girth, is infinitely expansive.

Still, infinitely expansive does not mean infinitely inclusive. One problem with applying the Bakhtinian model of popular festivity to Jonson's poetics is that as a whole Jonson's career makes no consistent effort to construct the anarchic, liberating social vision championed by Bakhtin, in which "no dogma, no authoritarianism, no narrow-minded seriousness can coexist" with popular festive forms (Bakhtin 3). To the extent that Jonson makes use of such a social vision, it is as a strategy of self-empowerment, not of general liberation: or, to be more precise, it is a strategy of general liberation played out metonymically within the authorial self. As Jonathan Haynes notes, "the opposition between popular festive and refined aristocratic cultures was still forming" in the seventeenth century "and should not be exaggerated" (97). As a result, Jonson is able to construct a poetics of centrifugal authoritarianism and centripetal polymorphism, in which the poet creates a slippery space for himself while seeking to impose rigorous canons of discrimination and behavior on others. Hence the selective concern with plagiarism, the energy spent on self-refashioning, the relatively muted but nonetheless manifest sympathy with labor and laborers, the concomitant and highly vocal antagonism to the meaner sort in general, and the highly ambivalent terms in which Jonson theorizes his own work/play: all of these matters may be related through Jonson's (non)metaphorical embodiments of the act of literary invention. Even the one critical proposition to which the poet would seem most consistently and crucially committed—the idea that writing is work—gets problematized in a pinch; Jonson's plays may be works, but there is little sense of him "strik[ing] the second heat / Vpon the *Muses* anuile" when he announces proudly, in the prologue to *Volpone*, that "fiue weekes fully pen'd" the comedy (*Volpone* Prologue.16). Such a comment certainly cannot—should not—countervail Jonson's repeated insistence on the laboriousness of his office, but it should suggest that even the firmest of his literary attitudes are subject to self-aggrandizing shifts of emphasis.

This chapter began by examining Jonson's surname for two major reasons. First, as itself a text subject to authorial digestion, the name usefully foregrounds Jonson's deep concern with the craft of making things from words. Moreover, since Jonson's name is, after all, Jonson's name, it signals the author's own commitment to reconceiving his personal identity and significance through the medium of his profession. To this latter degree, one may regard Jonson as the single most outstanding literary character in the Jonson canon. Himself a product of authorial labor, the author becomes one moving fiction among a host of others. Just as the others—Volpone, Subtle, Brainworm, and so on—remain subject to subsequent refictionalization through the media of performance, reading, and literary history, Jonson does, too. His work—even the work of his own name—becomes appropriable by others, and in the process of being appropriated, it resists Jonson's own insistence on the determinacy of his own authorial labor, inspiration, essence, and property.

To illustrate this argument one last time, I want to end where I began: with Jonson's surname itself. I had initially used it to reaffirm a fairly commonplace view of the distinction between Jonson and Shakespeare; Jonson's attempt to fix and control his identity through the materials of literary work would thus contrast with Shakespeare's seeming acquiescence in the processes of linguistic play. But this distinction grows more complicated in light of the editing to which Jonson's name became subject in the two centuries after his death. For the *h* that he sought so hard to exorcise from his life and work returned with the practice of printers in the 1630s, only to disappear again in the eighteenth century, when it became convenient for printers and readers to institute a typographical distinction between the Jo(h)nsons Ben and Samuel (Chute 19n.). Thus the very literary device that Jonson initially introduced as a means of marking his separateness from others reappears as a reminder that he is in fact not terribly separate at all—that there is more than one Jo(h)nson in the world, that more than one of them knows how to scribble, and that (to paraphrase Coleridge) there is a touch of Jo(h)nson in all of us to the extent that we as readers are responsible for sustaining the fiction of authorial integrity. As the other Johnson put it, fame is like a shuttlecock; it must be hit to remain in the air, and readers must do the hitting.

Borges's classic short story "Pierre Menard, Author of Don Quixote" offers a particularly resonant statement of the equivocal relation between author and reader—a statement, moreover, that applies to the distinction between Jonson's Jonson and Johnson's Jonson. Menard as author undertakes to reproduce perfectly what Menard as reader has processed in the past. The result, after much effort, is a letter-perfect replica of "the ninth and thirty-eighth chapters of Part One of *Don Quixote* and a fragment of the twenty-second chapter" (48). However, the very exactitude of Menard's typographical replication generates vast semiotic disparities:

> The fragmentary *Don Quixote* of Menard is more subtle than that of Cervantes. The latter indulges in a rather coarse opposition between tales of knighthood and the meager, provincial reality of his country; Menard chooses as "reality" the land of Carmen during the century of Lepanto and Lope. . . . [Menard] disregards or proscribes local color. This disdain indicates a new approach to the historical novel. . . . Equally vivid is the contrast in styles. The archaic style of Menard—in the last analysis, a foreigner—suffers from a certain affectation. Not so that of his precursor, who handles easily the ordinary Spanish of his time. (51–53)

In short, "The text of Cervantes and that of Menard are verbally identical, but the second is almost infinitely richer" (52). Borges's ironic deprecation of the original *Don Quixote* playfully explodes the notion that literary property or value can be assigned to a particular individual or text. Borges has taken to heart Jonson's idea—manifest in his use of alimentary motifs to figure his attitudes toward writing, reading, and literary property—that consumption is production, and vice versa. As a result, there is no space in Borges for a self-identical work of literature, or for a self-identical self.

"Pierre Menard" thus rehearses ex post facto the fate of Jonson's name (and the model of authorship it represents) within the Western hermeneutical tradition. Originally conceived as a marker of singularity, the name is generally ignored or (re)revised into a sign of nonoriginality. Yet when it reemerges in the eighteenth century, its very uniqueness is compromised in the gesture. The new Jonson arises from a literary dispensation committed to generalizing the old Jonson's peculiar emphasis on himself as the source of literary labor, products, and value. Or, to put things a different way, the idea of the literary professional, so unpopularly promoted by Jonson in his own lifetime, by the eighteenth century comes to appear natural and unavoidable, yet insofar as literary professionalism becomes an accepted, "natural" category, it ceases to be Jonson's own. In the eventual triumph of his ideas on authorship, Jonson must surrender—insofar as he ever really had it—the unique character of his literary identity. To win this game, as David Lodge has somewhere said, is to lose. But then, to lose is also to lose.

4
The Ordure of Things

JONSON IMAGINES WRITING AS A PROCESS of digestion, and he repeatedly thinks of his work as a banquet miraculously concocted through that process for the entertainment and improvement of his audiences:

> Truth sayes, of old, the art of making plaies
> Was to content the people; & their praise
> Was to the *Poet* money, wine, and bayes.
> . . . .
> Our wishes, like to those (make publique feasts)
> Are not to please the cookes tastes, but the guests.
> (*Epicoene* Prologue.1–9)

Still, Jonson does not always reroute the action of peristalsis in so generous and delightful a way. This study has already mentioned Captayne Hungry of Epigram 107, whose conversation acquires a distinctly excremental character. That same conversation, put to paper, results in the secret correspondence of Epigram 92 ("The New Crie"), generated by the "ripe statesmen" who are the object of that poem's satire. These worthies, the nondramatic equivalent of Sir Politic Would-Be, study

> the sundrie wayes
> To write in cypher, and the seuerall keyes,
> To ope' the character. They'haue found the sleight
> With iuyce of limons, onions, pisse, to write,
> To break up seales, and close 'hem.
> (25–29)

In doing so, not only do they superimpose the act of linguistic performance on that of urinary evacuation; they also conflate the functions of urine with those of such culinary staples as lemons and onions. In doing so, they elide the privy with the dinner table.

Scatology of this kind is central to Jonson's vocabulary of abuse. One could cite dozens of examples of it, some as pithy as the final sally of "To Inigo Marquess Would-Be" (*Ungathered Verse* 35.24)—"Wee'll haue thee styld ye Marquess of New-Ditch"—and some sustained, like the excremental badinage of *The Alchemist* and *Bartholomew Fair*, throughout entire plays. The recurrence of such material has generated much useful psychoanalytical criticism, the most prominent instances of which have been reviewed in the introduction to this book. On the other hand—even despite Gail Paster's outstanding discussion of the early modern medical significance of urine and excrement[1]—there has been relatively little effort to connect the psychoanalytical criticism of Jonson's work to the material and cultural disposition of human waste in Jacobean London. One aim of this chapter, therefore, is to attempt a modest historicization of Jonson's discourse of anality by surveying the cultural and infrastructural mechanisms available in Jonson's day for the disposal of feces, urine, dung, offal, and other assorted sewage.

In pursuing this interest, I hope to shed some light on the vagaries of Jonson's scatology as represented by the examples I have already given. On the most immediate level, for instance, Jonson's investment in excrement as a tool of abuse tends to implicate him in the excesses that he chastises. This argument has been advanced in classic form by Alvin Kernan, who views Renaissance satire in general as tending to a psychological fixation on vice that parallels the morbid fixations of the satirist's own subjects.[2] But the feculence of Jonson's writing is sufficiently bountiful, and sufficiently baroque, to suggest something more than the workings of an unhealthy moral imagination. When Justice Overdo inveighs against the possibility of alligators pissing on tobacco, and when Lickfinger describes Gondomar's Middletonian arsewipe, the excrementality of the language can only secondarily be described as abusive; its primary effect is not to heap contumely on a particular figure (Overdo? Tobacco? Tobacco smokers? Alligators?), but rather to inject an unexpected metamorphic vigor into the poet's own work. To this extent, Jonsonian scatology acquires the character of what Kenneth Burke has called "pure persuasion." It

> involves the saying of something, not for an extra-verbal advantage to be got by the saying, but because of a satisfaction intrinsic to the saying. It summons because it likes the feel of a summons. It would be nonplused if the summons were answered. It attacks because it revels in the sheer syllables of vituperation. It would be horrified if, each time it finds a way of saying "be damned," it really did send a soul to rot in hell. (*Rhetoric* 269)

From this standpoint, Jonson's scatology is closely connected to his fondness for enumeration and metonymy. The excrementality becomes an instrument of enumeration, prolonging the author's discourse and soliciting the audience's continued attention; it is part of what Jonas Barish has called Jonson's "amoral delight in the varied forms and shapes of language in the world" (260).

In short, Jonson's discursive universe is one in which alligators piss on tobacco and "ripe statesmen" write letters with piss, not simply as an expression of authorial censure, but also as a means of having fun. I know "having fun" is not a terribly precise phrase, and I must confess to be at a loss for a better one. To remain within Burke's terminology for a moment, the "fun" in question partly consists in the free-floating satisfaction of pure persuasion: the pleasure generated by the act of signification itself. But it also derives partly from the "principle of courtship" that functions as a precondition for any utterance whatever. As Burke observes,

In its essence communication involves the use of verbal symbols for purposes of appeal. Thus, it splits formally into the three elements of speaker, speech, and spoken-to, with the speaker so shaping his speech as to "commune with" the spoken-to. This purely technical pattern is the precondition of *all* appeal. And "standoffishness" is necessary to the form, because without it the appeal could not be maintained. (*Rhetoric* 271)

Jonson's scatological enumerations arguably function to maintain such distance vis-à-vis the audience by injecting an ongoing element of surprise into the poet's entertainment. A universe in which hungry captains utter excrement and marquesses derive their titles from sewage conduits, in which alligators urinate on tobacco leaves and newts float in ale bottles, in which Spanish counts cleanse their posteriors with the latest play quarto while would-be spies write messages in their own stale: such a world may be sufficiently unexpected, sufficiently distant from the experience of the audience, and yet also, in unexpected ways, sufficiently familiar to focus an audience's attention.

Moreover, Jonsonian scatology not only acquires a necessarily playful character; it also embodies and intensifies processes of cultural exploration that exist, in less pronounced form, off the page and outside the theater. When Gail Paster connects the opening line of *The Alchemist*—Subtle's contemptuous "I fart at thee" (1.1.1.)—to the folk-commonplace of the *proktos lalon* ("the speaking ass" [Paster 126]),[3] she points toward the complexity of this exploration. On one hand, Subtle's exclamation is clearly censorious in nature, constituting a refinement of the folk motif in which the farting in question is performed almost as a virtuoso activity, "deliberate and aggressive, signifying control, aim, the effectuality of will" (Paster 145). But underlying this virtuosity is the somatic uncontrol of the original folk motif itself, still available as a lightly inflected reference. And further, Subtle's use of the speaking asshole as a tool of condemnation opens up a space for exploration of his own body: a space in which the various terms of the anatomy become promiscuously interchangeable in their capacity for culturation and signification. Not only does Subtle's farting put others in their place; it also undoes the categorical distinctions that govern the farting body itself, opening up a smooth anatomical space in which one organ effectively becomes another, assuming the characteristics of the other and operating for and through it. Not only does the farting asshole speak for the whole body; when Subtle says, "I fart at thee," even if the actor playing the role accompanies the remark with an appropriate gesture of intestinal virtuosity, he nonetheless *says*, "I fart at thee." The functions of mouth and anus deterritorialize one another.

Given the Deleuzian theory that underlies this study, the conception of bodily space intrinsic to Subtle's words proves irresistibly interesting. As Deleuze and Guattari observe, arguing for a restructuration of images of the body such that a given organ "breaks into . . . or cuts off and receives the flow from another organ" (Canning 38), "Dismantling the organism has never meant killing yourself, but rather opening the body to connections . . . , circuits, conjunctions, levels and thresholds, passages and distributions of intensity" (*Plateaus* 160). Deleuze and Guattari are well aware that such connections are not dependent on the existence of a body of Deleuzian theory itself. On the contrary, Deleuzian theory develops largely as an ex post facto analysis of biological and cultural phenomena that instance the functioning of exploratory, nomad thought and that are in some cases at least as old as culture itself. For Jonson, I believe, scatology offers a point of departure for such thought, in part because the early modern English economy of sewage—the apparatus for conceiving, distributing, recycling, and disposing of sewage available in Jonson's day—was itself by no means as tidily compartmentalized as in twentieth-century England and America. If Jonsonian scatology offers readers a particularly inventive sense of self, it is a self made possible by the ordure of things in seventeenth-century England.

For a brief non-Jonsonian instance of this point: in 1596 Sir John Harington published his *Metamorphosis of Ajax*, thereby filling a much needed gap in the history of English letters. The book's declared purpose is to describe, for the first time in early modern Europe, the construction and operation of the flush toilet. Thus when Harington finally—after much preamble and general silliness—gets around to describing his invention, he contrasts it with the modes of waste disposal generally favored in sixteenth-century English houses:

The first and the ancientest, is to make a close vault in the ground, widest in the bottome, and narrower upward, and to floor the same with lime and tarris . . . : for if it be so close as no aire can come in, it doth as it were smother the savour. . . . Another way, is either upon close or open vaults, so to place the sieges or seats as behind them may rise tunnes of chimneys, to draw all the ill aires upwards: of which kind I may be bold to say, that our house of Lincolnes Inne, putteth downe all that have bene made afore it. (161–163)

Neither of these arrangements is adequate, in Harington's opinion, for neither genuinely moves the offending matter through and out of the living space. Instead, both aim primarily to deposit the contents of human bowels into the more capacious bowels of the buildings those human beings inhabit. Hence the mock eulogistic reference to Lincoln's Inn, guaranteed to make any senior bencher wince; one of the grand institutions of English law would appear, saving your reverence, to have been built upon a vast and ever expanding midden.

Harington exploits this insight with a certain glee; among his objections to the old ways of handling excrement, he notes explicitly that "in a Princes house where so many mouthes be fed, a close vault will fil quickly" (162). And indeed, early modern commentators suggest that once the privy vaults of such buildings were filled to overflowing, the denizens tended to load every rift with ore. As one country adage of the day observed, "A great housekeeper is sure of nothinge for his good cheare save a great Turd at his gate" (qtd. in Stone 562). The trick, for Harington, is to liberate such buildings from an economy of waste retention and connect them to an economy of waste expulsion instead, and by this measure Harington's work takes an important early step toward the segregationism that characterizes late and postmodern sanitary science. But at the same time, Harington's primary instrument for advocating this step forward is the sublimatory medium of the written word, which tends to overflow categories and limits, reveling in its own fecal extravagance. As Kelly Anspaugh has put it, Harington's "cloacal imperialism" is paralleled by a sensitivity to "*textual* imperialism"—an intense awareness of literary influence—as well (20).

Although the author's metamorphosed jakes seeks "to convey *away* both the ordure & other noisome things, as also the raine water that falles into the courts" of great houses (160, my italics), his prose describes—and in describing, helps to constitute—a process of excremental re-circulation from, to, and among the various texts of classical antiquity and European modernity. The author's fecal matter may be removed from sight by the local rainwater, but his book is to celebrate a piss pot with a classical name, derived from "the ancient house of AJAX" (69), and celebrated previously by Rabelais (68), Ovid (71), Martial (97), Saint Augustine (71), Sir Thomas More (101), John Heywood (102–103), and even Holy Writ itself (86–87). Precisely because of its innovative and exploratory nature, *The Metamorphosis of Ajax* is what Paster has called a deeply "self-divided text" (154): committed in part to a strenuous improvement of the mechanisms separating humanity from its own filth, but also inclined to a playful literary resurrection of the offending matter. Jonson's work takes advantage of a similar dynamic.

In his day, Harington was as noted for his epigrammatic wit as for his exploits in the field of sanitary engineering. He was more or less equally renowned, that is, for circulating filth on both the alimentary and the rhetorical levels. The latter measure of his fame descended, in turn, to the other great epigrammatist of the English Renaissance, Jonson, and therefore it is perhaps fitting that Jonson should conclude his only book of epigrams with the feculent mock epic "On the Famous Voyage"—a poem that itself concludes with a brief homage to "hi[m], that sung A-IAX" (196). The present chapter regards this work as marking a point of juncture between the scatological concerns of Harington and those of Jonson; as a result, I argue, Jonson's epigram invites readers to reexamine the much vexed issue of its author's anality, and to supplement the psychoanalytic embedment of that issue with information drawn from social history. In effect, I want to propose a revised notion of Jonson as an anal poet. Counter to Edmund Wilson's famous vision of him as a "constipated writer well primed with sack" (226), given over wholly to "the hoarding and withholding instinct" (218), I would suggest that the poet's anality—like Harington's before him—takes form in large part through tropes of deterritorialization and circulation. As a result, the author's rhetorical capacities function simultaneously as a supplement to, an alternative to, and a symbolic conduit for the ordure that Jonson's poetry represents. Furthermore, the scatology of "On the Famous Voyage" parallels a historical return to processes of waste management characteristic of Jonson's beloved antiquity.[4] And finally, the poem thus helps reshape Jonson's own reputation as an early neoclassicist,[5] for whom—to borrow a phrase from Roland Barthes—"language . . . was transparent, . . . flowed and left no deposit" (*Writing* 3). The resultant view extends Joseph Loewenstein's claim that the poet "has allowed his very body to leave an imprint on his creativity" ("Corpulence" 508), for the poet's body emerges as self-consciously constituted through the processes whereby its products are integrated into society as a whole.

The Excremental Vision

For psychoanalysis, of course, it has long been a truism that human waste is not simply a material phenomenon, and that individuals and societies must deal with it on both the physical and conceptual levels. Freud, Sandor Ferenczi, and Ernest Jones following Freud and Ferenczi, have traced this correspondence in detail through a series of conversions and equivalencies that they consider fundamental to the constitution of the adult ego.[6] On this view children grow out of an initial, jealous fascination with their own excrement by a combined process of sublimation and repression, gradually replacing the feces itself with such substitutes as mud, marbles, buttons, and coins. Mainstream Freudian analysis sees this sequence of displacements as exemplifying the principle that "the mind evolves from the body and . . . the body and its functions continue throughout life to influence how we feel and how we think" (Shengold 12). If therefore, as Loewenstein has argued, Jonson's body has left an imprint on his creativity, that imprint may partly be explained through Freudian models of anal substitution.

Such explanations have been proposed and debated more or less continuously ever since Wilson's original identification of anal motifs in the Jonson corpus. The present study seeks to contribute to this process by coordinating an analysis of the author's work with a consideration of the historical embedment of the excretory processes within Elizabethan and Jacobean social practice in general. In other words, I want to return to Freud's original claim that psychic ontogeny recapitulates phylogeny, for this claim, properly considered, must exert some influence on any assessment of the development of individual writers. If, as Freud argued, anal eroticism falls victim in individual cases to "the sexual repression which advances along with civilization" (*Civilization* 21:106), it is at least worth considering the precise forms this advance has taken before we characterize (or dismiss) a writer like Jonson as an anal neurotic. Moreover, in the case of early modern England, one encounters records of a society virtually consumed by tropes of anal retention, sublimation, and aggression. Jonson's anality, such as it is, deserves to be considered in the context of these records at least as much as it deserves to be evaluated in terms of twentieth-century psychoanalytic theory.

From this standpoint, David Riggs's thoughtful discussion of anal motifs in *The Case Is Altered* has helped to identify the waste-is-treasure equation as a point of contact between the formal preoccupations of Jonson's work and the historical circumstances of his upbringing as a bricklayer's stepson. When, for instance, the miserly Jacques de Prie hides his wealth within a pile of excrement (3.5), Riggs sees him as assuming the role of a "wicked stepfather" who, "carrying his scuttle full of horse dung, . . . resembles nothing so much as a bricklayer bearing a load of odorous mortar" (30). Thus, within the compass of *The Case Is Altered*, de Prie can serve as an outlet for Jonson's primal animosity: a fantasy substitute for "the man who married [Jonson's] mother and tried to make a bricklayer out of him" (31). This suggestive analysis only invites correction through its emphasis on the idiosyncratic aspect of Jonson's anality. As Trinh Minh-ha has remarked, "Wet dung remains an environmental potential. In many societies it serves to plaster earthen walls, protecting them from the weather" (54). Nor was this practice alien to early modern England, where plaster was often concocted out of a mixture of lime, sand, straw, and dung (which repelled wood-boring insects). Thus it is worth noting that as a bricklayer, Jonson (like his stepfather) would have come into close contact with manure on a regular basis, and the poet's association of brick-laying with dung-shoveling stepfathers, which at the distance of four centuries may seem positively febrile in its antagonism, may assume an almost matter-of-fact empiricism upon closer examination.

If Jonson was preoccupied with what we might call the social significance of the anus, he was not alone in that respect; nor should his interest in excremental matters be regarded merely as an outgrowth of unique family circumstances. Sir John Harington, for one, produces his own version of Jacques de Prie early in the *Metamorphosis of Ajax*:

an Hermit being carried in an evening, by the conduct of an Angell, through a great citie, to contemplate the great wickednesse daily and hourly wrought therein; met in the street a gongfarmer with his cart full laden, no man envying his full measure. (85)

The course of this tale is predictable. The hermit "stopt his nosthrils, & betooke him to the other side of the street," whereas "the Angell kept on his way, seeming no whit offended with the savour." Yet soon thereafter, "a woman gorgeously attyred, well perfumed, well attended with coaches" passed by, causing the angel to cringe and "hasten . . . him selfe away"; and thus the story concludes that "this fine courtesan laden with sinne, was a more stinking savour afore God & his holy Angels, then that beastly cart, laden with excrements" (85).

In effect, Harington's dung farmer can serve as a potential distraction for hermits and angels precisely because he is a distraction for Harington's readers in general. Occupying a necessary position in the social order, he exists outside that order at the same time, as the distinct point at which tropes of civilized waste disposal metamorphose into patterns of "beastly" waste retention. (Indeed, the London dung farmer tended to traffic more or less indiscriminately in both human and animal excrements, thereby further undermining his own status within culture.) Circumscribed by rituals of physical avoidance and required by law to do his work at night,[7] he toils his way forward with a "full measure" that arouses no one's envy, in large part because everyone has helped produce it. As a result, the dung farmer comes to stand metonymically for the ordure it is his job to collect; the process of conveying away our accumulated filth returns it to us in his new and more animate form.

This excremental return of the repressed seems to have taken various shapes in early modern English towns and cities. Thus, for instance, the large institutions of the land—great houses, universities, ecclesiastical and legal buildings, and so forth—constructed closed or open "vaults," to hold the filthy treasure of their respective inhabitants. As these receptacles filled, their contents were typically exhumed and conveyed away by dung farmers like the hapless fellow of Harington's anecdote. In other words, such latrines never really did the work they were designed for; rather than hiding away the users' excrement once and for all, they simply held it for later withdrawal, rather as a bank holds its own deposits. As for the withdrawal itself, it was scarcely a welcome sight, and was therefore relegated by statute to those hours of the evening when it could be most concertedly ignored. Yet the excremental holdings of Renaissance great houses tended to accrue interest in the form of a pervasive stench. Again and again, Harington complains about the odors of Renaissance latrines. He alludes to the "stately stinking privy in the Inner Temple" (173); he objects to the "infection or annoyance" of old-fashioned toilets on the ground that "*Sensus non falli-*

tur in proprio obiecto" [Sensation is not deceived in a thing that is near to it (163)]; and in an elegant combination of euphuistic prose and Aristotelian categories, he remarks that "Ajax was alwayes so strong a man, that this strength being an inseparable accident to him, doth now onely remain in his breath" (78). To this extent, *The Metamorphosis of Ajax* develops out of a system of waste management in which anal retention and anal expulsion remain at constant and frustrating loggerheads.

Beyond the privileged confines of great houses, on the other hand, the social mechanisms of anal retention assumed a much more aggressive form in early modern England. Animal excrement, human excrement, and various other kinds of solid waste were collected, occasionally amalgamated, occasionally sorted and distinguished for various purposes, and regularly saved for a wide range of uses throughout the English countryside. Recent historical research on the "relatively urban and compact" Lancashire town of Stuart Prescot, for instance, has traced out regular patterns of dung accumulation that would have been typical of many English towns and villages in the sixteenth and seventeenth centuries (King 444). From 1580 on, the inhabitants of Prescot enjoyed the statutory right "to pile solid waste products in the street near their doors for up to a week" (King 444). Moreover, citizens regularly left their middens on the street for much greater lengths of time, and could apparently secure the right to do so by paying "a fee, sometimes called a 'tax,' that went for street repairs" (King 444). Furthermore, citizens who wished to maintain a permanent (or semipermanent) dunghill on their property could "avoid the fee by piling dung on the back side of their residence" (King 444). These middens seem to have been largely (although not exclusively) composed of animal, as opposed to human, refuse, but (as Jonson's "On the Famous Voyage" itself attests) the distinction between animal excrement and human sewage tended to erode steadily as urbanization took its course.

Indeed, the fact that citizens were willing to pay a fee for the privilege of accumulating sewage suggests the pervasive presence of the waste-is-treasure motif in modes of early English household and city management. The fee was worth paying because the sewage was worth keeping. And kept it was. Contrary to the popular view of early modern streets (a view encouraged by the self-conscious urbanity of "Mac Flecknoe" and Swift's "City Shower") as clogged with discarded waste matter, such streets seem often to have been clogged with *non*discarded waste matter. Even William Shakespeare's father was fined a shilling in 1552 "for making a dungheap (*sterquinarium*) before his house in Henley Street," Stratford-upon-Avon

(Schoenbaum 7), and although John Shakespeare may not have regarded this midden as part of his overall estate, it was nonetheless clearly his. Similar stories abound—among them the case of William Conygrave of Southwark, haled into court in 1605 because he slaughtered hogs on his property, "and wth the filth & excrements Comminge of the said hoggs [did] much annoye & hurt all his neighbours . . . by raysing of great stinks & stenches."[8] Likewise, turning again to Stuart Prescot, we find that when the innkeeper Thomas Parr died in 1680 he held assorted turds in the value of £3 13s. 4d., or "four percent of his total worth" (King 447). Furthermore, "another eleven inventories of inhabitants of Stuart Prescot mentioned between 6d. and 20s. in dung and muck" (King 447).

In the case of Stuart Prescot, not only were individuals committed to the hoarding and recycling of solid waste; so was the municipality itself. The township reserved the right to confiscate and sell dung that was unclaimed or illegally piled (King 444). And in the nearby village of Ormskirk a "carter"—a professional relative of the "gongfarmer" in Harington's *Metamorphosis*—"was paid 5s. annually to carry away for his own use each Monday whatever 'small heaps and Cobbs of Dung' he found in the streets" (King 447). In short, "dung was a valuable commodity in pre-industrial society for improving soil fertility" (King 447), and for other functions as well. We have already had cause to mention the occasional value of dung as a plastering agent; likewise, during the production of woolen cloth, the wool was repeatedly washed and sprayed with urine (Singer 3:153, 169, 174). Urinary and fecal ingredients occasionally found their way into medicinal preparations—as, for instance, in the case of a remedy for ague recommended by the anonymous *Closet for Ladies and Gentlewomen*, which calls for "horse dung of a stone Horse [i.e., stallion], hot as you can get it from the horse," to be strained into a posset of white wine and drunk with "Methridate, . . . Cardus Benedictus water, and Vnicornes [i.e., narwhal's] horne" (sig. F4r). In addition, there is at least some evidence to suggest that laystalls were occasionally employed as landfills for marshland reclamation.[9] And as a final instance of the metamorphic utility of excremental matter, it is worth recalling that in the early sixteenth century Erasmus could refer disdainfully to the practice of brushing one's teeth with urine. For Erasmus, this is a Spanish custom (*Manners* 277; *De Civilitate* sig. A5r), and it may have been more imaginary than actual. Still, his reference to it in *De Civilitate* suggests that Erasmus, who was nobody's fool, found it credible enough. Such an imaginative use of one's own urine constitutes an extreme case of the tendency to retain and recycle sewage, but a case that is in keeping with the more general patterns of agrarian behavior already surveyed. When viewed against the backdrop of such activities, the practice—treated so scornfully by Jonson in "The New Crie" but actually advocated by Giambattista Porta (342, sig. Zz3v)—of writing secret script in urine hardly seems outrageous at all; it is more like business as usual.

However, the patterns of agrarian waste retention typical of England's farming communities do not necessarily apply to the increasingly urban landscape of seventeenth-century London and Westminster. If the townspeople of Prescot tended to treat their filth differently than did the inhabitants of great houses—hoarding it openly for agricultural use whereas the latter hoarded it privily for eventual removal—we may expect the exigencies of London life to generate a different accommodation between the imperatives of retention and excretion. Even the documents of Stuart Prescot indicate that local authorities had begun to react to population increases in the late seventeenth century by assuming a "less tolerant attitude" toward public health issues (King 454), and the question of how to handle large accumulations of fecal matter must have begun to trouble Londoners at a much earlier date. Records show that "even as far back as Edward I, the Fleet river was a nuisance" to Londoners (Ashton 15); Stow's *Survey of London* could note in the reign of Elizabeth I that the suburbs between the Tower and Wapping had recently developed into "a continuall streete, or filthy straight passage, with Alleyes of small tenements or Cottages" (Stow 2:71). In the reign of Henry VIII, moreover, the city's "main streets had been paved for the first time . . . , with runnels to permit sewage to escape more rapidly to the Fleet River and to the Thames" (Trent 83); and the relatively few buildings lucky enough to border one of the local rivers simply placed their privies directly athwart the water itself.

One obvious result of these arrangements was that different sorts of waste matter tended to commingle indiscriminately. Whereas rural communities seem to have made desultory efforts to distinguish between animal droppings (which regularly constituted fertilizer and building material) and human waste (which was sometimes used for fertilizer and sometimes not, depending on the authority consulted and the crops and soils in question),[10] no such distinction was worth pursuing in an urban environment. Human excrement, animal droppings, animal offal, and every sort of garbage thus tended to collect together in kennels and laystalls. A further consequence was the rapid pollution of the local waterways, particularly the Fleet, which had become a vast open privy by the end of the eighteenth century. Indeed, "in Charles Dickens's time it was still reasonable to describe the Thames itself as an enormous sewer that ebbed and flowed" (Trent 139). The pollution of the Fleet and related waterways had reached a crucial stage by the reign of James I; within a few years of the publication of "On the Famous Voyage," James's parliaments enacted a series of laws expanding previous provisions for cleansing of the city. The initial such statute, 3 James I, cap. 14, reaffirms, in more or less pro forma fashion, an old Henrician law establishing a local commission of sewers, but then follows a series of other acts without any precedent. Statute 3 James I, cap. 18 seeks to divert waters from outside the London area into the city itself, and entrusts this job to the commission of sewers; 4 James I, cap. 12 stipulates that the said waters be conveyed by closed vault rather than by open ditch; and 7 James I, cap. 9 provides that a closed waterway be built from Hackney marsh and the river Lea to "the King's College at Chelsey" (*Statutes at Large* 6). These laws, in turn, find an echo in the "nine Proclamations against spending the legal-term holidays in London . . . issued by King James between 1614 and 1627 [*sic*] . . . to curb the inordinate growth of the metropolis" (Stone 397). Taken as a whole, such legislation suggests a dawning awareness that London could not continue indefinitely to transact infrastructural business as usual.

In sum, Tudor and Stuart London, with its rapid population growth and concomitant municipal works, tended to rely upon the waste-disposal systems of the great houses, supplemented by the capacities of the local rivers. As the city's accumulated waste increased in mass, its agrarian value diminished, and city dwellers reacted by depositing enormous quantities of it into chamber pots and privy vaults, then into sewer conduits and laystalls, then into the local waterways—where it remained, stinking and congealing, until the nineteenth century. By then, the disadvantages of this system of waste management were manifest. The Fleet, whose vapors had long since taken on a life of their own, was roofed over in the mid-1700s (Edmund Wilson mistakenly believed this had been done in Jonson's time [228]); a series of cholera epidemics culminated in the Great Stink of 1858, when the odors of the Thames forced Parliament into recess; and as a result the London Metropolitan Board of Works began excavating an ambitious series of new sewer lines that would eventually divert the city's waste far downstream, to Beckton and Crossness. Likewise, in 1775, the Londoner Alexander Cummings took out a patent on Harington's old invention of the valve toilet, which grew steadily more common and came to be indisseverably associated, in popular memory, with the risible name of Thomas

Crapper (Palmer 22, 106). After three centuries of stench, neglect, and concerted fecal retention, Ajax had finally achieved his long-awaited metamorphosis.

    Thus we can trace a broad pattern, from English great houses to farming villages to London itself, of vacillation over how best to address the business of sewage disposal: whether by retention and sublimation, by expulsion and reaction formation, or by some uneasy amalgam of these processes. In general, the tendency to retain and sublimate seems to have done best in rural communities, whereas the impulse to expel and ignore gained greater vigor as London and other urban areas grew in size and importance. In addition, individuals seem to have explored at least one other model of how to do things with turds; the men and women of Renaissance England occasionally used the fruit of their bodies, in more or less deliberate ways, to counteract the imperatives of civilization and sociopolitical restraint. Or to be more blunt, people used their sewage for a kind of rebellious entertainment, often at the expense of others. This extension of Bakhtinian carnival, with literary antecedents that include the work of Aristophanes and Hipponax,[11] appears repeatedly in English legal records of the early modern period. Jonson himself alludes to the "grave fart . . . let in Parliament" in 1607 (108) to object to a proposal from the House of Lords. (The utterer of the fart in question was Sir Henry Ludlow, and his eloquence seems to have elicited some admiration.) Keith Thomas likewise recalls the 1598 case of a Cambridge man who allegedly disrupted church services with his "most loathsome farting, striking, and scoffing speeches" (192). Then there is the case of John Kibbitt, a servant in Leighe, Essex, who was charged on 2 October, 1630, "for that in prophane manner in tyme of the sermon upon a Sundaye, in the afternoon he did——in the church into the hat of one that sate by him" (Cockburn 252). And (for an early instance of like behavior) one wonders what could have been in the minds of Joan de Armenters and William de Thorneye when they "removed the privy-wall (*claustram*) and roof" from their tenement's single house of easement, "so that the extremities of those sitting upon the seats [could] be seen, a thing which is abominable and altogether intolerable" (Chew and Kellaway 79).

    Such behavior may comprise a special instance of the tendency to retain waste. However, to my mind, the impulse to make one's excrement part of the family estate is categorically distinct from the desire to rub one's neighbors' noses in filth. If that is indeed the case, then any reading of Jonson's "On the Famous Voyage" should identify, as an important part of the poem's historical context, at least three different, interrelated, and popular strategies for the cultural disposition of waste matter: the urge to retain and transform, the desire to expel and ignore, and the impulse toward carnivalesque *enmerdement*. The remainder of this chapter argues, first, that Jonson's work explores all three of these strategies to one degree or another; second, that in doing so it presages an exceptionally fertile notion of the cultural instrumentality of anal behavior; and third, that critics of Jonson have on occasion sought to narrow this fecundity in ways that fail to do justice to the poet's achievement as a whole.

A Tour of Fleet Ditch

The events of Jonson's "On the Famous Voyage" occur precisely in the heart of London's old-style sewage system, in the Fleet Ditch itself. As William Slights has recently observed, "this [sewage system] made up as large a part of the symbolic geography of Jonson's London as Mary Le Bow, or St Paul's" (114), and I would argue that the Fleet Ditch deserves to be regarded as the principal character of Jonson's poem. The poem's two mock heroes, Thomas Shelton (Medine 100–101) and Sir Christopher Heydon (Medine 103), undertake to sail a small boat up the ditch from its confluence with the Thames at Bridewell to its northern limit at Holborn Bridge. This itinerary traverses the full length of the Fleet itself; above Holborn, it took on various different names and arguably a different epistemological status as well. In its more rural reaches it was known as "the Hole-bourne, or stream in the hollow, referring to the deep valley of the lower part of its course" (N. Barton 29), and it was also called "the River of Wells, from the many wells or springs that fed it" (Sugden 194). Near Holborn, on the other hand, "it was called Turnmill Brook, from the mills on its banks" (Sugden 194). Finally, running parallel to and immediately beyond the old western walls of London, the north-to-south stretch of the ditch itself was defined by its contiguity to the city rather than by its relation to its source. Thus if, as Nicholas Barton has observed, "the history of the Fleet River has been described as a decline from a river to a brook, from a brook to a ditch, and from a ditch to a drain" (29), in Jonson's day this decline was apparent less as a temporal than as a spatial phenomenon. The ditch becomes for Jonson a geographical counterpart to the dung farmer of Harington's *Metamorphosis*: a liminal manifestation of the city that excludes it, and a space in which the city's accumulated, ignored filth may therefore reappear in new, disturbing forms.

As for those forms themselves, they are characterized by a grim, seriocomic tenacity. Offering an ironic corollary to what Katharine Maus has called the "law of the conservation of matter" in Jonson's work ("Economies" 66),[12] the Fleet Ditch functions almost as a repository of the city's collective unconscious. It is a place where nothing gets lost, and where things that one would like to lose have a habit of turning up again and again. Turds "languish . . . stucke vpon the wall" of the ditch (136), or, having been "precipitated downe the jakes," they nonetheless survive to swim "abroad in ample flakes" (137–138), or again they simply lie "heap'd like an vsurers masse" in the accumulated sludge—neither liquid nor precisely solid—of the ditch itself (139). These unsavory products of the alimentary tract, in turn, meet in the ditch an image of their former selves:

> Cats there lay diuers had beene flead, and rosted,
> And, after mouldie growne, again were tosted,
> Then, selling not, a dish was tane to mince 'hem,
> But still, it seem'd, the ranknesse did conuince [betray] 'hem.
> (149–153)

As the cats go through their various culinary incarnations and are consigned to the ditch, eaten or uneaten, so too the gaseous by-product of digestion finds its way to the same spot:

> Here, seu'rall ghosts did flit
> About the shore, of farts, but late departed,
> White, black, blew, greene, and in more formes out-started,
> Than all those *Atomi* ridiculous,
> Whereof old DEMOCRITE, and HILL NICHOLAS,
> One said, the other swore, the world consists.
> (124–129)

The metamorphic variety of the ditch is that of the world itself, in an alienated and repressed valence. Within the compass of the Fleet, dung meets meat meets flatulence, and the base elements of Democritean science are perpetually regenerated in the process.

Hence the mock-heroic character of Jonson's poem. Shelton and Heydon acquire a debased epic stature ("right able / To haue beene stiled of King ARTHVRS table" [23–24]) because the ditch itself is a congeries of figures and situations from Greco-Roman myth. A recrudescence of the classical underworld, populated by "ghosts . . . of farts," a Scylla-figure

"Ycleped *Mud*" (61), and sundry other literary atavisms, the landscape of "On the Famous Voyage" stands in relation to its enveloping cultural matrix as the Fleet Ditch stands in relation to the city of London. It is composed from pieces of floating, pagan debris that keep popping up incongruously amidst a thousand years of Christian repression. The ditch's counterpart to "bold BRIAREUS" (81), for instance, turns out to be an offal-laden barge, which does double duty on festival days as "the Lord *Maiors* foist" (120). Monsters from classical myth thus melt into the quotidian business of London waste disposal, which itself survives as a ghost (of farts?) in the Lord Mayor's pageant machine. Likewise, the spirit of "MERCVRY" rains down "*ab excelsis*" on the voyaging heroes (96), having himself been transformed into "potions, / Suppositories, cataplasmes, and lotions" for the treatment of venereal disease (101–102). And just as the Fleet Ditch harbors the cast-off elements of Democritean natural philosophy, so too it preserves those of Pythagorean metaphysics:

> But 'mongst these *Tiberts* [the discarded carcasses of
>   uneaten cats], who d'you thinke there was?
> Old BANKES the iuggler, our PYTHAGORAS,
> Graue tutor to the learned horse. Both which,
> Being, beyond sea, burned for one witch:
> Their spirits transmigrated to a cat.
>   (155–159)

Like the Lord Mayor's pageant barge and the messenger of the Roman gods, even the ghosts of a(n un)dead[13] mountebank and his performing horse get reprocessed by the retentive capacities of the ditch. Nothing there, or anywhere, goes to waste.

This tendency to rediscover and preserve discarded waste matter not only characterizes individual lines of Jonson's epigram; it reappears as the structural principle of the poem's overall narrative. Just as the filth in the Fleet refuses to go away (contrary to the adage that "this too shall pass"), so do the heroes of the famous voyage itself end up precisely where they started. Jonson's narrative supplies an appearance of purposeful motion, as the heroes embark from Bridewell Dock and head northward, moving through three major challenges on their way to Holborn, but the challenges themselves are never resolved, and the poem's ending, as James Riddell has observed, "is both obvious and otiose" (54). Instead, as Shelton and Heydon move from one obstacle to another—from the "monster, /

Ycleped *Mud*" (60–61) to a dung barge "So huge, it seem'd, they could by no meanes quite her" (86), and finally to their culminating vision of "Old BANKES the iuggler" (156)—the wording of the verse carefully renders their progress illusory. The mud refuses to go away and in fact is described in grosser detail at the end of the poem than at the beginning; the rubbish lighter not only seems, but is, too big to evade, for it will certainly reappear at the appropriate city pageant; and Bankes, both metempsychosal and inconveniently alive when Jonson describes him as dead, presents obvious problems for any notion of straightforward passing.

Under the circumstances, it is perhaps unsurprising that the heroes' itinerary should be further described via thoroughly confused anatomical analogies. When the "vgly monster, / Ycleped *Mud*" first appears, it does so "In the first iawes" of a strangely diffuse and unspecified body:

> But hold my torch, while I describe the entry
> To this dire passage. Say, thou stop thy nose:
> 'Tis but light paines: Indeede this *Dock*'s no rose.
>   In the first iawes appear'd that vgly monster,
> Ycleped *Mud*, which, when their oares did once stirre,
> Belch'd forth an ayre, as hot, as at the muster
> Of all your night-tubs, when the carts doe cluster,
> Who shall discharge first his merd-vrinous load:
> Thorough her wombe they make their famous road.
>
>   (57–65)

Against the stopped nose of the adventurer, Jonson's poem counterposes a landscape that is no landscape, described in a promiscuous confusion of body parts. A monster appears in the jaws of Bridewell Dock, belches forth air that is comparable to the feculent stench of an army of dung carts, and then opens her womb to the oncoming explorers. This riot of anatomical categories leaves the reader with no clear sense of geographical or bodily location. One pair of jaws (the dock's) opens to reveal another pair (the monster Mud's), which in turn exhale the odor of a thousand assholes while opening into a metaphorical uterus.

As for the conclusion of the heroes' exploit, it simply sends them "back, without protraction" to the spot from which their journey began (192). And the memorial Shelton and Heydon earn for themselves by thus traversing an endless river of sewage is itself clearly redundant, for "In memorie of [their] most liquid deed, / The citie hath since rais'd a Pyramide"

(193–194). That pyramid, correlative to the "vsurers masse" of ordure in the Fleet Ditch, was arguably there all along, only perhaps less lofty and fetid. Moreover, this fecal monument constitutes yet another piece of reprocessed and transfigured classical refuse; in recalling the Horatian "Exegi monumentum aere perennius / regalique situ pyramidum altius" [I have completed a monument more lasting than bronze, / And higher than the fabric of royal pyramids], the celebratory pyramid elides Jonson's verse with the very filth it describes and celebrates.

At least since the time of Swinburne, critics have deplored "On the Famous Voyage" as "a hideous and unsavoury burlesque" (Herford, Simpson, and Simpson 2:341), as "the plunge of a Parisian diver into the cesspool" (Swinburne 95), and as a "*morceau repugnant [de la] grossiereté rabelaisienne*" (Castelain 765n.). More recently, scholars like Wesley Trimpi, Peter Medine, and Bruce Smith have argued that Jonson's scatological epigram functions as a more or less broad-based condemnation of Jacobean London, its citizens, and various of its literary and social practices (Trimpi 97–98; Medine 97–98; Smith 109), while in at least one further case, "On the Famous Voyage" has been described as a deliberate exercise in self-parody (van den Berg 107). Each of these views has merit and can be defended at length, but their most particular interest derives from the fact that, despite their apparent incompatibility, they can nonetheless occupy the same literary space. Jonson's work can be characterized as literary satire, social condemnation, scatological burlesque, carnivalesque merriment, and as an effort at neoclassical purification, and criticism should be able to account for this multivalence as something other than mere paradox.

One way to explain this aspect of the poet's work may be to invoke the particular feature of the unconscious that Deleuze and Guattari have characterized as its "greatest art": the "art of molecular multiplicities" (*Plateaus* 27). The Deleuzian critique of Freud is very largely aimed at unseating the unitary principles of psychic organization that govern Freudian thought: the "familiar themes of *the* father, *the* penis, *the* vagina, Castration with a capital C" (*Plateaus* 27). Instead of seeking to reduce psychic organization to such recurrent and monolithic categories, Deleuze and Guattari emphasize a mode of psychoanalysis structured around "crowd phenomena" (*Plateaus* 30), which render individual enunciation illusory by constituting signification itself as multiple and dynamic. From this standpoint, "it should not be thought that it suffices to distinguish the masses and exterior groups someone belongs to or participates in from the internal aggregates that person envelops in him or herself. The distinction to be made is not at all between exterior and interior, which are always relative, changing, and reversible, but between different types of multiplicities that coexist, interpenetrate, and change places" (*Plateaus* 36). The distinctive flexibility of Jonson's work derives from its ability to coordinate sustained processes of ethical and satirical discrimination with themes and vocabulary that repeatedly place him on the wrong side of the discriminations he invokes. In the case of the poet's scatology, that flexibility would seem to be intrinsic to the very subject matter the poet has chosen, subject matter whose own cultural and material disposition is in flux during Jonson's career and for which "there are no individual statements, only statement-producing machinic assemblages" (*Plateaus* 36).

As Peter Stallybrass and Allon White have summarized matters,

> Jonson emphasized the notion of the "gathered self," which . . . presents such a closed face to the world that it is invulnerable to invasion and always remains "untouch'd." Yet within his writings Jonson also projected a self quite antithetical to this, the man "of prodigious waste," "laden with bellie," who knew "the fury of men's gullets." (78)

"On the Famous Voyage" develops out of a geographical space that itself encompasses this antithesis; testimony to "the fury of men's gullets," the Fleet Ditch likewise attests to the dramatic urbanization and concomitant repression that subtend the development of modern civilization in the West. The duality of Jonson's verse arguably arises from this fact, rather than from any unique predisposition to anal neurosis on the part of the poet himself. To put this case as simply as possible: Jonson writes the epic of a society trying to come to terms with its own sewage. If he cannot quite decide what to do with it all, if his thought wavers between the poles of sublimation, reaction-formation, and unrepressed revelry, at least he is not alone.

Jonson and the Psychoanalytic Tradition

Indeed, in "On the Famous Voyage" sublimation tends to enable reaction formation, and vice versa. Jonson's reformation of the abuses of Jacobean society depends not only on the existence of such abuses, but on his capacity to represent them in print; likewise, such representation justifies itself as a means of reprocessing actual filth through modes of literary substitution. Harington clearly understood this interdependence, and he made it the subject of a long introductory section to his *Metamorphosis*. Worried that readers might consider his work obscene, Harington insists repeatedly that it is in fact a means of combating obscenity, and that "He that would scorne a Physition, because for our infirmities sake, he refuseth not sometime the noisome view of our lothsomest excrements, were worthy to have no helpe by Physicke" (83). Yet by the same token, the *Metamorphosis* abounds in toilet humor of the silliest imaginable stripe, so that Thomas Nashe could speculate of Harington's work, "What shold moue him to [publish] it I know not, except he [m]eant to bid a turd in all gentle readers teeth" (5:195). Likewise, Jonson's scatology displays a pervasive awareness of the extent to which efforts at civilizing repression must founder upon "the anal priority of human beings" (Pops 27).

This observation may help explain the poem's placement at the end of the 1616 *Epigrams*—which Jonson himself, with perhaps an unintended fecal resonance, called "*the ripest of my studies*" (Herford, Simpson, and Simpson 8:25). After all, one governing concern of the epigrams is, in George Rowe's words, to establish "hierarchy and order out of ... confusion" (21), or, as Richard Helgerson has remarked, to demonstrate "the power of exclusion" by "heroically drawing the line" between virtue and vice, excellence and mediocrity (171). To this extent, the epigrams are an exceptionally repressive literary instrument; they exist for the purpose of tidying things up, sorting the acceptable from the unacceptable, the clean from the unclean. Yet this sustained effort culminates in a poem that manifestly challenges any such activity. As Bruce Smith has observed, "On the Famous Voyage" can scarcely even be called an epigram (109), and although it may lend itself to various modes of interpretation and categorization, it is unconfined by criteria of linguistic decorum or organizational clarity. Awaiting the reader at the promised end of Jonson's meticulous epideictic and satirical discriminations, this last poem sits like a pile of untreated garbage, and like the garbage it describes, it refuses to go away. It constitutes the external limit of Jonsonian classicism, both negating and necessitating all that has preceded it.

That Jonson should take pains to include this negation within the body of his work would suggest, at least, that he was sensitive to its status as the starting point for his own creativity. Various models of critical activity—including psychoanalytic, Bakhtinian, poststructuralist, and late feminist theories—have focused on the irreducible alterity of signification, and Jonson's literary exploration of the Fleet Ditch would seem, among other things, to be a self-conscious acceptance of the extent to which the poet's work is always already determined by the Other it must and yet cannot exclude. Bakhtin's work on Rabelais makes a similar point, although in the process it complicates its own foundational distinction between the classical and grotesque bodies. Discussing the presence of excremental images in late medieval billingsgate, Bakhtin remarks that

> each image is subject to the meaning of the whole; each reflects a single concept of a contradictory world of becoming, even though the image may be separately presented. Through its participation in the whole, each of these images is deeply ambivalent, being intimately related to life-death-birth. (149–150)

To think of scatology in such terms is necessarily to widen its frame of reference beyond the notions of bodily mastery/uncontrol and sexual repression/gratification that have typically governed Freudian discussions of anality, as well as Bakhtinian definitions of the classical and grotesque bodies. As Stephen Greenblatt has observed, the elements of excremental ritual may be most clearly distinguished by the fact that "they are not fully integrated, they defy hierarchical organization, they do not form a unified whole" (5).

The standard myth of Jonson as an anal neurotic fails in large part because it represents an unwarranted narrowing of this vision—a narrowing that is unjust both to Jonson and to the possibilities available to psychoanalytic theory. In 1908, when first introducing his views on anal eroticism, Freud concentrated on exploring the characteristics of what we now term the anal-retentive personality. These qualities—orderliness, parsimony, and obstinacy—exist, Freud argues, "as the first and most constant results of the sublimation of anal erotism" ("Character" 171). Yet even in this earliest brief study of the subject, Freud observes that sublimation is not the only way of dealing with the erotogenicity of the anal canal, out of which adult character traits may develop either as "unchanged prolongations of original instincts, or sublimations of those instincts, or reaction-formations against them" ("Character" 175). To be sure, Freud's terminology is itself untidy—and perhaps wisely so, for subsequent efforts, such as those of Ernest Jones (436), to distinguish completely between the psychic mechanisms of sublimation and reaction formation are not entirely satisfactory. Thus, although Freud groups orderliness, parsimony, and obstinacy together as instances of anal sublimation, in his very next paragraph he then redefines orderliness as "a reaction-formation against an interest in what is unclean and disturbing and should not be part of the body" ("Character" 172); moreover, his focus on the unstable categories of sublimation and reaction formation leads him away from the question of what constitutes an "original instinct" or its "unchanged prolongation." Even so, this earliest work on the subject of anality suggests sublimation to be only one of several interrelated, coextensive psychic mechanisms. And when Freud returns to the subject five years later, his linkage of anal erotogenicity with sadism complicates matters further ("Neurosis" 320–321).

As Sandor Ferenczi observed after Freud, "A part of anal-erotism is not sublimated at all, but remains in its original form. Even the most cultivated normal being displays an interest in his [*sic*] evacuation functions which stands in a curious contradiction to the abhorrence and disgust that he manifests when he sees or hears anything of the kind in regard to other people" (328). Indeed, Ernest Jones's "Anal-Erotic Character Traits" describes a whole panoply of disparate and sometimes mutually exclusive behavioral mechanisms as typical of anal eroticism. They include (but are not limited to) all forms of collecting (430), "giving-out" (432), cleaning (431), staining and contaminating (432), "sculpture, architecture, woodcarving, photography, etc." (433), and even grafitti writing (432). Given this impressive and incomplete catalog, one could reasonably ask what kind of behavior is *not* implicated in anal eroticism. Traditional notions of Ben Jonson as a "negative and recessive" personality (Wilson 221), "impoverished emotionally" (Pearlman 366) by his excremental fixations, effect a narrowing of psychoanalytic theory in which anality becomes synonymous with neurosis, and in which anal-erotic impulses find their satisfaction only via a kind of niggardly retention. It hardly need be added that such a reading of psychoanalysis is itself both grudging and retentive, leading to the construction of Ben Jonson as one of the two great anal basket cases of English literary history. (Swift deserves mention as the other.) But Jonson himself knew better than to accept such an impoverished vision.

On the contrary, Jonson's scatology performs multiple discursive functions, functions that access the significance of excrement on a whole series of different levels more or less simultaneously. There is, for instance, a delicious moment in *Volpone* when, after Mosca has conducted Voltore and Corbaccio through their initial visits with the fox, Corvino arrives. As Volpone reclines in bed, ostensibly blind and deaf, Mosca and Corvino rain insults on him:

>   MOS.   Would you once close
>   Those filthy eyes of yours, that flow with slime,
>   Like two frog-pits; and those same hanging cheeks,

>   Couer'd with hide, in stead of skin: (nay, helpe, sir)
>   That looke like frozen dish-clouts, set on end.
> CORV. Or, like an old smok'd wall, on which the raine
>   Ran downe in streakes. MOS. Excellent, sir, speake out;
>   You may be lowder yet: a culuering,
>   Discharged in his eare, would hardly bore it.
> CORV. His nose is like a common sewre, still running.
> MOS. 'Tis good! and, what his mouth? CORV. A very draught.
>   (1.5.56–66)

The aggression and censure manifest in this passage are only its most obvious features. More important by far is the way in which this extended abuse emphasizes the metamorphic capacities of Volpone's character. Having already transformed himself with his invalid disguise, Volpone employs his self-transformation not simply as an avenue to material self-aggrandizement, but also as a means of personal amusement, using it to eavesdrop on the conversation of his gulls ("O, I shall burst; / Let out my sides, let out my sides" [1.4.132–133]). That conversation, in turn, serves as continuing entertainment precisely through its determination to transfigure Volpone further via the capacities of metaphor. As his eyes turn to frog pits, his nose to a sewer, and his mouth to a cloacal pit, he and the audience observe the ongoing operation of the same principle of limitless transformation invoked later in the attempted seduction of Celia.

Of course it is this very metamorphic principle that relates Jonson to the antihero of his most successful play. In fact, Volpone represents a favorite pattern in Jonsonian character construction: that of the calculating, cynical observer, socially liminal or ambiguous, who sustains and exploits the misapprehensions of others not only for material advantage but also for personal sport. The three gallants in *Epicoene,* Quarlous and Winwife in *Bartholomew Fair,* Knowell Junior and Well-Bred in *Every Man in His Humour* all provide classic instances of this formula. For Jonathan Haynes, such characters supply a key to Jonson's own position vis-à-vis popular festivity and the popular stage, a position of simultaneous involvement and self-distancing. As Haynes summarizes, "On every level [Jonson] is willing to absorb the popular tradition, but unwilling to be absorbed by it" (134). If anything, I believe this principle can be extended to account for Jonson's position with respect to most of the other social groups for which he wrote and with which he interacted. As Robert Evans has shown, for instance, Jonson's relations with potential or actual patrons were as ambiguous and nervous as his relations with the popular tradition. Just as the poet's assertions of social independence ("He never esteemed a man for the name of a Lord" [Drummond 337]) simultaneously imply a transcendence of the realm of the sociopolitical while constituting a sociopolitical maneuver in and of themselves (R. Evans, *Patronage* 59–61), so Jonson's scatological vocabulary allows him to exploit the category of the excremental in various ways while simultaneously distancing himself from it. I believe this extraordinary linguistic opportunism—what I have already called self-assertion without self-limitation—is the most important feature of Jonson's life and work, more so even than his commitment to classical and humanist doctrines.

In *The Alchemist*, again, this same principle operates, although the standard form of Jonson's detached, manipulative gallant has been modified somewhat to permit the more verminous social standing of Subtle, Face, and Doll. Gail Paster's reading of this play's excremental vocabulary rightly draws attention to the aggression and censure intrinsic to Jonson's scatology. I would add, furthermore, that the scatology tends to achieve prominence in connection with the tropes of alchemical and supernatural transformation that dominate the play, and that provide a thematic parallel for the main characters' self-transformations and impostures. Thus when Face describes Subtle's dunghill origins he not only characterizes Subtle through images of bodily uncontrol such as hunger and constipation; he also reverses the order of digestion whereby healthy bodies are customarily sustained:

> But I shall put you in mind, sir, at *pie-corner*,
> Taking your meale of steeme in, from cookes stalls,
> Where, like the father of hunger, you did walke
> Piteously costiue . . .
> When you went pinn'd vp, in the seuerall rags,
> Yo'had rak'd, and pick'd from dung-hills, before day,
> Your feet in mouldie slippers, for your kibes,
> A felt of rugg, and a thin thredden cloake,
> That scarce would couer your no-buttocks.
> (1.1.25–37)

In effect, that is, Subtle is a creature for whom the standard rules of anatomy do not apply. He eats steam through his nostrils; he does not defecate; in fact, he has no buttocks at all; and he clothes himself with the moldy pickings of garbage heaps and dunghills. He is, in short, a phantasmagoric companion to the monsters of "On the Famous Voyage": a creature of the sewage conduit and cesspit, whose vitality and fascination derive in large part from his ability to escape efforts at social, anatomical, and sanitary containment. Like the dead cats in the Fleet Ditch, he refuses to disappear; like Freddy Krueger, he keeps coming back in ever more startling ways.

To this extent, Subtle should also be viewed in counterpoint to a figure like Jacques de Prie, the excremental emblem of filial resentment in *The Case Is Altered*. If, as Riggs and others have shown, de Prie functions as a surrogate stepfather, associated with dung and placed onstage as a focus for the poet's anal and oedipal aggressions, Subtle serves as something parallel but different: a reincarnation of the author himself, the lean and hollow-cheeked former resident of a London dunghill whose linguistic manipulations have propelled him to a busy trade at "the exact spot occupied by the Blackfriars Theater" (Riggs 171). This capacity for both personal and territorial metamorphosis then reappears when Subtle, "*disguised like a Priest of Fairy*" (3.5.1 s.d.), binds Dapper in rags and locks him in a privy, which does duty for the courtly anterooms in which Jonson himself, as patronage poet, must inevitably have cooled his heels many an hour. And similarly, in *Volpone*, the excremental imagery of abuse and entertainment undergoes at least one more strategic transformation. Corvino, who has heaped contumely on the supposedly blind and deaf Volpone, likening his nose to the "common sewre," is consigned at play's end to a pillory, where he himself is to be beaten blind for the entertainment of a vicious crowd armed with the products of Fleet Ditch:

> Yes,
> And, haue mine eies beat out with stinking fish,
> Bruis'd fruit, and rotten egges—'Tis well. I'am glad
> I shall not see my shame, yet.
>
> (5.12.139–142)

Deleuze and Guattari have criticized Freud for constantly reverting to arborescent, root-shaped notions of the meaning of behavior—for constantly reducing unconscious drives to a few monolithic principles such as oedipal aggression and castration anxiety. Instead, Deleuze and Guattari seek out rhizomatic forms of unconscious motivation: forms that tunnel, branch and multiply. In the breathtaking shifts and transformabilities of Jonson's scatological vocabulary, I believe just such a multiplicity is to be found.

Bread Upon the Waters

So far, this chapter has argued that the culture of excrement in early modern England displays concurrent and interrelated tendencies toward retention, exploration, and expulsion—or, in a more binaristic Freudian terminology, sublimation and reaction formation. Works like *Volpone*, *The Alchemist*, and "On the Famous Voyage," like their precursor in the work of Harington, exploit all these tendencies; in the process these works demonstrate an awareness of the ways in which such contradictory tendencies enable and depend on one another. Therefore Jonson's work helps us to revise, rather than simply to discard, traditional notions of Jonson himself as an anal poet. One is left with a Jonson whose fascination for the workings of the anus is neither impoverished nor unhealthy nor unique. If anything, it is marked by an extraordinary richness of range and capacity, encompassing the extremes of reaction formation through the poet's famous rage for order; of sublimation through his voluminous literary output as well as his notoriously bad temper; and of an unrepressed and unabashed interest in excrement for excrement's sake.

One could even go a step further in revising Jonson's reputation, for the poet's credentials as an anal neurotic are seriously affected by any effort to consider him within a wide range of competing personalities. The early modern period offers a rich variety of historical figures whose attitudes toward excrement were at least as pronounced as—and arguably more imbalanced than— Jonson's own, and who therefore stand in marked contrast to Jonson in terms of individual temperament and cultural significance. If one wants the anality of reaction formation, after all, there is always Elizabeth I, whose stinginess, meager diet, distrust of doctors, wicked temper, and inclination to micromanage the affairs of her courtiers were all legendary, even in her own day. For sublimation, one need only bury oneself in the logarithmically expanding piles of theological discourse that flowed from the pens of Luther, his detractors, and his followers. And for the fecal obsession in all its unrepressed glory, one may turn to Jonson's own prince and patron, James I, who earned an early reputation both for reveling in toilet humor and for fouling his hose under stress. Given this context, one can only admire the range and robustness of Jonson's commitment to exploring the strategies his culture had devised for the material and psychic disposal of excrement.

If the present analysis is correct, Jonson's fascination with the products of the alimentary tract cannot simply be deplored as a symptom of emotional morbidity, nor can it be dismissed as irrelevant to the poet's overall literary achievement. On the contrary, it constitutes a sustained inquiry into the conditions that make his achievement possible in the first place. Jonson's scatology may be viewed as robust or perverse, naive or satirical, but its outstanding quality is its capacity to remain within and outside all these categories at once. Like the waste it represents, Jonson's excremental verse refuses to be disposed of once and for all; it keeps coming back in different shapes that cannot be entirely ignored or dismissed, sublimated or repressed.

Indeed, if one wants a graphic historical instance of the failure of such sublimations and repressions, one need not turn to the English Renaissance at all. One might be tempted, for instance, to draw attention to Peru's recent cholera outbreak—an epidemic linked, like those of nineteenth-century London, to problems of public sanitation; but in fact there is more resonant matter at hand. The dung barge of Jonson's final epigram, or a vessel very like it, reappeared on the international scene in 1987, laden with more than three thousand tons of garbage from New York City and Long Island, and plying its way south through the Atlantic in search of a safe place to deposit its cargo. Ironically, the barge itself—the *Mobro*—and its attendant tugboat, the *Break of Dawn*, had set out in one more failed attempt to reconcile the imperatives of anal expulsion with those of retention and recycling. The vessels were initially engaged by the Alabama businessman Lowell Harrelson, and they were to bear their cargo to North Carolina, "where, after ripening for a time, it would give off methane gas, which could be sold at a tidy profit" (Logan 88).

The sequel to this venture is now nearly legendary. Six states and three nations rebelled at the prospect of being dungfarmers to the city of New York, and the *Mobro* eventually returned to Long Island in failure and disrepute. As it was shunted away from one prospective dumping ground after another, newscasts followed its daily progress, symbolically repatriating America's trash in America's living rooms, and demonstrating to all who wished to notice that the contents of Fleet Ditch cannot be ignored, buried, carted away, channeled downstream, or dumped in Third World nations. In fact, even the rhetoric of the event held its ironies. Johnny Carson, who had made predictable capital out of the garbage barge in his comedy monologues, was eventually informed by reporters that a good bit of the *Mobro*'s trash had come from a film studio—the Kaufman Astoria—of which he himself was part owner. Putting the best possible face on matters, a Carson spokesperson responded by quoting Ecclesiastes: "Cast thy bread upon the waters: for thou shalt find it after many days" (Logan 89–90). As Sir John Harington understood, Lincoln's Inn was built on this trash. Jonson knew it too.

5
Jonson's Crudities

FINALLY, THIS BOOK NEEDS TO OFFER some small account of Jonson's interest in those disorders that upset the usual course of digestion: the various constipations, diarrheas, indigestions, and vomits that populate the poet's work. To this end, I have chosen to concentrate on the last of these items, the vomiting, which is the disorder Jonson returns to most often and with the greatest brio. Vomiting occupies a prominent position, for instance, in *Poetaster*, where it serves both as a kind of medicine and as a mode of punishment. It reappears at the end of *Bartholomew Fair*; it surfaces briefly in *Discoveries* as a metaphor for Montaigne's use of his readings in other authors; and it provides a governing motif for Thomas Coryate's aptly named *Crudities*, a work to which Jonson contributed front matter of an appropriate character. In order to evaluate this recurrent interest in the production of vomitus, one arguably ought to examine the primary textual materials in question, consider their relation to each other and to the biographical matrix of which they are a part, and relate them to contemporary documents on the significance of the physical process they represent. This last chapter—less a chapter than a codicil, really, or perhaps an appendix—attempts to proceed in such a fashion.

I have already, on various occasions, touched briefly on the ways in which Jonson's alimentary discourse parallels and defines his relations to his contemporaries: Jonsonian digestion, for instance, offers the poet a way to subsume the artistic productivity of collaborators like Inigo Jones within his own professional corpus. But the issue of vomiting particularly impinges on Jonson's social negotiations. In *Poetaster*, for instance, the poet administers his emetic to a lightly fictionalized version of John Marston, whereas Jonson's use of the same motif in *Bartholomew Fair* arguably acquires a self-reflexive dimension. In both of these cases, I believe, the vomit in question offers an index to the ambiguities of the socioliterary situations that occasion it. Thus Jonson's interest in vomit supplies a final opportunity to explore the complex terms of the poet's literary self-construction.

In their efforts to revise notions of spatial and organizational relation, Deleuze and Guattari turn famously to the biological model of the rhizome. The rhizome, they argue, offers an alternative to the arborescent modes of cultural organization typical of Western thought. From the Great Chain of Being to genealogical catalogs and Linnaean taxonomies, the Western cultural tradition has worked in terms of vertical, hierarchical, self-enclosed systems based on the physical image of the tree, but the rhizome functions otherwise. As Ronald Bogue explains, "rhizomes . . . are non-hierarchical, horizontal multiplicities which cannot be subsumed within a unified structure, whose components form random, unregulated networks in which any element may be connected with any other element" (107). Rhizomes provide a biological illustration of the Deleuzian line of flight; crabgrass and blackberry brambles are virtually impossible to kill because they have no stable center of the kind that Western organizational patterns tend to seek and privilege. By the same token, the rhizome may offer a way to think of physical, spatial, and social relations that are constantly involved in both internal and external transformation.

Hence the rhizomic model may help explain many of Jonson's personal relationships, those with Marston and Coryate supplying excellent cases in point. One valuable line of Jonson scholarship has sought to contrast the poet's friendships with his enmities, thereby emphasizing the premium Jonson places on the artist's "integrity of the self, constant and positive behind his endlessly-shifting visors" (Duncan 155).[1] As Sara van den Berg remarks, "The idea of the one true self, centered, marks not only Jonson's praise of other people but also his vision of himself" (68). Certainly the persona of blunt Ben, steadfast and English, who "would not flatter though he saw Death" (Drummond 332), supports such an emphasis; likewise, the poet's relations with a limited number of specific individuals (e.g., Camden, Selden, and Cotton) suggest an unambiguous sedentarization of the social. But for others—many others—the record is far more complex, and as Robert Evans has shown, there is a distinct element of "insecurity at the heart of . . . many of [Jonson's] poems to patrons and friends" (*Patronage* 204). In keeping with this latter view, George Rowe has gone so far as to propose that Jonson's social and literary relations were governed by a species of "emulation," a turbulent process of establishing socioliterary affinities for the ultimate purpose of transcending and dissolving them:

The act of emulating is both a recognition of the importance of imitation and an attempt to imitate (compete) in such a way as to create (ultimately) difference rather than similarity, and so to establish hierarchy and order out of the imitative tendency toward equality and (potential) confusion. It is a particularly militant form of comparison whose final goal is contrast. (21)

Rowe's suggestive formulation, if divested of its commitment to a "final goal," may point toward the mobile, multivalent patterns of transformation that characterize the rhizomic model.

Moreover, in the case of the relationships I propose to examine here—the association with Marston on one hand and the more expansive relationship between the poet himself and the institutionalization of authority on the other—the alimentary imagery that frames Jonson's social interaction partakes of the same mobility as do the relationships themselves. One reason for this fact may be that the poet chose his alimentary motifs specifically to parallel or reflect the ambiguities of the social situations they represent. However, it seems more reasonable to regard the social and physiological fluidities of Jonson's work as parallel instances of a general discursive process: the process I have elsewhere called exploration, nomadism, or deterritorialization, whereby the poet stakes out microorganizational connections between apparently exclusive linguistic and social principles. From this standpoint, the oppositions intrinsic to Jonson's literary, political, moral, and even metabolic vocabularies exist, in very large part, precisely so that they may be brought into various kinds of conjunction. They serve as individual spots on Jonson's socioliterary terrain, to be placed in differing and malleable relation to each other as a given situation demands and the poet's own organizational abilities make possible.

Spurious Snotteries

The record of Jonson's relations with Marston is spotty, and largely overshadowed by the War of the Theaters, but even so it reveals a considerable measure of liquidity. At present, the standard view of matters is that Marston irritated Jonson by paying him the compliment of imitation; that the two men then fell out publicly, with Dekker entering into the fray on Marston's behalf; and that ultimately the affair was patched over in such a way as to permit some kind of public reconciliation.[2] At any rate, it is clear that Marston's allusions to Jonson in *Histriomastix* place the latter poet "in a highly favorable light" (Riggs 72); that after the War of the Theaters subsided, Marston could supply his *Malcontent* (1604) with an orotund and extremely complimentary dedication to Jonson; and that the two poets were on a sufficiently good footing to collaborate in 1604 on the script of *Eastward Ho*. Yet the reconciliation seems to have been no more stable than the quarrel; as late as 1618–1619, Jonson could proudly tell Drummond that "he beate Marston and took his pistoll from him" (Drummond 160), whereas Marston's preface to *Sophonisba* (1606) includes a derisive allusion to the self-conscious classicism of *Sejanus*. (Ironically enough, Marston had contributed dedicatory verses a year earlier to the 1605 quarto of *Sejanus*.) The record, in short, suggests a relationship of extreme volatility, capable of changing character at a moment's notice.

To this extent, Jonson's association with Marston may be viewed as typical of his connection with a wide variety of other individuals, from Inigo Jones to Thomas Coryate and even to the Shakespeare of the First Folio. Such figures occupy a smooth social space in which neither the courtly compliment of Jonson's patronage epigrams nor the blunt scorn of his disdain for Puritans and groundlings seems fully appropriate. Moreover, Jonson's relations to his professional peers, because of their constantly shifting and equivocal nature, may supply a better test of his political tact and discursive flexibility than do the relatively static relations between poet and monarch or pupil and master. For Jonson, Marston and his ilk are a resource to be exploited, as is James I or Camden, but the usefulness of people like Marston—and hence the proper manner of exploiting them—varies both diachronically and synchronically to a degree that James's and Camden's do not. In the case of Thomas Coryate, for instance, Jonson maintains an officially genial relationship that simultaneously displays undertones both of disdain and of something almost like envy. In the case of Marston, public expressions of hostility seem to have resulted from—and in turn demanded a renewal of—the more cordial relations to which Marston's dedication and the collaboration on *Eastward Ho* attest.

In any event, when Jonson castigates Marston's alter ego, Crispinus, in *Poetaster*, he does so with language that repeatedly invokes the functions of the digestive canal, but in highly ambivalent ways. Crispinus and the Dekker-surrogate Demetrius are charged with writing libels against the "full, and wel-digested" Horace (5.3.362), and the evidence entered against them, which comes from their own hands, employs imagery drawn from both ends of the alimentary tract. Crispinus/Marston's libel comes first, rooted in the notion that Horace's writing is a kind of linguistic slobber:

> *Rampe up, my* genius; *be not retrograde:*
> *But boldly nominate a spade, a spade.*
> . . . .
> *Teach thy* incubus *to poetize;*
> *And throw abroad thy spurious snotteries,*
> *Vpon that puft-up lumpe of barmy froth,*
> . . . .
> *Or clumsie chil-blain'd iudgement; that, with oath,*
> *Magnificates his merit; and bespawles*
> *The conscious time, with humorous fome, and brawles.*
> (5.3.275–288)

Crispinus's "spurious snotteries" contrive to present Horace as a mass of seething bubbles, bubbles that implicitly inform the poet from outside (they originate as "barmy froth," the gaseous by-product of beer fermentation) but that, upon digestion, return as the "humorous fome" with which Horace "bespawles" his listeners and readers. This passage supplies the *Oxford English Dictionary* with its earliest listing for the latter verb, which means "to spray with saliva"; in effect, says Crispinus, what you get from Horace is literary spittle, which in turn is simply regurgitated beer bubbles given a particular "humorous" form.

On one hand, this characterization is nicely in keeping with some of the nasty things that Dekker says about Jonson in *Satiromastix*. There, for instance, Horace/Jonson is described as spoiling for a literary food fight, and Sir Rees ap Vaughan can finally order him,

> When you Sup in Tauernes, amongst your betters, you shall
> sweare not to dippe your Manners in too much sawce, nor at
> Table to fling Epigrams, Embleames, or Play-speeches about
> you (lyke Hayle-stones).
> (5.2.328–331)

Yet at the same time, Crispinus's words echo Jonson's own self-description from the prologue to *Every Man out of His Humour*, where Carlo Buffone paints a picture of the poet dining in company in order to convert the supper-table talk into verse:

This [wine] is that our Poet calls *Castalian* liquor, when hee comes abroad (now and then) once in a fortnight, and makes a good meale among Players, where he has *Caninum appetitum*: mary, at home he keeps a good philosophicall diet, beanes and butter milke: an honest pure Rogue, hee will take you off three, foure or five of these, one after another, . . . and then (when his belly is well ballac't, and his braine rigg'd a little) he sailes away withall, as though he would worke wonders when he comes home. (Prologue.334–345)

For Dekker, Horace/Jonson writes libelous epigrams on his companions and then retails those epigrams among other companions at the supper table. For Carlo Buffone, the poet dines in company and then sails home to produce, perhaps, the epigrams to which Dekker will object. For Crispinus, Horace/Jonson drinks beer, rather than the "*Castalian* liquor" of *Every Man Out*, but nonetheless engages in much the same pattern of literary assimilation and regurgitation.

If anything serves to distinguish Jonson's good-humored self-characterization from the invidious attacks of Dekker and Crispinus, it would seem to be the character of the poet's social associations. Dekker's Sir Rees is obviously disgusted that Horace should behave as he does among his "betters," and Jonson's poetasters likewise resent Horace because "hee kept better company" than they (5.3.450). Carlo Buffone, on the contrary, describes Jonson as making his meal "among Players." (From this standpoint, it is also appropriate that Jonson himself should describe his dinner wine as "*Castalian* liquor," thereby characteristically promoting it to a new and more exalted ontological category, while Crispinus should replace it with the foamy scum from a beer keg.) This basic social distinction, in turn, finds another outlet in the dinner-table activities on which Dekker and Jonson choose to focus. For Dekker, Horace/Jonson offends when, dipping his manners in too much sauce, he seeks to enter the company of the great by libeling his true peers; for Jonson, the poet, inspired with Castalian liquors, enters humble company "once in a fortnight" and then returns, fortified with new literary insights, to his wonted abode. This latter characterization enables Jonson to relay the charge of social-climbing libel back onto his colleagues Dekker and Marston. In *Poetaster*, Crispinus and Demetrius force their way into the exalted company of Horace, Virgil, and Augustus in order to read their libelous squibs.

On one level, when Crispinus describes Horace as a "lumpe of barmy froth" that "bespawles / The conscious time," the imagery of slobber and regurgitation gives shape to the poetasters' conviction that Horace is out of his proper social place. The confusion of dining with writing, together with the failure of the literary digestive canal to process its meat and drink properly, suggests a disruption of metabolic order that parallels Horace's supposed disruption of the social. Roughly the same view is then reiterated by Demetrius, from an entirely different alimentary perspective, when he describes Horace as "*A* critic, *that all the world bescumbers* [i.e., beshits] / *With* satyricall *humours, and* lyricall *numbers*" (*Poetaster* 5.3.304–305). In this latter case, as Horace confuses the place of writing with the place of excrement, he ends up transforming the court of Augustus into a metaphorical privy.

But *Poetaster* exists not only to refute such charges, but also to demonstrate their almost infinite utility. Much of Jonson's play is a blatant reversal of the attacks leveled at the poet by Crispinus, Demetrius, and their historical originals. The "apologeticall Dialogue" appended to *Poetaster*, for instance, is obsessed with the kind of language introduced above. In it, the Author denounces the "black vomit" that flows from his detractors' pens (37); he likens Dekker's and Marston's audiences to "the barking students of Beares-Colledge, / [That] swallow vp the garbadge of the time / With greedy gullets" (45–47); he describes his literary enemies as "Fellowes of practis'd, and most laxatiue tongues, / Whose empty and eager bellies, i' the yeere, / Compell their braynes to many desp'rate shifts" (89–91); and he concludes by referring obliquely to Marston and Dekker as "vncleane birds, / That make their mouthes their clysters, and still purge / From their hot entrailes" (219–221). In each of these cases, Jonson associates his detractors with the same confusions of bodily category and alimentary function that have elsewhere been applied to him. In particular, the references to "laxatiue tongues" and oral clysters suggest a coalescence of the invidious imagery directed at Horace by Crispinus and Demetrius: an imaginative aggregate of the oral and anal functions in which regurgitation implies defecation, and vice versa.

But language of this sort not only reverses the invective of Marston and Dekker; it also, quite naturally, complicates efforts to distinguish between the various antagonists in the War of the Theaters. As Dekker, Marston, and Jonson bescumber one another in verse, they dramatize their intimate interrelation as much as any differences that might obtain between them. As Riggs has noted, Jonson's "attempt to create the impression that he really was . . . 'the English Horace,' while Dekker and Marston were mere hacks, was so successful that one tends to overlook the basic similarities between the poet and the poetasters" (78). I would merely add that Jonson's success as a self-promoter came largely after—and partly as a consequence of—the War of the Theaters, and therefore would necessarily be more obvious to twentieth-century interpreters than to the audiences that first viewed *Poetaster* and *Satiromastix*. Indeed, it is a crowning irony that the quarrel between Jonson and Marston apparently originated out of a compliment one poet paid the other, eventually resolving itself into another set of compliments entirely. Within this context, the Poetomachia arguably functions less as a dramatic war, with clear winners and losers, than as a mutually useful moment of self-dramatization. To this extent, the War of the Theaters needs to be viewed as a cooperative literary endeavor, not terribly different from the collaboration on *Eastward Ho*, for example.

This is not to say that the War of the Theaters did not give rise to some very genuine animosities. Jonson's beating of Marston surely involved an element of powerful and spontaneous rage. But the beating may easily be regarded as an outgrowth of the self-promotional conflict dramatized by the poets onstage. From this standpoint, it becomes an early modern equivalent of the fights that regularly punctuate professional hockey games and that, as Roland Barthes has shown, likewise supply an integral part of the spectacle at popular wrestling matches.[3] At the very least, it must be granted that Jonson's insistently martial self-characterization seems to have answered the poet's own perceived literary needs; whatever else they may be, Jonson's epigrams on soldiers—like his boasts to Drummond about *spolia opima*—are part of a calculated literary performance. In other words, instead of viewing the War of the Theaters as a personal quarrel that gave rise to literary recriminations, one might just as well regard it as a literary event that ultimately demanded a certain amount of personal animus. This formulation comes close to George Rowe's claim that the War of the Theaters was generated by the "annoying similarity" of the participants (68); I would go farther, however, and suggest that the War of the Theaters itself generated the very similarity it sought to correct.

At the level of its recurrent alimentary imagery, *Poetaster* certainly suggests that the War of the Theaters was a more complicated affair than can be explained by any model of straightforward antagonism. When the Author of the "apologeticall Dialogue" describes Dekker and Marston as creatures of "laxatiue tongue," thereby regurgitating Crispinus's and Demetrius's charges against Horace, which in their turn reprocess charges made by both Dekker and Jonson in other plays, the mewling and puking constitute a gesture of artistic solidarity far more persuasive than Marston's compliments in *Histriomastix* and *The Malcontent*. It is a gesture repeated in the crowning moment of *Poetaster*, when Horace administers an emetic to Crispinus in order to "purge / His braine, and stomack" (5.3.393–394). As Crispinus vomits forth the inferior poetic language of Marston, he belches up the language of Jonson's own parodies as well:

> CRIS. O, I shall cast vp my—*spurious—snotteries—*
> HORA. Good. Againe.
> CRIS. *Chilblaind*—o—o—*clumsie—*
> . . . .
> GALL. Who would haue thought, there should ha' beene such a deale of filth in a *poet*?
> CRIS. O—*barmy froth—*
> CAES. What's that?
> CRIS.—*Puffy—inflate—turgidous—ventositous.*
>
> (5.3.483–494)

There may be additional irony in the fact that George Ruggle's university play *Ignoramus* (1615) recycles this entire pattern of emetic recycling with a scene in which its title character "vomits up one strange [legal] term after another" (Evans, *Contexts* 93)—a scene that Robert Evans has described as a "compliment" to Jonson (*Contexts* 94). In any case, it is not, in my opinion, sufficient to describe such moments as a lapse of Jonson's better judgment, fostered by the heat of a personal quarrel. The mudslinging (or, in this case, vomit slinging) is far too self-conscious for that. At the very moment when *Poetaster* most triumphantly proclaims Horace's difference from his enemies, the markers of that difference acquire an irresolvably mixed, ambiguous character. Likewise for Crispinus's punishment itself; Horace administers his emetic to Crispinus before the poetasters are formally convicted of libel, and the emetic itself is officially introduced as an exercise in physic, rather than a judicial sentence ("CAESAR is carefull of your health, CRISPINVS; / And hath himself chose a physician / To minister vnto you" [5.3.399–401]). But Horace's tender concern for his enemy's health preempts the more conventional moments of judgment and punishment that conclude plays like *Volpone* and *Every Man in His Humour*. After seventy lines of Crispinus's literary retching, the poetasters are handed something like a suspended sentence. Virgil assigns Crispinus a program of "faire abstinence," dietary and literary, "in place / Of a strict sentence" (5.3.558–561), while Demetrius, at Horace's behest, receives "A mitigation" of the corporal punishment that would ordinarily be his "iuster doome" for libel (5.3.570–574).

In other words, Horace's exercise in physic both displaces and refocuses the punitive impulses of his play. As a result, it supplies audience and author alike with an ambiguous exchange that nicely parallels the ambiguities of language, motivation, and complicity that characterize the War of the Theaters. Under the circumstances, it is small wonder that the theatrical competition between Jonson and the poetasters has generally been viewed as a wash;[4] the very discursive weapons and tactics with which the Poetomachia was waged guaranteed the maintenance of fluid interchange—as opposed to the establishment of any stable difference—between the principals involved. Ironically, Jonson does in the end manage to differentiate himself from his foes in the War of the Theaters, but only by coming close to announcing his own surrender. When, in the "apologeticall Dialogue," Polyposus reveals that many spectators consider Jonson to have been "hit, and hurt" by *Satiromastix* (41), the poet's disarming frankness manages what all the theatrically contrived vomit in the world could not: to make him look more human, more vulnerable, and more sympathetic than his detractors.

Finally, it is Jonson's determination to have matters both ways—or, more accurately, all ways—that moves him beyond the free-flowing resemblances and regurgitations of the Poets' Quarrel. Of course, Jonson offers the vision of a "hit, and hurt" author only to snatch it back at once. The Author responds to Polyposus's remark with one of the more nauseating alimentary images in the Jonson canon:

> POL.　　The Multitude . . .
> . . . thinke you hit, and hurt: and dare giue out
> Your silence argues it, in not reioyning
> To this, or that late libell?
> 　　　　　AVT. 'Lasse, good rout!
> I can affoord them leaue, to erre so still:
> And, like the barking students of Beares-Colledge,
> To swallow vp the garbadge of the time
> With greedy gullets, whilst my selfe sit by,
> Pleas'd, and yet tortur'd, with their beastly feeding.
> 　　　　　　　　　　(40–48)

Still, the Author's retraction doesn't quite retract; he remains "tortur'd" with the beast multitude's feeding, and the expression of pleasure supplements that torture without mitigating it. But not only does Jonson proclaim his own injury while simultaneously renewing the assault on his opponents; this passage adds still another layer to the discursive palimpsest of the War of the Theaters by effectively declaring war on the audience as well. The "black vomit" of Dekker and Marston has become their spectators' food, which those spectators in turn recycle among each other as the common cry that Jonson has been hit, and hurt.

The Culture of Emesis

So the action of Jonsonian vomit expands in various directions at once. On one hand, it involves larger and larger numbers of people: first Marston, then Marston and Dekker, then Marston and Dekker and their audiences, and implicitly—given his participation in the common satirical/alimentary gestures of the Poetomachia—Jonson himself. On the other hand, it positions the poet ambiguously vis-à-vis the objects of his satire; vomiting, after all, is simultaneously a restorative and a punitive—and arguably even a repatriative—process. Still further, the emotional overcoding of the poet's self-dramatized reaction to the literary regurgitations of his detractors is such that Jonson himself emerges hurt yet aloof, "pleas'd, and yet tortur'd," from the welter of vomitus that is his and his competitors' work.

This can be the case, in part, because the action of vomiting takes on a series of competing significations in the physical vocabulary of seventeenth-century England. Helkiah Crooke, for instance, associates vomit with excretion much as does Jonson when he speaks of the poetasters' "laxatiue tongues"; in fact, vomiting and excretion are closely interrelated, operating as unhealthy and healthy processes of alimentary expulsion, respectively. According to Crooke, "The naturall motion" of expulsion "is . . . double, *One According to, another Against nature*" (166, sig. P5v). The latter occurs when the fibers of the esophagus, stomach, and so forth

> do gather them selues from below vpward . . . and in this motion the wind, the Chylus, and the excrements are auoyded by the vpper parts, nothing by the lower although such euacuations be prouoked by sharpe Clisters. . . . *Hippocrates* acknowledgeth a threefold cause of this depraued motion, *Inflammation, a confirmed oppilation or stopping, & sometimes a slight exulceration.* (166, sig. P5v)

Walter Cary offers a similar, albeit narrower, explanation; continual vomiting is induced either "when the first veines, which receiue the nutriment from the stomach, are stopped" or "when the bodie is long bound, and the excrement verie hard"—in either case the intestinal tract thus being blocked (sig. B8v). Philip Barrow explains that "the disposition to vomit . . . is a naughty & wicked motion of the expulsive vertue of the stomack, . . . caused of a vicious humour" (102, sig. H3v). Gail Paster has drawn attention to the ethical overlay of phrases like "depraued motion" and "vicious humour" (Paster 78–84), and we need not return to that aspect of the physiology presented here. For present purposes, certain other points are more interesting.

First, Crooke, Cary, and Barrow all perceive the actions of alimentary expulsion *per orem* and *per anum* to be intimately interrelated. On one hand, they exist in a kind of specular complementarity; vomit is defecation's evil twin, coming into play when the more normal and healthy route of digestive extrusion has been blocked or disrupted. But this relation of specularity is at once complicated by the fact that some authorities believe certain manipulations of the anus to exert an emetic effect on the nasoesophageal tract; for instance, Crooke can note that "*Rhasis* is of opinion, that Clisters may ascend vnto the stomacke, and are often cast out by the Nosethrills" (Crooke 166, sig. P5v). Crooke himself disagrees, but even so he acknowledges that in certain limited conditions, an enema can transcend its humble origins and reappear through the mouth. Thus he can speak of the "lamentable and odious disease called *Ileos* or *Miserere mei Deus*, wherein the seate or fundament is so closed, that a Needle cannot be thrust into it, and if any Clisters bee with much ado administered, they are incontinently suckt vp" (166, sig. P5v). (The condition Crooke describes here would almost certainly be a severe obstruction of the lower intestine, an ailment that frequently causes sufferers to vomit their excrement. In such cases the functions of mouth and anus trade place with frightening literality.)

Still further, the products of the lower end of the alimentary tract were often introduced into the emetic infusions administered to the upper end—infusions that seem to have produced both vomit and stools on an indiscriminate basis. Shakespeare's son-in-law, John Hall, for instance, records treating one Rogers of Stratford, who "did labour of vomiting, jaundice, stopping of the courses, and bleeding at the nose" with a series of emetic infusions (Hall 127, sig. G4r). The first, consisting of "*syrup of violets half a spoonfull*," produced "seven vomits, and five stools"; thereafter Hall administered a mixture of "*Sarsaparilla*" and a "*laxatiue powder of Seny*," which together "purged very well," then finally a preparation of *"the white of hens dung in white wine with sugar"* (Hall 127, sig. G4r). In short, it is not by accident that enemas and emetics (together with bleedings) are two of the three great purgative staples of early modern physic. Early modern medicine presents a model of the human body in which fiddling with the mouth may or may not affect the anus, and vice versa, depending on the condition of the body in question, the constitution of the purge being administered, and the avenue and circumstances of administration. The relation between oral and anal expulsion is an extremely unstable and ambiguous one, so much so that F. David Hoeniger has recently combined enemas and emetics into a single category as "the other chief therapeutic way," aside from bloodletting, whereby early modern physicians could "remove obstructive substances or offending humors from the body" (242). Thus, when Jonson refers to Dekker and Marston as "vncleane birds, / That make their mouthes their clysters, and still purge / From their hot entrailes," the association of oral and anal purgation—indeed, the casual yet complex superimposition of one upon the other—arguably derives in part from a medical vocabulary, well represented by Crooke and others, that itself encourages such superimposition.

In addition, it is worth noting that Crooke and his contemporaries tended to view vomit primarily as a symptom of certain metabolic disorders: for instance, bowel obstructions (*"a confirmed oppilation or stopping"*), gastroenteritis and related ailments (*"inflamation"*), and ulceration. This is doubtless a reasonable way to present the matter, but it places early modern medical practice in a distinctly ambivalent light. Consider, for instance, Hall's treatment of Rogers of Stratford, described above. Hall is interested in addressing a complex of symptoms of which the foremost is vomiting; he does so, in effect, by inducing more vomiting. Moreover, as Lucinda Beier observes, such treatment was not only employed in response to specific ailments; it was part of the standard regime of early modern English preventive medicine: "Emetics or 'vomits' . . . were used for prophylactic as well as curative purposes. Traditionally, the English thought it good to take physic at least once a year, usually in the spring, whether they were ill or not" (62). The result is, from the twentieth-century viewpoint, a peculiar spectacle indeed: generations of Englishmen and women vomiting on a regular basis in order—among other things—to avoid vomiting on a regular basis.

This peculiarity may be explained, at least in part, by culture-specific notions of what constitutes effective physic. As Beier observes,

The question of whether or not a remedy "worked" was understood very differently [in early modern England] than it would be by a twentieth-century sufferer. The seventeenth-century medicine-taker expected a preparation to show its strength by producing an immediate result—usually in the form of multiple bowel movements or vomits. Thus, the fact that a remedy "wrought well" had nothing to do with whether or not it cured the sufferer's symptoms. Indeed, prophylactic medicine was expected to "work" in the absence of illness. (169–170)

Beier's remarks are borne out by even a cursory reading of seventeenth-century medical casebooks. Yet by the same token, it is patently silly to divorce the administration of medicine from curative purposes altogether, and, as we have already seen, vomit is repeatedly described by early modern physicians as an unnatural action symptomatic of specific kinds of illness.

This conflict can only be resolved by expanding the physical signification of emesis so as to assign it a therapeutic value in addition to its status as evidence of morbidity. In the process, we find ourselves once more on shifting semiotic ground: ground of precisely the sort upon which *Poetaster* is acted out. The social multivalence of Crispinus's vomiting—it is at once an index of the poetaster's illness, evidence of the efficacy of Horace's medicine, an act of charitable therapy, and the climactic gesture of punishment in the play—is subtended by a similar multivalence in the early modern medical vocabulary. It stands to reason that these two levels of discursive ambiguity reinforce, and are in turn reinforced by, the personal ambiguities—the instabilities of compliment and cooperation, invective and reconciliation—that comprise the biographical background to the War of the Theaters.

Bartholomew Fair and the Oral Purge

Finally, I want to turn to one of the other moments in Jonson's career when vomit rises to the poet's occasion. This event, the climactic emesis of *Bartholomew Fair*, may provide a particularly good subject with which to end the present study, for *Bartholomew Fair* offers the full gamut of Jonsonian alimentary gestures in an exceptionally limited and tightly interrelated focus. If, as I noted at the end of the introduction to this work, Jonson handles the various alimentary functions in ways that both invite and resist segmentation, *Bartholomew Fair* offers the classic case in point. To begin with, Jonson's comedy is a sustained literary embodiment of the desire for food, and the original motive force of its plot is a pregnant woman's longing to eat roast pork. Frances Teague, among others, has remarked on the "pattern of eating and drinking" that structures the play (46). Jonas Barish has viewed this "persistent appearance of food and drink" as "expressive of [an] omnipresent carnality" (228), and Anne Barton has noted that "almost everyone in this comedy has been hungry, swallowing down roast pig, gingerbread, Catherine pears, bottle ale, women, money and property with indiscriminate greed" (*Jonson* 214). The appetitive theme of the play is manifest and pervasive, encompassing much more than the quotidian act of eating; here, as much as anywhere, Jonson is concerned to cross the borders that ostensibly separate eater from eaten and edible from inedible.

Perhaps somewhat less obtrusive, but nonetheless inextricably linked to the imagery of food and drink, is the play's preoccupation with the excretory processes. Peter Stallybrass and Allon White have observed, for instance, that the figure of Ursula the pig woman, around whom "food, drink, sex, urine, and even property . . . constantly circulate" (65), offers a focal point for ongoing patterns of transformation in her play. But other such foci proliferate, too. One of the passages with which this book began, Justice Overdo's speech on the evils of ale and tobacco, associates "the fome of the one, and the fumes of the other" (2.6.2) with the consumption of newt-bodies and alligator urine. Joan Trash's gingerbread, made of "stale bread, rotten eggs, musty ginger, and dead honey" (2.2.9–10), is one more example of the decomposing food that keeps finding its way into Jonsonian representations of city life; to this extent it parallels the flayed and roasted cat bodies of "On the Famous Voyage" and the moldy piecrust that sustains Penniboy Senior in *The Staple of News*. Gail Paster is right to claim that Ursula the pig woman is archetypally feminine in her somatic liquefaction and uncontrol (36–37), but she is not the only leaky vessel in her play. Even her roast pigs are capable of weeping (2.4.58–59). Among the regulars at Ursula's pig booth is a pimp named after a chamber pot, and the only urinary receptacle in Jonson's fair—carefully located in the pig booth itself—is a "cut-down beer bottle" (Slights 148). One of the play's recurrent catch lines is the cheerful expletive "turd i' your teeth" (1.4.53; 1.5.16; 3.4.44; etc.); this asseveration is then replaced, in the puppet-play that ends the comedy, by such elegant formulas as "*Kisse the whore o' the arse*" (5.4.339). Jonson's fair abounds with alimentary entertainment that is always distilling into various kinds of excreta. The poet seems determined to make his characters urinate, defecate, sweat, weep, and drool where they eat.

Given this highly indecorous context it is perhaps surprising that *Bartholomew Fair* also offers its audience a sustained exploration of the question of table manners. The character of Humphrey Wasp and the vapors-game played ad nauseam by the regulars at Ursula's pig booth are the two representational vehicles for this theme. As guardian of the nitwit Bartholomew Cokes, Wasp embodies—in theory, at least—the Erasmian commitment to *civilitas*. His main business in Jonson's play is to supervise the wayward behavior of his charge, behavior Wasp himself ascribes to an overly liberal education:

> His [i.e. Cokes's] foolish scholemasters haue done nothing,
> but runne vp and downe the Countrey with him, to beg
> puddings and cake-bread, of his tennants, and almost spoyled
> him, he has learn'd nothing, but to sing *catches*, and repeat
> *rattle bladder rattle*, and *O, Madge*.
> (1.4.72–76)

The puddings and cake bread through which Cokes exercises his folly at home are replaced, in turn, by the sundry delicates of the city and the fair, all of which interfere with Wasp's efforts to control his pupil:

> If [Cokes] goe to the *Fayre*, he will buy of euery
> thing. . . . And then he is such a Rauener after fruite! you
> will not beleeue what a coyle I had, t'other day, to
> compound a businesse betweene a *Katerne*-peare-woman, and
> him, about snatching!
> (1.5.113–120)

Cokes's childishness manifests itself repeatedly in his inability to discipline his appetite, and his behavior—neglecting conversational skills, grasping greedily after food as soon as it appears—provides a virtual antitype of the comportment advocated by Erasmus in *De Civilitate*.

But Wasp's own efforts to enforce the Erasmian ideal of *civilitas* are themselves decidedly uncivil. Indeed, where Cokes represents a principle of ungoverned appetite, Wasp is one of those late Jonsonian characters for whom—as Katharine Maus has put it—"the inclination to discipline has become a private whim" (*Inwardness* 148). At the fair, he finds himself drawn toward increasingly irascible and confrontational behavior in his attempt to govern his charge. When Cokes stops in midgambol, mesmerized by Justice Overdo's temperance speech, Wasp sputters in semicoherent rage, urging his ward forward: "Why will you heare him? because he is an Asse, and may be a kinnne [*sic*] to the *Cokeses*?" (2.6.18–19). But the fool is unmoved, and so Wasp's efforts at governance grow increasingly inarticulate and violent, eventuating first in an effort to carry Cokes away forcibly (2.6.96–100) and then, when that expedient fails, in an assault upon Justice Overdo himself (2.6.146–154). What starts out as an effort to discipline a simpleton ends up as a small riot.

In the first chapter of this study, I argued that Jonson's vocabulary of convivial behavior (and of manners in general) exhibits a decidedly interventionist character. In *Bartholomew Fair*, the figure of Wasp gives us a parody of that very approach to the regulation of behavior; it is almost as if Wasp were a study in self-caricature. And that is, indeed, what he may be, at least to an extent. According to David Riggs, *Bartholomew Fair* may bear the marks of Jonson's own experience as the erstwhile tutor to Sir Walter Raleigh's son (206–207):

> This Youth being knavishly inclyned, among other pastimes (as the setting of the favour of Damosells on a Cod piece) caused him to be Drunken & dead drunk, so that he knew not wher he was, therafter laid him on a Carr which he made to be Drawen by Pioners through the streets, at every corner showing his Governour streetched out & telling them that was a more Lively image of ye Crucifix then any they had. (Drummond 296–302)

The spectacle of Jonson, intoxicated and inert before his scapegrace pupil, certainly suggests that the poet's efforts to regulate manners could have their limits. Likewise, Wasp's increasingly testy efforts to control Cokes merely infect the governor himself with the ward's vice of poor self-control. Robert Watson has characterized Jonson's later plays as "a flag of surrender" (10), a capitulation to the various modes of literary taste and social behavior that the poet had spent a good portion of his life attempting to reform. *Bartholomew Fair*, with its implicit parody of Jonson's own reformational tendencies, may provide encouragement to this view.

As a consequence of such parody, Wasp becomes an ideal participant in the vapors game that governs social interaction at Ursula's pig booth. This game exhibits the Jonsonian interventionist tendency at its logical point of degeneration. Barish is right to claim that the game, in which "*euery man . . . oppose[s] the last man that spoke: whethe[r] it concern'd him, or no*" (4.4.27–38 s.d.), "codifies contradictoriness into a formal rule" (217), but one might just as well say that the game makes a formal rule of correction. That is why Wasp is so good at it; his own zeal to amend the behavior of others, hardened in the fire of Cokes's imbecility, now finds its proper scope in a general reformation of manners. In fact, if Wasp is partly a parody of Jonson himself, the vapors game may perhaps be taken as a parody of the very concept of civility. I have already argued that Jonson's work contributes, in self-conscious and mobile ways, to the progressive expansion of the category of distasteful behavior that Norbert Elias identifies as a prime element of the European history of manners. In the vapors game, this expansion has reached its inevitable limit; everything that anyone does or says is automatically offensive to someone else, and therefore subject to correction. Just as *Bartholomew Fair* elides urine and excrement with food and drink, it manages to generate, out of the motive force behind courteous behavior, a distinctively squalid social mess.

At the same time, the vapors game gives us something more, too. It returns us to the governing rhetorical dynamic of the War of the Theaters, a dynamic that discovers in mutual antagonism a twisted kind of solidarity. After all, the act of opposing whatever one's fellows have said proceeds from two necessary assumptions: first, that one has fellows to oppose, and second, that the opposition is worth the effort it demands. As a result, the vapors game places its players in a peculiar interdependence. The respondent reproduces, in specular form, the words he has just heard, and the overall effect of the game is thus to produce a strange kind of echo poetry:

> KNO. He is i' the right, and do's vtter a sufficient vapour.
> CVT. Nay, it is no sufficient vapour, neither, I deny that.
> KNO. Then it is a sweet vapour.
> CVT. It may be a sweet vapour.
> WAS. Nay, it is no sweet vapour, neither, Sir, it stinkes, and I'le stand to't.
> WHI. Yes, I tinke it dosh shtinke, Captaine. All vapour dosh shtinke.
> WAS. Nay, then it do's not stinke, Sir, and it shall not stinke.
> CVT. By your leaue, it may, Sir.
> WAS. I, by my leaue, it may stinke, I know that.
>
> (4.4.54–65)

In a passage like this, the meaning of the words is both nugatory and irrelevant; in fact, the words take on a life almost wholly independent of their lexical value. The vapors game staggers on and on like a drunken round of "Frere Jacques," with the participants sharing their language as they do Ursula's roast pig and bottle ale.

In this respect, the vapors game provides perhaps the culminating treatment of a subject that fascinated Jonson throughout his career: the social ambiguity of the convivial moment. Again and again, Jonson brings his characters together for moments of silly game-playing structured around food and drink, and the resulting onstage behavior has a strangely mixed quality to it. We have already considered Ovid's banquet in *Poetaster*, with the widely disparate reactions it occasions in characters and audiences. *Cynthia's Revels* offers another version of the same situation; the mock duel of manners staged between Amorphus and Asotus in that play (5.3), like the recurring word games, serves to emphasize the participants' vacuity. But it also paves the way for a later and parallel contest between Amorphus and Mercury (5.4), while functioning as the prelude—almost an extended antimasque, in fact—to the masque of Crites with which the play ends. In *Bartholomew Fair*, the model of convivial interaction provided by the vapors game contrasts with—but also prepares for and in its unifying capacities may actually inspire—Justice Overdo's concluding supper invitation. When Overdo issues his invitation "*Ad correctionem, non ad destructionem; Ad aedificandum, non ad diruendum*" (5.6.112–113), we may glimpse something of the same reformist zeal that led Wasp to the pig booth and the vapors game. To correct, not to destroy; to build up, not to tear down: these are fine sentiments, and they have motivated both Wasp and Overdo himself throughout the play, but for that very reason they provide a decidedly inconclusive conclusion to what has gone before. That inconclusiveness is then famously intensified when Bartholomew Cokes accepts Overdo's dinner invitation in the comedy's final line: "Yes, and bring the *Actors* along, wee'll ha' the rest o' the *Play* at home" (5.6.114–115).

As for Overdo himself, he provides the prime example in *Bartholomew Fair* of the processes of readerly assimilation and digestion that Jonson associated with literary production. Within five lines of his first appearance onstage, Overdo is Englishing Horace—or "my *Quint. Horace*" (2.1.5), as the justice prefers to call him. Nor is it accidental that this process of literary reproduction accompanies a similar process of visual reconstruction; Overdo's first echo of Horace (drawn from Satire 1.3.26–27, "Tam cernis acutum, / quam aut aquila aut serpens Epidaurius") denies the possibility of penetrating the disguise he has donned in order to observe the criminal activity of the fair covertly. Thus when Overdo declares, "Faine would

I meet the *Linceus* now, that Eagles eye, that piercing *Epidaurian* serpent . . . that could discouer a Iustice of Peace . . . vnder this couering" (2.1.4–7), he confronts his auditors with a remarkable series of interpenetrating impostures. Here is a character who speaks as if he were Horace but looks as if he were a local lunatic, who evidently believes that he and Horace are in some sense compatriots while equally believing that onlookers will not possibly be able to distinguish his intrinsic justiciary identity from his assumed identity of madman, and who thus calls in question the extent to which identity can be regarded as intrinsic and unassumed in the first place. Jonson famously observed that "our whole life is like a *Play*: wherein every man, forgetfull of himselfe, is in travaile with expression of another. Nay, wee so insist in imitating others, as wee cannot . . . returne to our selves" (*Discoveries* 8:597). This remark provides the admonitory counterpart of the poet's concomitant advice "to make choise of one excellent man above the rest, and so to follow him, till he grow very *Hee*" (*Discoveries* 8:638). Overdo, by following Jonson's precept in respect of the latter passage, risks incurring the poet's censure in respect of the former.

Indeed, Overdo may very well have swallowed Horace whole. The justice's first words are Englished Latin, and his last—the invitation to dine "*Ad correctionem, non ad destructionem*"—are Latinized English. In between, Overdo has a habit of invoking classical models for all sorts of behavior, as he does, to singularly unedifying effect, when placed in the stocks for disturbing the peace:

> *Adam*, thou art aboue these batteries, these contumelies. *In te manca ruit fortuna*, as thy friend *Horace* saies; thou art one, *Quem neque pauperies, neque mors, neque vincula terrent*. And therefore as another friend of thine saies, (I thinke it be thy friend *Persius*) *Non te quaesiveris extra*.
> (4.6.96–101)

The last of these Latin tags is particularly appropriate. Persius counsels us not to seek ourselves beyond ourselves, yet the patterns of Jonsonian imitation espoused by Overdo, and absurdly illustrated in this passage, suggest that the very notion of selfhood can be a function of textuality, that—in Overdo's case, at least—the quotation utters the man rather than vice versa. In effect, Overdo's Latinisms, hurled about with such unconsidered abandon, help place him in the company of Ursula's customers, with their vapors game. In both cases, the characters' language has taken on a life of its own, leaping the bounds of individuality, purposiveness, and interpretive determinacy.

Bartholomew Fair thus offers its audiences the full repertory of Jonsonian alimentary gestures, all arranged in the most intricate and multivalent patterns. The play's treatment of ingestion, excretion, the cultivation of courteous behavior, and the assimilation of literary material amounts to a massive program of statement and self-interference, in which the patterns of difference that govern a particular alimentary category are exploded in such a way that the different categories themselves come to be intimately interrelated. One effect of this development is to add immeasurably to the chaotic atmosphere of the play as a whole. *Bartholomew Fair* has always been famous for the sheer volume of the white noise it generates, and the play's alimentary materials add substantially to this aspect of the work. It is thus perhaps a crowning irony that such chaos should be built on a framework of neoclassical purity. As Anne Barton has noted, "much modern criticism of the play [has] stigmatized it as ill-plotted and congested . . . , when its unobtrusive ordering is in fact one of its greatest and most hard-won triumphs" (*Jonson*, 197).[5] In Patricia Parker's formulation, the "masterfully controlled matter" of Jonson's play comprises an "expanded body" that encompasses and overwhelms even so vast and appetitive a figure as Ursula herself (25).

Into the midst of his play's elaborate cacophony, Jonson then interjects two moments of climactic revelation. Both involve the bodily functions; both constitute what one might call the silencing of oracles; and yet both simultaneously represent the triumph of noise over silence and of nonsense over sense. The first of these climactic moments comes in the puppet play, which culminates the day's activities at the fair and which the Puritan Zeal-of-the-Land Busy seeks in prophetic fashion to disrupt. The consequences of this disruption are famously brilliant; Busy is sucked into theological debate with the Puppet Dionysius, who defends the practice of theatrical entertainment against the range of Puritan complaints adduced by Busy. In the process, the puppet also draws Busy—another reformist in the mold of Overdo and Wasp—into one more echo of the vapors game:

> BVS. I say vnto thee, Idoll, thou hast no *Calling*.
> PVP. D. *You lie, I am call'd* Dionisius.
> . . . .

BVS. I meane no *vocation, Idoll*, no present lawfull *Calling*.
PVP. D. *Is yours a lawfull Calling?*
. . . .
BVS. Yes, mine is of the Spirit.
PVP. D. *Then* Idoll *is a lawfull* Calling.
. . . .
BVS. Yet, I say, [your] *Calling*, [your] Profession is prophane, it is prophane, *Idoll*.
PVP. D. *It is not prophane*!
. . . .
BVS. It is prophane.
PVP. *It is not prophane.*
BVS. It is prophane.
PVP. *It is not prophane.*

(5.5.52–74)

In this case, as in the others already considered, the impulse to reform—to assert and to hierarchize difference—itself constitutes a gesture of rhetorical unanimity. It is altogether typical of Jonson's literary strategies that a character like Busy should repeatedly discover counter-signifying capacities within his language, which consistently escapes his efforts to use it as an instrument of social discrimination. The same model of counter-signification, played out upon the space of the body, likewise governs the Puppet Dionysius's last rebuttal of Puritan arguments against the theater. When Busy famously declares to the puppets, "My maine argument against you, is, that you are an *abomination*: for the Male, among you, putteth on the apparell of the *Female*, and the *Female* of the *Male*" (5.5.98–100), he grounds his antitheatricalism, in the best tradition of British common sense, upon the givenness and irrefutability of sexual difference. The Puppet Dionysius, in turn, lifts his gown, revealing an absence of genitals—and hence of the biologically constructed difference between male and female—in the very space that grounds Busy's argument; in effect, where Busy expects to see sex, he instead discovers gender. As a result, the terms of Busy's argument are absorbed by a prior ambiguity that both enables and exceeds the argument itself. Jonson's interest in the linguistic articulation of gender—elsewhere made manifest by the transvestism of *Epicoene* and *Volpone*—returns here in ways that parallel the poet's concern with alimentary instabilities.

Thus it is appropriate that this moment of sexual indefinition should find a counterpart in the vomiting that ends Jonson's play. Where Busy's efforts to organize the world are met with a deafening burst of sexual static, Justice Overdo's efforts are rewarded with a massive wave of culinary feedback. Like Busy, whose final silencing has just been witnessed by Jonson's audience, Overdo seeks to impose order on social confusion—in this case the confusion of Ursula's pig booth. The effort to establish this order plays itself out in various ways; as he builds to an intended climax in the distribution of justice, Overdo literally moves the other characters around onstage, forcing them to take positions that correspond with the judgments he is about to deliver. Moreover, Overdo not only positions his fellows onstage, he also tells them how to comport themselves. When Cokes enters in confusion, seeking his betrothed, Overdo commands him to join his mother and be silent: "If this graue Matron be your mother, Sir, stand by her, *Et digito compesce labellum*" (5.6.20–21). He declares his intention to "rescue" Grace "out of the hands of the stranger" Winwife, extricating her from Winwife's clutches even as he speaks. He extols his own labors and discoveries, and then proceeds to strip off the velvet masks worn by the pig-booth prostitutes. Encountering his own wife drunk among the whores, Overdo is "*silenc'd*" (5.6.67–71 s.d.) in his turn, and the process that begins with the justice silencing Cokes—telling Cokes to press his lips with his finger—repatriates itself on the terrain of Overdo's own body.

In this context, Mistress Overdo's vomit takes on a wide range of different dramatic functions. On one hand, it ironically accords with Overdo's desire to reduce the play's other characters to an overawed silence; the justice's exposure of enormities deprives one character after another of the ability to speak, until it takes as its ultimate victim the justice's own wife. But by the same token, Mistress Overdo's sickness provides a rhetorical statement—obviously a comment of sorts on her husband's self-important speechifying. Denied the option of verbal rebuke, the mouth transforms itself from a speaking machine to a vomiting machine and continues with business as usual. By the same token, if we think of the play's society in somatic terms of the sort familiar to early modern English political theorists,[6] Mistress Overdo's vomiting session constitutes a rebellion—or at least a rejoinder—aimed at the head of the body politic by the belly, with the head—Overdo—deprived of its articulateness by the untimely reappearance of the belly's contents. Likewise, the very mixedness of the belly's contents constitutes a refutation of the order so sedulously imposed upon society by Overdo. In response to the justice's painstaking efforts to organize character groups, to govern their comportment, and to correct their transgressions, the final visual spectacle of the play is a basinful of crudities: half-digested food, awash in an alimentary soup.

But beyond these more or less obvious readings of the vomiting session, there is at least one more. Mistress Overdo's emesis is not simply gastrointestinal; it is also literary. It constitutes a resurgence of the vomiting motif already explored by Jonson in *Poetaster*, and now situated in an entirely different social context with a substantially different object.

To this extent, the sickness of *Bartholomew Fair* further exploits the semiotic multivalence of the emetic gesture. We have already noted that one strength of the oral purgation in *Poetaster* is its symbolic motility. It is simultaneously an expression of Horace's mastery over the arts of Apollo, a means of theatrical humiliation directed at the hapless Crispinus, a surrogate for judicial punishment, a confirmation of Crispinus's illness, and—ostensibly, at least—a gesture of kindly solicitude. In Mistress Overdo's case, I do not think it accidental that this same gesture now rebounds upon the judicial apparatus of which, in *Poetaster*, it serves as an extension. The result is a considerable realignment of theatrical sympathies, a realignment that might even be viewed as Jonson's response to the relative failure of his efforts in the War of the Theaters.

In *Poetaster*, Crispinus's therapy constitutes, among other things, a symbolic identification of author-surrogate with surrogate prince; Horace, by chastising Crispinus as he does, occupies the position both of Augustan court poet and of Augustan court enforcer. He becomes, among other things, *Poetaster*'s equivalent of Justice Overdo, performing his works "in Iustice name, and the Kings" (2.1.1). By the same token, the crudities vented by Crispinus constitute an all-encompassing figure of deformity—medical and moral, literary and legal—to be made subject to the multiform disciplinary capacities of the court through the court's instrument, Horace/Jonson. In *Bartholomew Fair*, on the other hand, the metamorphic character of these deformities has escaped containment by any hands. No longer subject to the punitive dispensation of poet or magistrate, Jonson's crudities fly in the face of even the most concerted reformers, becoming the reformational instrument of an altogether disembodied intelligence. One effect of this transformation is to distance the play from the very forms of authority that animated Jonson's earlier work, and that, in the earlier work, first evoked the emetic gesture with which the later play concludes. Jonson's vomit has—if I may be forgiven the phrase—reterritorialized itself in ways that imply the reterritorialization of the poet's own satirical allegiances. Instead of serving as the functionary of a particular social or political institution—the court, the kingdom, the classical literary canon—the satirical voice of *Bartholomew Fair* takes on a playful, self-reflexive, and completely elusive character. It is as if Jonson had heard the music of the spheres, and it sounded like someone retching.

The Raw and Undigested

I began this chapter by calling it a codicil of sorts, and I certainly do not want to lend too much interpretive weight to the esophageal discomforts of Crispinus and Mistress Overdo. Such matters are, at most, ancillary to the farther-reaching issues of social intercourse, conspicuous consumption, literary digestion, and scatology addressed in preceding parts of this book. Still, the present chapter takes courage from the example of Graham Hammill, who has recently described the anal purge as a metabolic analogue to Baconian epistemology. As Hammill argues, the "repetition of expurgation" is central to Bacon's work and thought, providing "a formal structure whose most critical, epistemological effect is the revision and reconstruction of knowledge, and whose most critical sexual effect is the cathexis and eroticization of the purged male anus" (246).

As is well known, Jonson felt considerable enthusiasm for Baconian philosophy, and the poet's own emphasis on observation and imitation arguably parallels the Baconian dynamic of epistemological purgation. Just as Bacon's readers must be "purged" of their "idols" in order to grasp "the complexities of experimental science" (Hammill 237), so the processes of Jonsonian imitation aim, as I have already argued, to purge the aspiring author of his or her own literary idiosyncracies so as to replace them with an originally external model of literary subjectivity. But the moments of vomiting we have just considered, despite their obvious medical character as purgation, operate differently, with much greater ambivalence, than does the logic of anal expulsion. Far from consigning one's aliment to the sewer, vomit returns it to the table like Thomas Coryate's crudities or Montaigne's reading, "raw and undigested" (*Discoveries*, 8:586), ready for further recycling. Far from betokening openness and receptivity, the oral purge may very well signify the body's absolute blockage and inability to process meats. Far from being an unequivocally salutary and natural function, the act of emesis cuts across the categories of illness and health in an unstable, paradoxical way.

To this extent, Jonson's crudities correspond to the Deleuzian notion of the desiring machine. For Deleuze and Guattari, the body is conditioned by a series of machinic operations, each of them "a *system of interruptions* or breaks," each of them functioning adjacent to and in the same space with others, and each one "related to a continual material flow . . . that it cuts into" (*Anti-Oedipus* 36). Thus, for instance, "the mouth of the anorexic wavers between several functions: its possessor is uncertain as to whether it is an eating-machine, an anal machine, a talking-machine, or a breathing-machine" (*Anti-Oedipus* 1). Likewise, in the vomiting scenes from *Poetaster* and *Bartholomew Fair*, Jonson treats the mouth as a multiplicity of functions, connected to different but superimposed material flows of food, language, and medication. The result is grotesque, perhaps amusing or even trivial, but it is most certainly not static, unilinear, or univocal. Instead, I take it to be representative of Jonson's work at its best: constantly in motion, crossing boundaries, discovering new landscapes and resources within the most apparently familiar terrain.

Conclusion

> The one thing that the world will never have enough of is outrageousness.
> —Salvador Dali

It is time now to take stock, and I must immediately admit that this book has proven nothing. Nor has it tried to, if by proof one refers to the linear organization of interrelated premises so as to lead to a single predetermined conclusion. Instead, this book has proceeded, in an episodic and experimental manner, from two observations: first, that Jonson, as scholars regularly note, was a past master at having all aspects of a situation or dilemma his way; and second, that Jonson was indefatigably given to notions of movement, kinesis, energy, and exploration. As Alexander Leggatt has remarked, the poet's work is pervaded by the "fear that a human being can become a dead thing" (48), by a suspicion that "the sensual world is a world asleep" (60), and by a particular loathing of the sluggard and the time server: those who "are not normally corrupt, but normally inert" (49). As for Jonson's sense of himself, perhaps it is sufficient to recall that the motto he inscribed in his books was "*Tamquam explorator.*" In the present work, I have sought to investigate my sense that Jonson's discursive agility—his ability to exploit to his own advantage the ambiguities of a given social, political, or literary situation—is a function of his commitment to movement and exploration.

My choice of subject matter, in turn, has been a logical extension of my efforts to comprehend the Jonsonian poetics of mobility. Jonson himself attests, in the conversations with Drummond, to his propensity for reconfiguring the static body into new and extraordinary forms: "He heth consumed a whole night in lying looking to his great toe, about which he hath seen tartars & turks Romans and Carthaginions feight in his imagination" (Drummond 322–324). Immediately preceding this famous anecdote is another, demonstrating a further imposition of the social onto the somatic via the protocols of dining: "Being at ye end of my Lord Salisburie's table with Inigo Jones & demanded by my Lord, why he was not glad

My Lord said he yow promised I should dine with yow, but I doe not, for he had none of his meate, he esteamed only yt his meate which was of his owne dish" (Drummond 317–321). And immediately preceding this anecdote is the equally famous one, already discussed in Chapter 3, about Jonson's draining of the communion cup. For Drummond's Jonson, in short, the body could clearly be a negotiable construct: something to be composed, recomposed, explored, and adapted according to the capacities of the imagination and the limits imposed by external circumstances. Moreover, the body's negotiations and resources, particularly as they accrue around the alimentary functions, provided a crucial test case for the poet's capacity to make meaning in and through the world at large. As W. H. Herendeen has recently argued, "The body provided an image of art and reality that haunted Jonson's imagination" and that is itself characterized by "a strategic tension . . . between form and fluidity, definition and meaninglessness, being and nonbeing" (Brady and Herendeen 14–15).

In examining the development of Jonson's alimentary vocabulary, I have sought to cast my net fairly wide: to consider, for instance, the poet's use of classical convivial materials, the politics of conspicuous consumption, the infrastructural landscape of Jacobean London, and certain aspects of Renaissance medical practice and physiological theory. My focus on Jonsonian texts has, in turn, been fairly wide-ranging and deliberately unconstrained by considerations of genre, chronology, or the relative critical importance of major and minor works. Although I have tried not to neglect such literary monuments as *Volpone*, *The Alchemist*, *Bartholomew Fair*, and "To Penshurst," I have also sought to concentrate on some of the least-discussed, least-appreciated items in the Jonson canon: the *Leges Conviviales*, for instance, as well as "On the Famous Voyage." I have done this out of the conviction that there is something to be gained by divorcing Jonson from his marmoreal reputation as the grandfather of English neoclassicism. A book that concentrates on the poet's mobility, his trickiness and double-dealings, ambiguities and cross-negotiations, arguably needs to disencumber itself from the apparatus of the literary grand tradition. After all, even so self-consciously conservative a critic as Eliot could complain that Jonson's work has been "damned by the praise that quenches all desire to read the book," "afflicted by the imputation of the virtues which excite the least pleasure," and—the unkindest cut of all—"read only by historians and antiquaries" (65).

In the seventy-five years since Eliot wrote those words, Jonson's academic reputation has been bolstered immeasurably by a series of brilliant and deftly researched scholarly books, the least of which far surpasses, in its way, anything I could possibly do here. But there is little evidence to suggest that Jonson has become a more popular playwright for the broad generality of readers and theatergoers. Richard Allen Cave, for instance, has recently complained about the "current lack of a readily accessible, reasonably priced, sound edition of the Complete Plays" (178); scholars are currently working to remedy this lack, but the relative belatedness of the remedy itself says much about Jonson's current literary status. In performance, Jonson's plays have not drawn the same level of attention or general enthusiasm as Shakespeare's or Marlowe's. Faustus has his Olivier, Hamlet his Mel Gibson, Benedick and Beatrice their Branagh and Thompson, but until Keanu Reeves can be persuaded to play Volpone, something more remains to be done to popularize Jonson on the stage and screen.

The present study cannot pretend to repair this deficit. But it can at least suggest some of the ways in which Jonson's was an interactive art: an art in constant motion, and an art that achieved through its motion a constant, contradictory, opportunistic, and alogical connection with the world of its readers and listeners. One of the crushing ironies of Jonson's career is that his cherished classicism—itself the subject of many fine scholarly studies and appreciations—developed out of a humanist historical sense that regarded the past as being alive in the present. Yet in many ways that same classicism has helped give Jonson's own plays the aspect of dead things—dusty museum pieces or, in Jonas Barish's description of *Cynthia's Revels*, "great fossilized dinosaur[s]" (121). On the other hand, recent politicized scholarship has sought to counter the poet's classicism with an emphasis on his engagement in contemporary issues, usually subsumed within the quasi-mystical Foucauldian category of power relations. In this book, I have chosen to work against a Deleuzian theoretical background in part because Deleuze and Guattari are, like Jonson, so manifestly committed to the pervasive presence of the past; in part because unlike other poststructuralist theoreticians they are profoundly uninterested in questions of power; and in part because of their determination to speak across the boundaries that traditionally separate academic discourse from popular discourse and high culture from low culture.

In choosing to ground my work in so idiosyncratic a theoretical matrix, I have run a real risk. Readers sympathetic to theory may object to Deleuze and Guattari as unfashionable or even lunatic fringe, whereas antitheorists will doubtless object to them as theory. But years ago, C. S. Lewis began his *Preface to "Paradise Lost"* by claiming that, as a Christian, he was uniquely qualified to explicate a major Christian epic. By the same token, the lunatic fringe (Deleuze and Guattari would call them "schizo") elements of Deleuzian theory may be particularly appropriate for reading a poet who was—and I mean this in the best possible way—clearly something of a lunatic himself. As Drummond observed of him, he was "oppressed with fantasie, which hath ever mastered his reason, a generall disease in many poets" (Drummond 692–693). He seems to have been a borderline alcoholic, and he was capable of aggressive behavior—such as the killing of Gabriel Spencer—which would lead in twentieth-century America to swift and certain institutionalization. One of the tremendous achievements of Jonson's life and art is to have constructed a venue within which his volatile, unstable personality could coexist with, and even thrive on, the surrounding world. I believe Deleuzian theory—with its unconcern for linear thought, its disregard for static forms of being and perceiving, its unexpected humor and repeated irreverence—speaks particularly well to this aspect of the poet's productivity. Indeed, Deleuzian theory shares with Jonson's work a commitment that may perhaps be best summarized by the epigraph to these concluding remarks—Dali's claim that the world can never have enough of the outrageous.

It may be objected that this treatment of Jonson scants the frequent tone of moral solemnity in his work—that so multivalent and opportunistic a vision of Jonson fails to do justice to the poet's affinity for "unequivocal statement" or his concern to "protect the integrity" of his "poetic self" (Duncan 119). But even the most sober academic studies of Jonson have been of differing minds about his high seriousness. For Alexander Leggatt, for instance, Jonson's habit of "passing solemn judgments on trivial vices" often trivializes and vitiates his own work (178); for Michael McCanles, on the other hand, the poet seems to be a kind of ethical number cruncher, slicing moral distinctions so thinly that virtue finally comes to consist in the act of multiplying the discriminations themselves. In other words, Jonson's concern for personal integrity itself seems to take on the aspects of a mutable, multivalent construct. For this reason, I am inclined to view it as one among the poet's many strategies for professional self-construction and self-aggrandizement: an important and often used strategy, but nonetheless, like the others, one to be ignored or de-emphasized as soon as it threatens to limit the author's own abilities.

In fact, if the separate chapters of this study are unified by any governing insight, it is into Jonson's relentless rage for self-expansion. As a dictator of table manners in the *Leges Convivales*, he propels himself into a legislative space that comprehends all relations between host and guest while finding its own proper rhetorical expression in a timeless, placeless legal Latin. Celebrating the pleasures of the table, he develops a volatile poetics in which the vocabulary of conspicuous consumption is constantly melting into that of temperance, and vice versa. As a theorist of writing, he employs alimentary metaphors for literary production and consumption so as to destabilize the boundaries between such categories and in the process authorize a uniquely expansive vision of himself as artist. Writing in the scatological tradition, he produces a poem that is encyclopedic in its scope, discovering a kind of *faeces rerum* within mountebanks and performing horses, Lord Mayor's barges and parliamentary debates, and ultimately within the poet's own work. This gesture—in which the poet reaches out to the world in order not so much to embrace it as to engulf it—is a central feature of Jonson's art, concomitant with the "literary imperialism" investigated by scholars like Robert Watson.

The poet's girth may be the obvious physical emblem of this literary self-expansion, but it is important to note that his ever increasing waistline itself comprehends and enables a wide range of different significations. It can be a visual expression of the "fullness" that Richard Peterson considers central to the poet's appropriations of the classical tradition (31); it can be, as Joseph Loewenstein has observed, a kind of metaphysical defense mechanism, an effort "to shore up a fugitive being within a bulwark of flesh" ("Corpulence" 501); it can signify ill health and joviality at the same instant; it can implicate the poet in the culinary excesses of Jacobean courtly society; and so on. Not only is Jonson's body constantly getting bigger; the meaning of its getting bigger is getting bigger itself.

In his amusing work on class in America, Paul Fussell has produced a tongue-in-cheek anatomy of twentieth-century Western social relations that reflects the importance of Jonson's self-expansive literary project. For Fussell, the essence of the twentieth-century American class system is complication. Classes, subclasses, and quasi classes proliferate, and Fussell contents himself with enumerating the nine most basic ones: the Top Out-of-Sight, Upper, Upper Middle, Middle, High-Proletarian, Mid-Proletarian, Low-Proletarian, Destitute, and Bottom Out-of-Sight (46), all distinguished by a combination of external characteristics that include income, occupation, education, appearance, and so forth. In addition to these categories, however, Fussell also proposes another, called "Class X," which he describes as "a floating class with no permanent location in this hierarchy" (47). Distinguished by its ability to mingle with all the other classes at will, Class X consists of "well-to-do hippies, 'artists,' 'writers' (who write nothing), floating bohemians, politicians out of office, disgraced athletic coaches, residers abroad, rock stars, 'celebrities,' and the shrewder sort of spies" (47). (One might as well add journalists and academics to the heap.) Class X is located, in effect, in something like the professional space staked out by Jonson's own life and art.

In the end, it is unimportant whether this class anatomy corresponds to any reality quantifiable by social scientists; Fussell's own account attests to its availability as an imaginary construct—in a sense, perhaps, as a social ideal. It is also, on the level of social organization, a construct quite similar to the cultural and somatic ones encouraged by Jonson's use of alimentary motifs. Insofar as Jonson's alimentary imagery provides the somatic equivalent for a set of social aspirations, those aspirations would seek not to undo class distinctions, nor to identify with a single distinction to the exclusion of others, nor even to amalgamate with the entirety, but rather to superimpose on the body a new distinction that comprehends all others while being finally reducible to none. Insofar as this is the case, the models of alimentary activity presented in the introduction to this book—the jealous, overly tidy aggression of traditional anal neurosis, the ideal of Bakhtinian carnivalesque communion, and the notion of alimentary behavior as a metaphorical representation for larger cultural crises and transitions—all participate in and contribute to our understanding of Ben Jonson's art. The art itself, however, is emphatically not reducible to any one of these models, nor even to a combination of all three.

Finally, one may well wonder if an academic study of Jonson's work does not—through its own limitations of audience and occasion—subject the poet to the very kind of social and intellectual containment the work itself so energetically escapes. To this objection I have little reply, other than to express my belief that the experience of reading Jonson, and of participating in the processes of cultural production that Jonson represents, is in itself so rich and rewarding that it is worth enduring a measure of labor and vexation along the way. If this study has offered new insight into even a single minor aspect of the poet's productivity, it will have accomplished my heart's desire. Even if it has not, perhaps it has managed to keep you reading. That in itself is an achievement I believe Jonson would not have completely despised.

Notes

Introduction

1. In a lengthy footnote on these same lines from Epigram 101, Joseph Loewenstein accepts Gognard's reading while making the case against an alternative interpretation proposed by Thomas Greene:

> His [Greene's] paraphrase would run something like this: "I shall make no other written representations of anticipated dishes; if I should manage to provide another dish, a dish that even I do not anticipate, it will be up to the pastry to represent ('show of') it." I find this reading problematic, first because the preceding four lines have been concerned, not with the menu, but with what will be read at table. Moreover, Professor Greene's reading produces some slight problems of construction. . . . Gognard's does not do so. . . . Gognard's Jonson is coyly making one of his few promises—there will be pastry—but the promise is buried in the apodosis of a *conditional* statement. And, of course, the promised pastry may, in fact, be stained with ink. ("Corpulence" 513–514 n. 10)

Ian Donaldson offers a helpful additional gloss, reading the line in question to mean that "the cook may produce a pastry surprise, but Jonson will not produce a surprise reading" (*Ben Jonson* 661).

2. Giambattista Porta, for instance, describes a preparation "of the herb called Tobacco, namely of the juice thereof, and the ashes of Cockle shells" that is used in the New World to stave off "hunger, thirst, [and] weariness" (147, sig. Y2r). Sir Hugh Plat refers to a similar practice in his *Sundrie New and Artificiall Remedies Against Famine* (sig. D2v). Also see Knapp 138.

3. Fumerton begins her discussion of Jonson's masques by noting that their proper place lay in the venue of the cook" (111) and by describing them as "the crowning development of a long tradition of banqueting cuisine and architecture" (112). This view of matters presents an obvious challenge for Jonson's efforts to privilege the poetic element in courtly entertainment.

4. The work of Wilson, Pearlman, and Riggs is of great importance to this study, and I offer the present remarks as an extension, rather than as a censure, of these authors' substantial achievements. In fact, I strongly believe that one way to strengthen and refine the claims of anus psychology as an instrument for interpreting Jonson's verse is to reexamine the original manner in which Freud developed his theory of anal eroticism. Wilson, for his part, defines anal eroticism by referring not

to Freud, but rather to William Healy, A. F. Bronner, and A. M. Bowers's *Structure and Meaning of Psychoanalysis* (Wilson 217–218). Pearlman never quotes Freud, and his one bibliographical reference to Freud is a general citation of "Character and Anal Erotism" in a single footnote (Pearlman 365). Even Riggs's massive and brilliant biography introduces the subject of anal eroticism without a single quotation from or specific reference to Freud's writings (Riggs 31). The present book hopes to further the dialogue on Jonsonian anality by situating the important work of Wilson, Pearlman, and Riggs in closer relation to that of Freud.

5. Brown's extensive discussion of anality and psychoanalytic theory, although not specifically focused on Jonson, is sufficiently relevant to merit brief mention here. Unfortunately, Brown neglects Jonson when he describes Swift as a writer for whom "the anal function . . . is unique in Western literature" (179). In fact, Brown's response to the critical reception of Swift's scatological writings deserves quotation with respect to Jonson:

> If personal immaculateness, ambition, and the championship of righteous causes are neurotic traits, who shall 'scape whipping? . . . Common humanity makes us turn in revulsion against . . . the psychoanalysts. By what right do they issue certificates of lunacy? . . . We can only save ourselves from their madness by admitting that we are all mad. Psychoanalysis deserves the severest strictures, because it should have helped mankind to develop this kind of consciousness and this kind of humility. (184–185)

It is unfortunate that Brown, who recognizes the difficulties inherent in the pejorative view of anal eroticism, should then go on to regard anal-erotic behavior as a limited stage of personal and cultural development:

> Archaic man is preoccupied with . . . the transformation of genital impulses into that aim-inhibited libido which sustains the kinship systems in which archaic life is embedded. . . . The pregenital impulses, all the fantastic wishes of infantile narcissism, express themselves in unsublimated form. . . . Hence archaic man characteristically has a massive structure of excremental magic. (299)

Mary Douglas has criticized this latter position at length (116–120); here one may simply note that it tends to circumscribe and delimit a psychoanalytic concept that, by Brown's own earlier admission, should be kept general.

6. See Donaldson's *The World Upside-Down* (37–45) for the argument that Jonson employs rituals of festive misrule as the organizing principle of his comedy *Epicoene*. Those rituals have received considerable attention from cultural historians in the past twenty years; see, for instance, Davis, *Society and Culture* 105–119.

7. Bakhtin himself finds exceptions to the rule of the classical bodily canon "in the ancient forms of Doric comedy, in 'satyric' drama, in Sicilian comic forms, in the works of Aristophanes, in mimes and the *Atellanae*," as well as in "Hippocrates, Galen, Pliny, in the symposia, in Athenaeus, Macrobius, Plutarch, and other writ-

ings of nonclassical antiquity" (28 n. 10). Later in his work, as will be noted, Bakhtin contrasts the grotesque banquet tradition with that of the classical symposium. The result is an equivocation about the canonical status of certain Greco-Roman literary works (e.g., the comedies of Aristophanes, Martial's convivial epigrams, and the dialogues of Lucian) that were crucially important influences on Jonson.

8. Maus's remark deserves to be quoted at length: "While it is usual to eat a piece of an animal, and not the whole thing, here this humdrum fact is made to seem unusually disturbing. Sir Epicure is typical of Jonson's characters in connecting consumption with despoliation, and with the competitive displacement of other claimants, the fetal piglets, for the same resource" ("Economies" 72). To this extent, Mammon's sow's paps derange the body's territory along at least two competing and coextensive axes. Superimposing the act of dining on that of suckling and thus invoking a new territorial function for the nursing mouth, they also refigure Mammon as piglet by placing him in the position of deriving his sustenance from a maternal teat.

9. The most detailed recent assessment of early modern authorial property rights is Mark Rose's work on the subject. Surveying early modern European attitudes toward printing rights, Rose concludes that

> in the seventeenth century . . . there may have been some feeling that authors should have the right to control the first publication of their writings. But in England at any rate no clearly defined set of authorial rights existed, and English authors had no obvious form of redress if books were published without their permission. Indeed, the very concept of "author" was still incompletely developed. Not only was the modern notion of the author as an autonomous creator, the producer and first proprietor of original works, not yet formed, but even the Renaissance notion of the author as an individuated authority was often problematic. (25)

Beyond Rose's work, Elizabeth Eisenstein also gives the matter of authorial property rights some attention, arguing that the advent of the printing press foregrounds questions of authorial origination (1:79–85). Loewenstein ("Script in the Marketplace") and Timothy Murray have both brought recent attention to bear on Jonson's particular contributions to the development of copyright and authorial editing in England.

10. See Herford, Simpson, and Simpson 11:1.

11. David McPherson has noted that Jonson was rereading—and annotating—his copy of Martial at least as late as 1619 (11), almost a decade after the close paraphrases of Martial in the *Epigrams*. Drummond observes that Jonson "insisted in that of Martia / vitam quae faciunt Beatiorem" (108–109) and, again, "the Epigrame of Martial Vin Verpum he Vantes to expone" (610). Also see Revard 140–150, Whipple 384–406, and Robert Wiltenburg's discussion of Jonson's debt to Martial in the *Epigrams* (Wiltenburg 49–56).

12. Birt ponders the relations between Martial and his booksellers at some length, concluding that the booksellers' access to the poet's work must have been governed by some sort of seniority or collective bargaining:

Jedenfalls muss, wenn Martial in seinem ersten Buch seinen Käufer an drei vershiedene Handlungen, sowohl an den Atrectus wie an den Secundus wie an den Valerianus verweist, jede dieser Handlungen rechtmassig in Besitz der Examplare sein, die sie verkauft; entweder nur Einer, Valerianus, war der Viervielfältiger und gab das Buch nach Vereinbarung an Sortimentshandlungen ab, oder die Viervielfaltigung war von den dreien auf gemeinsamen Kosten ausgefuhrt worden. (359–360)

[In any case, since in his first book Martial refers to his booksellers at three different shops, not only Atrectus but also Secundus and Valerianus, each of these shops must be properly an example of who sold the books; either only one, Valerianus, was the copyright-owner and gave the book out per an agreement on retail distribution, or else the copyright was encumbered by all three at a common cost.]

Such uncertainty, and the speculation it elicited, could naturally be of interest in relation to the uncertainties accruing around the notion of copyright in early modern Europe.

13. Burke's remarks are worth recalling at length:

Why not extend . . . analysis of proverbs to encompass the whole field of literature? Could the most complex and sophisticated works of art legitimately be considered somewhat as "proverbs writ large?" . . . The point of view might be phrased this way: Proverbs are *strategies* for dealing with *situations*. In so far as situations are typical and recurrent in a given social structure, people develop names for them and strategies for handling them. Another name for strategies might be *attitudes*. . . . One tries, as far as possible, to develop a strategy whereby one "can't lose." One tries to change the rules of the game until they fit his own necessities. Does the artist encounter disaster? He will "make capital" out of it. If one is a victim of competition, for instance, if one is elbowed out, if one is willy-nilly more jockeyed against than jockeying, one can by the solace and vengeance of art convert this very "liability" into an "asset." (*Forms* 296–298)

Burke's argument has been criticized for imparting more deliberateness and organization to the social functionality of literature than is proper, but these charges do not impair the usefulness of his remarks for an appraisal of Jonson's life and work. The social and professional pressures surrounding Jonson are sufficiently powerful, distinct, and unpredictable to make Burke's position relevant to the present analysis.

14. F. J. Fisher has analyzed patterns of food production for Tudor and Stuart London. In the process, he has noted that during the early seventeenth century "the area from which the city obtained its food was growing, and . . . by 1640 it was large" (65). As a result, the London food market "gave a definite stimulus to English agriculture" (66) during the early modern period. London's "increased demands for food were, quite clearly, not met to any noteworthy degree by larger supplies from abroad. . . . The conclusion, therefore, seems inevitable that there was an

important net increase in the output of English agriculture" and "in certain commodities this increase is beyond all doubt" (66–67). Fisher cites Samuel Hartlib to the effect that market-gardening first began to flourish in England during the first decade of the seventeenth century, and goes on to note the importance of "the work . . . of specialists working enclosed holdings by intensive methods" (69). All in all, Fisher's analysis thus agrees with those of Everitt and Appleby in charting the rapid development of an early modern English industry based on the commodification of food. As a result of this industry, Fisher concludes, "city retailers won a new importance and an increasing control over the trade in agricultural produce . . . and a powerful impetus was given to the forces that were working for the commercialisation of agriculture in England at large" (79). It is at least conceivable that the concern of Epigram 3 with the retail trade in books and groceries derives in part from developments of the sort documented by Fisher, Appleby, and Everitt.

Chapter 1

1. The comparison deserves to be made on at least two different levels. First, as both Leah Marcus and Patricia Fumerton have recently pointed out, the masques were the site of all sorts of loose behavior, involving drink, sexual indecorum, brawling, and more (Marcus 120–126; Fumerton 161–162). Consider Dudley Carleton's account of the performance of *The Masque of Blackness* (1605):

> In the cumming owt, a banquet which was prepared for the king in the great chamber was ouerturned table and all before it was skarce touched. It were infinit to tell you what losses there were of chaynes, Jewels, purces, and such like loose ware. and one woeman amongst the rest lost her honesty, for which she was caried to the porters lodge being surprised at her business on the top of the Taras. (Herford, Simpson, and Simpson 10:449)

Second, as Fumerton adds, this misbehavior occurred in connection with a courtly event—the masque—that dramatized itself as a sort of "secular annunciation" (156), repeatedly eliding royal subjectivity with divinity.

2. To this extent, my reading of Martial agrees with Robert Evans's claim that "much more than Martial's poems, 'Inviting a Friend' conveys a sense of the supper as a refuge from a world of power games and political intrigue" (*Patronage* 207). However—despite my general tendency to defer to Evans—I believe this view requires further clarification. As I argue, the "refuge" that Jonson's poem constructs is a consequence of the host's infinite expansion and empowerment, whereas the convivial space of Martial's source epigrams is distinguished by its tendency to exempt the poet from any sense of public authority or responsibility. Hence, as Evans himself notes, Jonson's notions of convivial refuge are unavoidably politicized.

3. Cf. *Lives of the Twelve Caesars*, Domitian 4.5:

> He [Domitian] . . . in the course of one of his shows in celebration of the feast of the Seven Hills gave a plentiful banquet, distributing large baskets of vict-

uals to the senate and knights, and smaller ones to the commons; and he himself was the first to begin to eat. On the following day he scattered gifts of all sorts of things to be scrambled for, and since the greater part of these fell where the people sat, he had five hundred tickets thrown into each section occupied by the senatorial and equestrian orders.

[Inter spectacula muneris largissimum epulum Septimontiali sacro, cum quidem senatui equitique panariis, plebei sportellis cum obsonio distributis initium vescendi primus fecit; dieque proximo omne genus rerum missilia sparsit, et quia pars maior intra popularia deciderat, quinquagenas tesseras in singulos cuneos equestris ac senatorii ordinis pronuntiavit.]

The distribution of gifts to a scrambling crowd would particularly seem to emphasize the emperor's superiority. The distinction between the dole of food to knights and senators on one hand and to the commons on the other would likewise underscore differences in social rank.

4. See *Ambition and Privilege* for Whigham's basic formulation:

The pressure from below of . . . able young men attempting to enter the ruling elite . . . caused the established aristocracy much anxiety. . . . The first employment of courtesy literature was the repression of such mobility. . . . However, . . . the circulation of the texts would have had to have been restricted for the recuperation to be effective. . . . [Hence] courtesy literature seems effectively to have discouraged social humility and aroused ambition. (18–20)

5. Agnew applies his analysis of market capitalism to Jonson's work with a brief examination of *Bartholomew Fair*, which he regards as "an illustration of the aggregate utility of a competitive market" (120): a scene of organized chaos in which market interaction "divert[s] private vices to the public benefit" (120). Stallybrass and White extend the focus on *Bartholomew Fair* with their important discussion of the play's relation to the dynamics of early modern fair activity (27–79). Fumerton draws attention instead to Jonson's masques and the extent to which they figure anxieties regarding the nature of alien goods and manners—anxieties also introduced into late Jacobean England by the East India Company (169–206).

6. As Herford and the Simpsons note (8:653–654), the 1692 folio of Jonson's works describes the *Leges Convivales* as having been "Engraven in Marble over the Chimny, in the APOLLO of the *Old Devil Tavern* at *Temple-Bar*." Likewise, the verses "Over the Door at the Entrance into the Apollo" were "painted on a panel" for public display (8:654).

7. See, for instance, Plutarch's observation in the *Moralia* that

The first obligation of one who is invited [to supper] and himself asks others is to be careful not to ask too many. . . . Of course it is merely to make fun of us [i.e., Delphic priests such as Plutarch himself] that people say, "Who offers sacrifice at Delphi must buy meat for himself"; but this is really what happens to those whose guests, whether strangers or friends, come with a lot of "shadows," like Harpies, to carry off and make spoil of the feast. (9:65–67)

Also see Horace's Satire 2.8, which describes Maecenas as bringing two *umbrae* with him to a dinner engagement (2.8.21–22).

Chapter 2

1. This is not the place to enter into a lengthy discussion of the possible nature or role of ideology in the construction of early modern English literary texts; however, Jonson's work can clearly be said to participate in ideological activity insofar as it embodies the statements and practices through which an established social order ascribes identity to the individuals who comprise it. Since the first ideological practice to which I refer is the ritual of communion, it is perhaps worth recalling Tony Bennett's remark that "The celebration of communion might . . . be regarded as quintessentially ideological. It consists of a practice of signification which, inscribed in ritual form and housed within the ideological apparatus of the church, produces the consciousness of the communicant: that is, produces him/her as, precisely, the subject of a religious consciousness" (113). Of course, there are other ways in which the rituals of eating and drinking may be organized to individual consciousness and self-consciousness. The bulk of this present chapter focuses upon such rituals in their secular and courtly, rather than their sacred, form.

2. For one more example, Leggatt claims that Epigram 101 distinguishes "between mere self-indulgence and the conviviality of civilized men" (117), who avoid "self-display" and "the dangers of drink" (116, 117).

3. Although Loewenstein's work on "Inviting a Friend to Supper" gives relatively little attention to the social valences of Jonson's overeating, it deals admirably with an issue the present chapter does not address: the poem's classical influences. Loewenstein reviews Jonson's sources in Martial, arguing that Jonson adapts Martial to a Renaissance economy of the marketplace: "The movement toward modernity in Jonson's imitation of Martial involves the recognition of middlemen. . . . The economic drama of Jonson's feast is located precisely in the interstices of Martial's: between Martial's (often foreign) agriculture and his domestic cuisine, we find Jonson's marketplace" ("Corpulence" 498). In this sense Epigram 101 both exploits and plays against the economics of mediation. Repeating and reprocessing Martial's work, it seeks to create a space where no further such repetitions shall occur, where "our cups" shall not "make any guiltie men." Thus we may see Jonson's own indebtedness to classical texts as another instance of the ambiguities implicit in his social presence.

4. "Jonson was the impoverished stepson of a London bricklayer, yet he aspired to a place in a noble household; he had made his mark as a satirist, yet he wanted to be taken into the establishment . . . ; he was a fiercely independent individual, yet he was putting his services at the disposal of his social superiors" (Riggs 64).

5. As Riggs has pointed out, the view of Jonson as a "priggish social climber" was current even in the poet's own day (Riggs 64). In twentieth-century criticism, this aspect of Jonson's achievement has often been read to exclude any possibility of sympathy for, or identification with, values other than the conservative ones of the traditional aristocracy. Thus K. W. Evans, for instance, has traced Jonson's affiliations with the ideal prince tradition and concluded from them that "Jonson's thought has little in it that anticipates the future" (264). Dale Randall offers a somewhat more qualified statement of the same position: "Jonson, like James, believed in an old-fashioned paternalistic monarchy with a wise and good king at the top of a fixed social hierarchy. Neither James nor Jonson saw, or at least admitted seeing, that such an idea was anachronistic [by the early seventeenth century]" (163). Although I agree with these scholars' evaluation of Jonson's investment in traditional aristocratic social and political values, I do not agree that this investment forestalls any possibility of the poet's imaginative identification with opposed or emergent ideological constructs.

6. William Blissett, for one, has argued that the theatrical failure of *Catiline* derives from its embodiment of a republican political ideology—"*potestas in populo, auctoritas in senatu*" (102)—that was at odds with the standard Jacobean political investment in "an anointed monarch with royal prerogative and a parliament representing the estates of the realm" (102).

7. Albert Tricomi identifies *Sejanus* with a wide range of Jacobean anticourt drama, arguing that "In *Sejanus*, reformist, homiletic history is *Jonson's* truth" (77) and that "against the absolutism of Caesar (to whom contemporary princes such as James [I] routinely compared themselves)," Jonson "championed the heroes of the Roman Republic and of the Senate" (73).

8. Of course, the conspicuous consumption of prominent nobles dwarfs that of Jonson's "Inviting a Friend to Supper," yet spectacular use of food becomes more and more an option for the emergent seventeenth-century middle class. Goody notes that from the sixteenth century forward, changes in English cuisine "were related to the changing nature of social stratification in England, and especially to the increasing dominance of the middle class. Their concern with status was greatly aided by the use of printed books [and] manuals [that] helped them breach the hierarchical organisation of cuisine" (152). In this spirit Jean Latham describes a feast served on 13 Jan. 1660 at the home of Samuel Pepys: it included "oysters, a hash of rabbits, lamb and [a] chine of beef. . . . Then came 'a great dish of roasted fowl cost me about 30s, and a tart, and then fruit and cheese.'" Latham concludes with Pepys's telling remark, "My dinner was noble and enough" (14–15).

9. See Fumerton 122–126, 133–134.

Chapter 3

1. For full transcripts of the documents in question, see Chambers 2:90–95 and 154–180. The six signatures have been photographically reproduced in G. Blakemore Evans et al. 1696.

2. In their facsimile edition of *Shakespeare's Plays in Quarto*, Michael Allen and Kenneth Muir reproduce twenty-three title pages, thirteen of which mention Shakespeare by name. Of these thirteen, ten give the now regular spelling, one (Q1 of *Hamlet*) gives "Shake-speare," one (*Lear*) gives "Shak-speare," and one (*The Two Noble Kinsmen*) gives "Shakspere."

3. See de Grazia 86–87 for a summary of Malone's efforts to standardize Shakespeare's name on the basis of his signature. De Grazia notes the obvious problem with such efforts when she asks, "If each of the signatures consisted of different letters and of differently formed letters, how could any one be singled out as the original" of "a typographically-regularized name?" (87).

4. I have based these and the following figures on the historical survey of Jonson's early texts included in Herford, Simpson, and Simpson 9:3–159. Herford and the Simpsons list seventeen quarto (and one octavo) editions of Jonson's plays before 1669, together with the folios of 1616 and 1640 and the abortive printing of 1631. Of these, the editions prior to 1605 never give "Ionson" or "Jonson" on the title page. Beginning with the quarto *Sejanus*, "Ionson" and "Jonson" appear uninterruptedly until 1631, by which time Jonson's age and ill health seem to have partly impaired his ability to supervise printing. The quarto editions of Jonson's masques follow the same trend.

5. See Herford, Simpson, and Simpson 1:217–249. Of these records only one—Jonson's 1621 warrant for the reversion of the mastery of the revels (1:237–239) spells Jonson's name without the *h*. In addition, there is one document—a 1621 deed of assignment (1:236–237)—that bears Jonson's signature with the *h*. I take this to be the exception that proves the rule.

6. Partridge 41–55. Partridge particularly notes that "the language of the last decade of the 16th C and the first quarter of the next was undergoing fairly rapid modification" (8), that "indications of this are found . . . in the increased use of *'s* for the possessive genitive" (8), and that "no passage from Shakespeare could offer the wealth of interest . . . for the student of the possessive genitive" that Jonson's work affords (45). Since one point of this chapter is that Jonson's distinctive contributions to English literary history include a developing emphasis on authorial labor and property, these remarks are certainly worthy of mention.

7. "A nerve-stimulus, first transcribed [*ubertragen*] into an image [*Bild*]! First metaphor! The image again copied into a sound! Second metaphor! And each time he [the creator of language] leaps completely out of one sphere right into the midst of an entirely different one. . . . What, therefore, is truth? A mobile army of metaphors, metonymies, anthropomorphisms; . . . truths are illusions of which one has forgotten that they *are* illusions, . . . coins that have their obverse effaced and now are no longer of account as coins but merely as metal" (Nietzsche 178–180).

8. Of Boccaccio's *De genealogia deorum*, in which the author "discusses the position of . . . humanism with regard to the age," Burckhardt remarks that "we must not be misled by his exclusive references to *poesia*, as closer observation shows that he means thereby the whole mental activity of the poet-scholars" (1:214). This concept of "whole mental activity" would of course authorize Jonson's conflation of oratory and poetry. However, other modes of distinction are available, as in Bartolommeo Facio's *De viris illustribus liber*, which "divides . . . famous men into

nine classes, nearly all of them prefaced by remarks on their distinctive qualities," and two of which happen to be the Poets and the Orators (Burckhardt 1:159n.). Jonson's ambiguity in *Discoveries* seems to stem from an attempt to move between these two opposed modes of nomenclatural division.

9. See Harold Ogden White for a summary of theoretical statements on this subject. In White's view, the dominant (although not the only) Renaissance attitude toward plagiarism and imitation elides literary property with literary value; thus "the writer who transforms what he takes from his predecessors into 'as much and as good' is not in debt to his sources" (127). This conflation of categories tends to expand the scope of a given argument, rather than narrowing the avenue of inquiry. In the process, this conflation arguably supplies an example for the much broader and more aggressive equivocations that characterize Jonson's literary theory.

10. The *Oxford Latin Dictionary* cites Ovid's *Heroides* 13.50 and Martial 8.15.2 and 8.65.1 as instances of this usage. Lewis and Short's *Latin Dictionary* multiplies examples, noting that when taken in the active sense *redux* is "mostly an epithet of Jupiter and of Fortuna, in the poets and in insc[riptions]" (s.v. redux 1).

11. Richard Newton thus notes the "closed coherence" that is one of the folio's distinctive features and that lends Jonson's work a "coercive authority, both critical and moral, to which [it] challenges . . . readers to submit" (35). Joseph Loewenstein, following Timothy Murray, describes the folio as "transhistorical and, frequently, . . . antioccasional," promoting a sense of "text as antitheater" (Loewenstein, "'Multitudinous Presse'" 182), and likewise encouraging "Jonson's contentious jealousy of his own cultural authority" ("'Multitudinous Presse'" 183). Jennifer Brady similarly ascribes to the folio "a place and status outside 'the time of the body and its voice'" (196).

12. In addition, compare Richard West's prefatory poem to Jacques Ferrand's *Erotomania*, which disapproves of dedicatory verses' habitual claim that such-and-such a "Play / Exceeds all Johnson's Works" (sig. B7r; qtd. in Bradley and Adams 270); and Suckling's "Sessions of the Poets," in which Jonson claims "he deserv'd the Bayes, / For his were calld Works, where others were but Plaies" (21–22; qtd. in Herford, Simpson, and Simpson 11:499). Also note attempts, like that of John Eliot, to reinscribe the value of Jonson's writing within traditional patronage relations and thereby discount Jonson's own agency as author. Eliot, commenting on Jonson's various epigrams to Richard, Lord Weston, Lord High Treasurer, remarks that "they return'd you *Ben* as I was tould, / A certain sum of forty pound in gold: / The verses then being rightly understood, / His Lordship not *Ben Johnson* made them good" (sig. B6r; qtd. in Herford, Simpson, and Simpson 11:406).

13. British Museum MS. Harley 6057, f. 30; qtd. in Herford, Simpson, and Simpson 11:385.

14. D. H. Craig has brought together a good deal of the matter on Jonson's literary borrowings. See especially 91–92, 102, 122, 234, 262, and 358–359.

15. John Sweeney thus writes matter-of-factly of the "deep . . . aggression" and "hostility" that Jonson displayed toward his popular audiences (13, 35, 123). Katharine Maus observes that "as his career proceeds, [Jonson] portrays his audience in less and less flattering ways" (*Roman Frame* 149), and Peter Stallybrass and Allon

White note the urgency with which Jonson's plays insist on "the abyss between the author and the vulgar" (69).

16. Cf. Jonson's translation of Horace's *Ars poetica* 440–441 (627–628 in Jonson's translation): "Blot all: and to the anvile bring / Those ill-torn'd Verses, to new hammering" (in Herford, Simpson, and Simpson 9).

Chapter 4

1. Paster suggestively argues that the aggressive anality of Face and Subtle is made possible by a developing "desire to appear before the world without blemish, to conceal any marks that might signify a history of syphilis or other infectious disease" (146). This argument certainly agrees with the views advanced in the present study; however, it naturally pays primary attention to medical and sexual discourse, whereas the present work is more interested in the infrastructural mechanisms of early modern London sewage disposal.

2. Kernan makes this point early on: "The author of satire always portrays the grotesque and distorted, and concentrates to an excessive degree on the flesh. . . . The most unpleasant details appearing in literature are to be found in satire: Juvenal's pathic who tells us in explicit and revolting terms about his relationship with his patron, the descriptions of the excrementary functions of the Yahoos, Trimalchio's purge in *The Satyricon*, Rochester's pictures of the amorous pleasantries of King Charles and his mistresses" (11). As a result, "In no art form is the complexity of human existence so obviously scanted as satire. The satirist is out to persuade us that vice is both ugly and rampant, and in order to do so he deliberately distorts, excludes, and slants. . . . Inevitably when he dips into the devil's broth in order, he says, to show us how filthy it really is, he gets splattered" (23–24). Kernan does credit Jonson with softening these characteristics of satire, but they nonetheless remain integral to his literary vision.

3. See Curtius for the classic description of this motif, which "appears as early as in the hagiographic comedy of the Merovingian period. The body of St. Gangolf works miracles. A woman who is told of this cries: 'Sic operatur virtutes Gangulfus, quomodo anus meus.' This was avenged: the designated organ immediately emitted an 'obscenus sonus.' This happened on a Friday. During all the rest of her life the woman could not speak a word on Friday but that it was followed by a detonation" (435). Curtius includes this tale under the general rubric of "kitchen humor," under which he also lists certain related motifs.

4. It is of at least incidental interest that Harington's new jakes was apparently a reinvention of technology used by the Minoans (Palmer 14). Neither Jonson nor Harington could have known this particular fact; however, both authors were distinctly interested in classical civilizations that made more than an incidental investment in matters of sanitary engineering.

5. In the most influential description of Jonson as a stylistic neoclassicist, Wesley Trimpi relates the Jonsonian plain style to a Ciceronian rhetoric whose "lan-

guage will be pure . . . , plain and clear" (60). Similarly, Judith Gardiner notes that "Jonson's 'plain style' throughout the epigrams is fairly consistent, with its frequent use of abstract diction, unobtrusive imagery, functional figures of sound and rhythm, simple rhetorical structures, and highly articulated syntax" (52). And Richard Flantz credits Jonson with "helping to establish in England . . . a plain-style genre modeled on Latinate forms" (59).

6. See Freud, "Character and Anal Erotism" and "The Disposition to Obsessional Neurosis" (1908 and 1913 respectively), Ferenczi, "The Ontogenesis of the Interest in Money" (1914), and Jones, "Anal-Erotic Character Traits" (1918).

7. Ernest Sabine mistakenly believed this ordinance to be of Restoration origin (317). However, Anthony Munday's enlargement of Stow's *Survey of London*, published in 1633, lists among the "Statutes of the Streets of this City" the provision that "No Goungfermour shall carry any Ordure till after nine of the clocke in the night" (Stow 1633, sig. 3L2v).

8. London Public Record Office Assize 35, 47/5, m. 40.

9. Stow notes, for instance, that by his time Finsbury Fields had been drained and "made main and hard ground, . . . since the which time, also the further grounds beyond Fensbury Court have been so overheightened with Laystalls of dung, that now three windmills are thereon set" (Stow 1908, 2:71) and that Moorditch had become "a verie narrow, and the same a filthie channell, or altogither stopped up for Gardens planted, and houses builded thereon" (Stow 1908; 1:19). Moreover, since David Riggs tentatively identifies the bricklayer Robert Brett as Jonson's stepfather, it is worth noting that a lease of 1586 mentions a "little garden made over the sewer by Robert Brette" in Hartshorn Lane (qtd. in Riggs 10). A handwritten archivist's note in the London Guildhall Record Office copy of Geoffrey Cumberledge's *The Corporation of London* adds that even into the early 1900s refuse was removed from London to "marshland at Rainham, 130 acres having been purchased in 1903 of John Abbott for L23,411" (Cumberledge 129).

10. Hugh Plat contends that "all excrements as wel of man as beast, serue to fatten & inrich the earth" (*Jewel-house* 15, sig. B4r). James Donaldson, writing roughly a century later, lists the principal forms of fertilizer as "Dung of Cattle, Ashes, Lime, Marle, and Sea-ware" (20, sig. D2v). Gervase Markham takes a middle route, advocating "mans ordure" for the treatment of barren clay (*Farewell to Husbandry* 41, sig. F1r) and for raising "rootes or Cabbages" (*English Husbandman* 204, sig. Dd2v), but recommending differently constituted fertilizers for a wide range of other soils and crops. It is a nice question just how closely the average farmer would have attended to such distinctions.

11. Jeffrey Henderson's survey of obscene language in Greek comedy naturally pays close attention to Aristophanes, who, according to Henderson, uses scatology "primarily in slapstick routines," as "a way to degrade a character" (54), and in the construction of "scatophagous insults" (192). George Rowe, in turn, has argued convincingly that Jonson is indebted to Aristophanes for a vocabulary of competition and aggression (105–112)—the very vocabulary of which Aristophanes' scatology was an integral part.

12. Maus argues that "the fundamental principle of what I shall call Jonson's

'satiric economy' might, anachronistically, be called the law of the conservation of matter. In the comedies and the satiric epigrams, he represents a world that contains a predetermined quantity of substance, a quantity not subject to increase" ("Economies" 66). This world, in which "nothing is created and everything is endlessly recycled" ("Economies" 73), arguably leads to the patterns of fecal metamorphosis prominent in "On the Famous Voyage."

13. Herford and the Simpsons note that Jonson refers to Bankes in *Every Man Out* (IV.vi.60) as well as in the present poem, that records indicate Bankes was still alive in 1625, and that he became a vintner in Cheapside (11:32).

Chapter 5

1. Also see Thomas Greene's influential essay "Ben Jonson and the Centered Self" for an important treatment of this theme. Greene explicitly contrasts Jonson's fixed morality with the character of Volpone, which he identifies with "Protean man, man without core and principle and substance" (337). By now it may be clear that I am uncomfortable with Greene's commitment to such moral fixities and oppositions.

2. For this account of the relations between Jonson and Marston, see Riggs 72–84 and Miles 49–51. Chute takes a more starkly oppositional view of matters (96–103).

3. See Barthes's classic essay in *Mythologies*, "The World of Wrestling," which argues that the "passions" exhibited by professional wrestlers develop as a consequence of the semiotic context within which the wrestling match itself unfolds. As Barthes explains, "It is . . . easy to understand why out of five wrestling-matches, only about one is fair. . . . In actual fact a fair fight is nothing but an exaggeratedly polite one: the contestants confront each other with zeal, not rage; they can remain in control of their passions, they do not punish their beaten opponent relentlessly, they stop fighting as soon as they are ordered to do so" (*Mythologies* 22). This behavior would be inconsistent, Barthes argues, with wrestling's self-presentation as "a sort of mythological fight between Good and Evil" (*Mythologies* 23), and Barthes's theatrical analysis of wrestling may certainly have some value for pugilistic theatrical displays like the War of the Theaters.

4. Chute, for instance, remarks that the War of the Theaters "had come to a disastrous end," although, as she adds, "no one was to conclude from this that Jonson had lowered his banner and had been defeated in his attempt to adapt classical drama to the Elizabethan stage" (103). Riggs observes that Dekker's *Satiromastix* "scored a number of palpable hits" against Jonson and that "despite the brilliance with which he conducted his side of the quarrel, Jonson failed to win a clear-cut victory" (84). According to Miles, the "apologeticall Dialogue" appended to the published version of *Poetaster* comprised "a valiant attempt to cover [Jonson's] retreat" from the War of the Theaters (61). She also notes that both sides were clearly injured by the quarrel: "Marston was silent for over two years while Jonson did not write another comedy for nearly four" (62).

5. See Peter Womack 50–54 for a good account of the plot structure and observation of neoclassical unities in *Bartholomew Fair*.

6. This ubiquitous commonplace has received frequent attention and, given *Bartholomew Fair*'s clear preoccupation both with bodily and social relations, it is obviously germane to the present reading. See Tillyard 94–99 for a selection of early modern texts dealing with the theme.

Bibliography

PRIMARY SOURCES

Athenaeus. *The Deipnosophists*. Trans. Charles Burton Gulick. 7 vols. London: William Heinemann, 1951.
Aubrey, John. *Aubrey's Brief Lives*. Ed. Oliver Lawson Dick. Ann Arbor: University of Michigan Press, 1962.
Barrow, Philip. *The Method of Physick*. London, 1634.
Cary, Walter. *A Briefe Treatise, called Caries Farewell to Physicke*. London, 1583.
Chew, Helena, and William Kellaway, eds. *London Assize of Nuisance, 1301–1341: A Calendar*. Chatham, England: W. and J. Mackay, 1973.
A Closet for Ladies and Gentlewomen. London, 1608.
Cockburn, J. S., ed. *Calendar of Assize Records, Essex Indictments, Charles I*. London: Her Majesty's Stationery Office, 1982.
Crooke, Helkiah. *Mikrokosmographia. A Description of the Body of Man*. London, 1615.
[Curteys, Richard.] *A Sermon preached before the Queene's Maiestie . . . the 14. Day of Marche. 1573*. London, 1573.
Dekker, Thomas. *Dramatic Works*. Ed. Fredson Bowers. 3 vols. Cambridge: Cambridge University Press, 1952.
Donaldson, James. *Husbandry Anatomized*. Edinburgh, 1697.
Drummond, William. *Informations be Ben Johnston to W. D. when he came to Scotland upon foot*. In *Ben Jonson*, ed. C. H. Herford, Percy Simpson, and Evelyn Simpson. Vol. 1 Oxford: Clarendon Press, 1925. 128–178. 11 vols.
Dryden, John. *The Works of John Dryden*. Ed. H. T. Swedenberg et al. 18 vols. Berkeley: University of California Press, 1971.
Eliot, John. *Poems or Epigrams, Satyrs, Elegies, Songs and Sonnets*. London, 1658.
Erasmus, Desiderius. *De Civilitate Morum Puerilium*. Milan, 1539.
———. *On Good Manners in Boys*. Trans. Brian McGregor. In *The Collected Works of Erasmus*, ed. J. K. Sowards. Vol. 25. Toronto: University of Toronto Press, 1985. 269–289. 27 vols.
Felltham, Owen. *Lusoria: Or Occasional Pieces*. London, 1661.
Ferrand, Jacques. *Erotomania, or, A Treatise . . . of Love, or, Erotique Melancholy*. Oxford, 1645.
Ford, John. *'Tis Pity She's a Whore*. Ed. Derek Roper. Manchester: Manchester University Press, 1975.
Hall, John. *Select Observations on English Bodies*. London, 1657.
Harington, Sir John. *A New Discourse of a Stale Subject, Called the Metamorphosis*

of Ajax. Ed. Elizabeth Story Donno. New York: Columbia University Press, 1962.
Herodotus. *Herodotus*. Trans. A. D. Godley. 4 vols. London: William Heinemann, 1920.
Horace. *Horace: Satires, Epistles, Ars Poetica*. London: William Heinemann, 1961.
Jonson, Ben. *Ben Jonson*. Ed. C. H. Herford, Percy Simpson, and Evelyn Simpson. 11 vols. Oxford: Clarendon Press, 1925–1952.
Lucian. *Lucian*. Trans. A. M. Harmon. 8 vols. London: William Heinemann, 1913.
Manningham, John. *The Diary of John Manningham of the Middle Temple, 1602–1603*. Ed. Robert P. Sorlien. Hanover: University Press of New England, 1976.
Markham, Gervase. *Markhams Farewell to Husbandry*. London, 1620.
———. *The English Husbandman*. London, 1635.
Martial. *M. Val. Martialis Nova Editio. Ex Museo Petri Scriverii*. Leyden, 1619. Ben Jonson's copy, now in the Folger Library.
———. *Epigrams*. Trans. Walter C. A. Ker. 2 vols. London: William Heinemann, 1930.
Middleton, Thomas. *The Selected Plays of Thomas Niddleton*. Ed. David L. Frost. Cambridge: Cambridge University Press, 1978.
Nashe, Thomas. *The Works of Thomas Nashe*. Ed. R. B. McKerrow. 5 vols. Oxford: Basil Blackwell, 1958.
Parrot, Henry. *Laquei ridiculosi: Or Springes for Woodcocks*. London, 1613.
Plat, Sir Hugh. *The Jewel-house of Art and Nature*. London, 1594.
———. *Sundrie New and Artificiall Remedies Against Famine*. London, 1596.
Pliny. *Natural History*. Trans. H. Rackham. 10 vols. London: William Heinemann, 1947.
Plutarch. *Plutarch's Lives*. Trans. Bernadotte Perrin. 11 vols. London: William Heinemann, 1948.
———. *Plutarch's Moralia*. Trans. Edwin L. Minar. 15 vols. London: William Heinemann, 1961.
Porta, Giambattista. *Natural Magick*. London, 1658, Reprint, New York: Basic Books, 1957.
Statutes at Large. 67 vols. London: King's Printer, 1767–1866.
Suckling, Sir John. *The Works of Sir John Suckling*. Ed. T. Clayton and L. A. Beaurline. 2 vols. Oxford: Clarendon Press, 1971.
Suetonius. *Lives of the Twelve Caesars*. Trans. J. C. Rolfe. 2 vols. London: William Heinemann, 1930.
Vicary, Thomas. *A Profitable Treatise of the Anatomie of Mans Body*. London, 1577.
Winstanley, William. *The Lives of the Most Famous English Poets*. Ed. William Riley Parker. Gainesville, Fla.: Scholars' Press, 1963.
Wits Recreations Augmented, with Ingenious Conceites for the Wittie, And Merrie Medecines for the Melancholic. London, 1641.

SECONDARY SOURCES

Abrams, M. H., et al., eds. *The Norton Anthology of English Literature*. 2 vols. New York: W. W. Norton, 1968.

Agnew, Jean-Christophe, *Worlds Apart: The Market and the Theater in Anglo-American Thought, 1550–1750*. Cambridge: Cambridge University Press, 1986.
Allen, Michael, and Kenneth Muir. *Shakespeare's Plays in Quarto*. Berkeley: University of California Press, 1981.
Anspaugh, Kelly. "Ulysses upon Ajax? Joyce, Harington, and the Question of 'Cloacal Imperialism'." *South Atlantic Review* 60.2 (1995): 11–29.
Appleby, Joyce. *Economic Thought and Ideology in Seventeenth-Century England*. Princeton, N. J.: Princeton University Press, 1978.
Ashton, John. *The Fleet: Its River, Prison, and Marriages*. London: T. Fisher Unwin, 1889.
Bakhtin, Mikhail. *Rabelais and His World*. Trans. Helene Iswolsky. Bloomington: Indiana University Press, 1984.
Barbour, Richmond. "'When I Acted Young Antinous': Boy Actors and the Erotics of Jonsonian Theater." *PMLA* 110.5 (1995): 1006–1022.
Barish, Jonas. *Ben Jonson and the Language of Prose Comedy*. Cambridge, Mass.: Harvard University Press, 1960.
Barthes, Roland. *Writing Degree Zero*. Trans. Annette Lavers and Colin Smith. New York: Farrar, Straus and Giroux, 1968.
———. *Mythologies*. Trans. Annette Lavers. New York: Hill and Wang, 1972.
Barton, Anne. "*The New Inn* and the Problem of Jonson's Late Style." *English Literary Renaissance* 9 (1979): 395–418.
———. *Ben Jonson, Dramatist*. Cambridge: Cambridge University Press, 1984.
Barton, Nicholas. *The Lost Rivers of London*. London: Leicester University Press, 1962.
Bate, Jonathan. *Shakespeare and the English Romantic Imagination*. Oxford: Clarendon Press, 1986.
Beier, Lucinda. *Sufferers and Healers: The Experience of Illness in Seventeenth-Century England*. London: Routledge and Kegan Paul, 1987.
Bennett, Tony. *Formalism and Marxism*. London: Methuen, 1979.
Birt, Theodor. *Das Antike Buchwesen in seinem Verhaltniss zur Literatur*. Berlin: W. Hertz, 1882, Reprint, 1959.
Blissett, William. "Roman Ben Jonson." In *Ben Jonson's 1616 Folio*, ed. Jennifer Brady and W. H. Herendeen. Newark: University of Delaware Press, 1991. 90–110.
Bogue, Ronald. *Deleuze and Guattari*. New York: Routledge, 1989.
Borges, Jorge Luis. *Ficciones*. Ed. Anthony Kerrigan. New York: Grove Press, 1962.
Bourdieu, Pierre. *Outline of a Theory of Practice*. Trans. Richard Nice. Cambridge: Cambridge University Press, 1977.
Bradley, Jesse Franklin, and Joseph Quincy Adams. *The Jonson Allusion-Book*. New Haven, Ct.: Yale University Press, 1922.
Brady, Jennifer. "'Noe Fault, but Life': Jonson's Folio as Monument and Barrier." In *Ben Jonson's 1616 Folio*, ed. Jennifer Brady and W. H. Herendeen. Newark: University of Delaware Press, 1991. 192–216.
Brady, Jennifer, and W. H. Herendeen, eds. *Ben Jonson's 1616 Folio*. Newark: University of Delaware Press, 1991.
Bristol, Michael. *Carnival and Theater*. New York: Methuen, 1985.

Brock, D. Heyward. *A Ben Jonson Companion*. Bloomington: Indiana University Press, 1983.
Brooks, Jerome. *The Mighty Leaf: Tobacco Through the Centuries*. Boston: Little, Brown and Company, 1952.
Brown, Norman O. *Life Against Death: The Psychoanalytic Meaning of History*. Middletown, Ct.: Wesleyan University Press, 1959.
Burckhardt, Jacob. *The Civilization of the Renaissance in Italy*. Trans. S. G. C. Middlemore. 2 vols. New York: Harper and Row, 1958.
Burke, Kenneth. *The Philosophy of Literary Forms*. Baton Rouge: Louisiana State University Press, 1941.
———. *A Rhetoric of Motives*. Berkeley: University of California Press, 1969.
Burt, Richard. *Licensed by Authority: Ben Jonson and the Discourses of Censorship*. Ithaca, N.Y.: Cornell University Press, 1993.
Canning, Peter M. "Fluidentity." *SubStance* 13.3/4 (1984): 35–45.
Castelain, Maurice. *Ben Jonson, l'homme et l'oeuvre*. Paris: Hachette, 1907.
Cave, Richard Allen. *Ben Jonson*. London: Macmillan, 1991.
Chambers, E. K. *William Shakespeare: A Study of Facts and Problems*. 2 vols. Oxford: Clarendon Press, 1930.
Champion, Larry. *Ben Jonson's "Dotages."* Lexington: University of Kentucky Press, 1967.
Chute, Marchette. *Ben Jonson of Westminster*. New York: Dutton, 1953.
Craig, D. H. *Ben Jonson: The Critical Heritage, 1599–1798*. London: Routledge, 1990.
Cumberledge, Geoffrey. *The Corporation of London: Its Origin, Constitution, Powers, and Duties*. Oxford: Oxford University Press, 1950.
Curtius, Ernst. *European Literature in the Latin Middle Ages*. Trans. Willard Trask. Princeton, N.J.: Princeton University Press, 1953.
D'Arms, John. "The Roman *Convivium* and the Idea of Equality." In *Sympotica: A Symposium on the "Symposion."* Ed. Oswyn Murray. Oxford: Clarendon Press, 1990. 308–320.
Davis, Natalie Zemon. *Society and Culture in Early Modern France*. Stanford, Calif.: Stanford University Press, 1975.
———. "Beyond the Market: Books as Gifts in Sixteenth-Century France." *Transactions of the Royal Historical Society* 5th ser. 33 (1983): 69–88.
de Grazia, Margreta. *Shakespeare Verbatim: The Reproduction of Authenticity and the 1790 Apparatus*. Oxford: Clarendon Press, 1991.
Deleuze, Gilles, and Guattari, Felix. *Anti-Oedipus: Capitalism and Schizophrenia*. Trans. Robert Hurley et al. Minneapolis: University of Minnesota Press, 1983.
———. *Kafka: Toward a Minor Literature*. Trans. Dana Polan. Minneapolis: University of Minnesota Press, 1986.
———. *A Thousand Plateaus: Capitalism and Schizophrenia*. Trans. Brian Massumi. Minneapolis: University of Minnesota Press, 1987.
Donaldson, Ian. *The World Upside-Down: Comedy from Jonson to Fielding*. Oxford: Clarendon Press, 1970.
———, ed. *Ben Jonson*. New York: Oxford University Press, 1985.

Donovan, Kevin. "Jonson's Texts in the First Folio." In *Ben Jonson's 1616 Folio*, ed. Jennifer Brady and W. H. Herendeen. Newark: University of Delaware Press, 1991. 11–37.
Douglas, Mary. *Purity and Danger: An Analysis of the Concepts of Pollution and Taboo*. New York: Frederick A. Praeger, 1966.
Duncan, Douglas. *Ben Jonson and the Lucianic Tradition*. Cambridge: Cambridge University Press, 1979.
Dutton, Richard. *Ben Jonson: To the First Folio*. Cambridge: Cambridge University Press, 1983.
Eisenstein, Elizabeth. *The Printing Press as an Agent of Change*. 2 vols. Cambridge: Cambridge University Press, 1979.
Elias, Norbert. *The History of Manners*. Trans. Edmund Jephcott. New York: Pantheon Books, 1978.
Eliot, T. S. *Essays on Elizabethan Drama*. New York: Harcourt Brace, n.d.
Evans, G. Blakemore, et al., eds. *The Riverside Shakespeare*. Boston: Houghton Mifflin, 1974.
Evans, K. W. "*Sejanus* and the Ideal Prince Tradition." *Studies in English Literature* 11 (1971): 249–264.
Evans, Robert. "Jonson's EPIGRAMMES I-III." *The Explicator* 45.2 (1987): 7–10.
———. *Jonson and the Contexts of his Time*. Lewisburg, Pa.: Bucknell University Press, 1994.
———. *Ben Jonson and the Poetics of Patronage*. Lewisburg, Pa.: Bucknell University Press, 1989.
Ferenczi, Sandor. *Sex in Psycho-Analysis*. Trans. Ernest Jones. New York, 1950.
Ferguson, Arthur B. *The Articulate Citizen and the English Renaissance*. Durham, N.C.: Duke University Press, 1965.
Fish, Stanley. "Authors-Readers: Jonson's Community of the Same." *Representations* 7 (1984): 26–58.
Fisher, F. J. *London and the English Economy, 1500–1700*. London: Hambledon Press, 1990.
Flandrin, Jean-Louis. "Distinction Through Taste." In *A History of Private Life*, ed. Roger Chartier, trans. Arthur Goldhammer. Vol. 3. Cambridge, Mass.: The Belknap Press of Harvard University Press, 1989. 264–307. 3 vols.
Flantz, Richard. "The Authority of Truth: Jonson's Mastery of Measure and the Founding of the Modern Plain-Style Lyric." In *Classic and Cavalier: Essays on Jonson and the Sons of Ben*, ed. Claude J. Summers and Ted-Larry Pebworth. Pittsburgh, Pa.: University of Pittsburgh Press, 1982. 59–75.
Foucault, Michel. *Discipline and Punish: The Birth of the Prison*. Trans. Alan Sheridan. New York: Pantheon, 1977.
———. *The History of Sexuality: Volume 1*. Trans. Robert Hurley. New York: Vintage, 1980.
Freud, Sigmund. "The Disposition to Obsessional Neurosis: A Contribution to the Problem of Choice of Neurosis." In *The Standard Edition of the Complete Psychological Works of Sigmund Freud*, trans. James Strachey. Vol. 12. London: Hogarth Press, 1958. 315–326. 24 vols. 1953–74.

---. "Character and Anal Erotism." In *The Standard Edition of the Complete Psychological Works of Sigmund Freud*, trans. James Strachey. Vol. 9 London: Hogarth Press, 1959. 167–175. 24 vols. 1953–74.

---. *Civilization and Its Discontents*. In *The Standard Edition of the Complete Psychological Works of Sigmund Freud*, trans. James Strachey. Vol. 21. London: Hogarth Press, 1961. 57–145. 24 vols. 1953–74.

Friedberg, Harris. "Ben Jonson's Poetry: Pastoral, Georgic, Epigram." *English Literary Renaissance* 4 (1974): 111–136.

Fumerton, Patricia. *Cultural Aesthetics: Renaissance Literature and the Practice of Social Ornament*. Chicago: University of Chicago Press, 1991.

Fussell, Paul. *The Boy Scout Handbook and Other Observations*. New York: Oxford University Press, 1982.

Gardiner, Judith Kegan. *Craftsmanship in Context: The Development of Ben Jonson's Poetry*. The Hague: Mouton, 1975.

Gardiner, Judith Kegan, and Susanna S. Epp. "Ben Jonson's Social Attitudes: A Statistical Analysis." In *Drama in the Renaissance: Comparative and Critical Essays*, ed. Clifford Davidson. New York: AMS Press, 1986. 84–102.

Gaskell, Philip. *A New Introduction to Bibliography*. Oxford: Clarendon Press, 1974.

Gognard, Roger. "Jonson's 'Inviting a Friend to Supper.'" *The Explicator* 37.3 (1979): 3–4.

Goldberg, Jonathan. *James I and the Politics of Literature: Jonson, Shakespeare, Donne and Their Contemporaries*. Baltimore, Md.: Johns Hopkins University Press, 1983.

Goody, Jack. *Cooking, Cuisine, and Class: A Study in Comparative Sociology*. Cambridge: Cambridge University Press, 1982.

Greenblatt, Stephen. "Filthy Rites." *Daedalus* 111.3 (1982): 1–16.

Greene, Thomas. "Ben Jonson and the Centered Self." *Studies in English Literature* 10 (1970): 325–348.

---. *The Light in Troy: Imitation and Discovery in Renaissance Poetry*. New Haven, Ct.: Yale University Press, 1982.

Hammill, Graham. "The Epistemology of Expurgation: Bacon and *The Masculine Birth of Time*." In *Queering the Renaissance*, ed. Jonathan Goldberg. Durham, N. C.: Duke University Press, 1994. 236–252.

Hawkes, Terence. *That Shakespeherian Rag: Essays on a Critical Process*. London: Methuen, 1986.

Haynes, Jonathan. *The Social Relations of Jonson's Theater*. Cambridge: Cambridge University Press, 1992.

Helgerson, Richard. *Self-Crowned Laureates: Spenser, Jonson, Milton, and the Literary System*. Berkeley: University of California Press, 1983.

Henderson, Jeffrey. *The Maculate Muse: Obscene Language in Attic Comedy*. New York: Oxford University Press, 1991.

Herendeen, W. H. "A New Way to Pay Old Debts: Pretexts to the 1616 Folio." In *Ben Jonson's 1616 Folio*, ed. Jennifer Brady and W. H. Herendeen. Newark: University of Delaware Press, 1991. 38–63.

Herford, C. H., Percy Simpson, and Evelyn Simpson, eds. *Ben Jonson*. 11 vols. Oxford: Clarendon Press, 1925–1952.

Hill, Christopher. *The Century of Revolution, 1603–1714*. London: Cardinal, 1974.
Hinman, Charlton, ed. *The First Folio of Shakespeare*. New York: W. W. Norton, 1968.
Hoeniger, F. David. *Medicine and Shakespeare in the English Renaissance*. Newark: University of Delaware Press, 1992.
Hunter, William B., Jr., ed. *The Complete Poetry of Ben Jonson*. New York: W. W. Norton, 1963.
Jackson, Gabriele Bernhard. *Vision and Judgment in Ben Jonson's Drama*. New Haven, Ct.: Yale University Press, 1968.
Jardine, Alice. "Woman in Limbo: Deleuze and his Br(others)." *SubStance* 13.3–4 (1984): 46–60.
Johnson, A. W. *Ben Jonson: Poetry and Architecture*. Oxford: Clarendon Press, 1994.
Johnson, Samuel. *Selected Poetry and Prose*. Ed. Frank Brady and W. K. Wimsatt. Berkeley: University of California Press, 1977.
Jones, Ernest. *Papers on Psycho-Analysis*. Baltimore, Md.: William and Wilkins, 1949.
Kelly, William Blackwood. "Interdicted Subjects: Marlowe's Drama as Minor Literature." Diss. University of South Florida, 1995.
Kernan, Alvin. *The Cankered Muse: Satire of the English Renaissance*. New Haven, Ct.: Yale University Press, 1959.
King, Walter. "How High Is Too High? Disposing of Dung in Seventeenth-Century Prescot." *Sixteenth Century Journal* 23.3 (1992): 443–457.
Knapp, Jeffrey. *An Empire Nowhere: England, America, and Literature from "Utopia" to "The Tempest."* Berkeley: University of California Press, 1992.
Latham, Jean. *The Pleasure of Your Company: A History of Manners and Meals*. London: Black, 1972.
Leggatt, Alexander. *Ben Jonson: His Vision and His Art*. London: Methuen, 1981.
Leinwand, Theodore. "Negotiation and New Historicism." *PMLA* 105.3 (1990): 477–490.
Licht, Meg. "Elysium: A Prelude to Renaissance Theatre." *Renaissance Quarterly* 49.1 (1996): 1–29.
Lloyd-Jones, Kenneth. "Erasmus and Dolet on the Ethics of Imitation and the Hermeneutic Imperative." *International Journal of the Classical Tradition* 2.1 (1995): 27–43.
Loewenstein, Joseph. "The Script in the Marketplace." *Representations* 12 (1985): 101–114.
———. "The Jonsonian Corpulence, or The Poet as Mouthpiece." *ELH* 53.3 (1986): 491–518.
———. "Printing and 'The Multitudinous Presse': The Contentious Texts of Jonson's Masques." In *Ben Jonson's 1616 Folio*, ed. Jennifer Brady and W. H. Herendeen. Newark: University of Delaware Press, 1991. 168–191.
Logan, Andy. "Around City Hall: Everything That Rises." *The New Yorker* 15 June, 1987: 82–90.
Marcus, Leah. *The Politics of Mirth: Jonson, Herrick, Milton, Marvell, and the Defense of the Old Holiday Pastimes*. Chicago: University of Chicago Press, 1986.
Marotti, Arthur. "All About Jonson's Poetry." *ELH* 39.2 (1972): 208–237.

Marx, Karl. *The Letters of Karl Marx*. Trans. Saul Padover. Englewood Cliffs, N. J.: Prentice Hall, 1979.
Massumi, Brian, "Preface" to *A Thousand Plateaus: Capitalism and Schizophrenia*, by Gilles Deleuze and Felix Guattari. Minneapolis: University of Minnesota Press, 1987. i–xv.
Maus, Katharine. *Ben Jonson and the Roman Frame of Mind*. Princeton, N.J.: Princeton University Press, 1984.
——— . "Facts of the Matter: Satiric and Ideal Economies in the Jonsonian Imagination." In *Ben Jonson's 1616 Folio*, ed. Jennifer Brady and W. H. Herendeen. Newark: University of Delaware Press, 1991. 64–89.
——— . *Inwardness and Theater in the English Renaissance*. Chicago: University of Chicago Press, 1995.
McCanles, Michael. *Jonsonian Discriminations: The Humanist Poet and the Praise of True Nobility*. Toronto: University of Toronto Press, 1992.
McPherson, David. "Ben Jonson's Library and Marginalia: An Annotated Catalogue." *Studies in Philology* 71.5 (1974):1–100.
Meagher, John. *Method and Meaning in Jonson's Masques*. Notre Dame, Ind.: University of Notre Dame Press, 1966.
Medine, Peter. "Object and Intent in Jonson's 'Famous Voyage'." *Studies in English Literature* 15 (1975): 97–110.
Miles, Rosalind. *Ben Jonson: His Life and Work*. London: Routledge, 1986.
Miller, David Lee. "Writing the Specular Son: Jonson, Freud, Lacan, and the (K)not of Masculinity." In *Desire in the Renaissance: Psychoanalysis and Literature*, ed. Valeria Finucci and Regina Schwartz. Princeton, N.J.: Princeton University Press, 1994. 233–260.
Murray, Oswyn. "Symposium and Genre in the Poetry of Horace." *Journal of Roman Studies* 75 (1985): 39–50.
Murray, Timothy. "From Foul Sheets to Legitimate Model: Antitheater, Text, Ben Jonson." *New Literary History* 14.3 (1983): 641–664.
Newton, Richard. "Jonson and the (Re-)Invention of the Book." In *Classic and Cavalier: Essays on Jonson and the Sons of Ben*, ed. Claude J. Summers and Ted-Larry Pebworth. Pittsburgh, Pa.: University of Pittsburgh Press, 1982. 31–55.
Nichols, J. G. *The Poetry of Ben Jonson*. New York: Barnes and Noble, 1969.
Nietzsche, Friedrich. "On Truth and Falsity in their Ultramoral Sense." In *The Complete Works of Friedrich Nietzsche*, ed. Oscar Levy. Vol. 2. Edinburgh: Foulis, 1910–13. 174–268. 18 vols.
Orgel, Stephen. *The Jonsonian Masque*. Cambridge, Mass.: Harvard University Press, 1965.
——— , ed. *Ben Jonson: The Complete Masques*. New Haven, Ct.: Yale University Press, 1969.
Orgel, Stephen, and Roy Strong. *Inigo Jones: The Theatre of the Stuart Court*. 2 vols. Berkeley: University of California Press, 1973.
Palmer, Roy. *The Water Closet: A New History*. Newton Abbott, England: David and Charles, 1973.
Parfitt, George. *Ben Jonson: Public Poet and Private Man*. New York: Barnes and Noble, 1976.

Parker, Patricia. *Literary Fat Ladies: Rhetoric, Gender, Property*. London: Methuen, 1987.
Partridge, A. C. *The Accidence of Ben Jonson's Plays and Masques: With an Appendix of Comparable Uses in Shakespeare*. Cambridge: Bowes and Bowes, 1953.
Paster, Gail Kern. *The Body Embarrassed: Drama and the Disciplines of Shame in Early Modern England*. Ithaca, N.Y.: Cornell University Press, 1993.
Patton, Paul. "Conceptual Politics and the War-Machine in *Mille Plateaux*." *SubStance* 13.3–4 (1984): 61–80.
Pearlman, E. "Ben Jonson: An Anatomy." *English Literary Renaissance* 9 (1979): 364–394.
Peterson, Richard. *Imitation and Praise in the Poems of Ben Jonson*. New Haven, Ct.: Yale University Press, 1981.
Pinto, V. de Sola. *Sir Charles Sedley, 1639–1701: A Study in the Life and Literature of the Restoration*. London: Constable and Company, 1927.
Pops, Martin. "The Metamorphosis of Shit." *Salmagundi* 56 (1982): 26–61.
Quaife, G. R. *Wanton Wenches and Wayward Wives: Peasants and Illicit Sex in Seventeenth-Century England*. New Brunswick, N.J.: Rutgers University Press, 1979.
Randall, Dale. *Jonson's Gypsies Unmasked: Background and Theme of "The Gypsies Metamorphosed."* Durham, N.C.: Duke University Press, 1975.
Ranum, Orest. "The Refuges of Intimacy." In *A History of Private Life*, ed. Roger Chartier, trans. Arthur Goldhammer. Vol. 3. Cambridge, Mass.: The Belknap Press of Harvard University Press, 1989. 206–263. 3 vols.
Revard, Stella. "Classicism and Neo-Classicism in Jonson's *Epigrammes* and *The Forrest*." In *Ben Jonson's 1616 Folio*, ed. Jennifer Brady and W. H. Herendeen. Newark: University of Delaware Press, 1991. 138–167.
Revel, Jacques. "The Uses of Civility." In *A History of Private Life*, ed. Roger Chartier, trans. Arthur Goldhammer. Vol. 3 Cambridge, Mass.: The Belknap Press of Harvard University Press, 1989. 166–205. 3 vols.
Riddell, James. "The Arrangement of Ben Jonson's *Epigrammes*." *Studies in English Literature* 27 (1987): 53–70.
Riddell, James, and Stanley Stewart. *Jonson's Spenser: Evidence and Historical Criticism*. Pittsburgh, Pa.: Duquesne University Press, 1995.
Riggs, David. *Ben Jonson: A Life*. Cambridge, Mass.: Harvard University Press, 1989.
Rose, Mark. *Authors and Owners: The Invention of Copyright*. Cambridge, Massachusetts: Harvard University Press, 1993.
Rowe, George. *Distinguishing Jonson: Imitation, Rivalry, and the Direction of a Dramatic Career*. Lincoln: University of Nebraska Press, 1988.
Sabine, Ernest L. "Latrines and Cesspools of Mediaeval London." *Speculum* 9 (1934): 303–321.
Schoenbaum, Samuel. *Shakespeare's Lives*. Oxford: Clarendon Press, 1991.
Shapiro, James. *Rival Playwrights: Marlowe, Jonson, Shakespeare*. New York: Columbia University Press, 1991.
Shengold, Leonard. *Halo in the Sky: Observations on Anality and Defense*. New York: Guilford Press, 1988.

Shields, David. "Anglo-American Clubs: Their Wit, Their Heterodoxy, Their Sedition." *William and Mary Quarterly* 51.2 (1994): 293–304.
Simon, André, ed. *The Star Chamber Dinner Accounts*. London: George Rainbird, 1959.
Singer, Charles, et al. *A History of Technology*. 3 vols. Oxford: Clarendon Press, 1957.
Siraisi, Nancy. *Medieval and Early Renaissance Medicine: An Introduction to Knowledge and Practice*. Chicago: University of Chicago Press, 1990.
Slights, William. *Ben Jonson and the Art of Secrecy*. Toronto: University of Toronto Press, 1994.
Smith, Bruce. "Ben Jonson's *Epigrammes*: Portrait-Gallery, Theater, Commonwealth." *Studies in English Literature* 14 (1974): 91–109.
Stallybrass, Peter, and Allon White. *The Politics and Poetics of Transgression*. Ithaca, N.Y.: Cornell University Press, 1986.
Stivale, Charles. "The Literary Element in *Mille Plateaux*: The New Cartography of Deleuze and Guattari." *SubStance* 13.3–4 (1984): 20–34.
Stone, Lawrence. *The Crisis of the Aristocracy, 1558–1641*. Oxford: Clarendon Press, 1965.
Stow, John. *The Survey of London: Conteyning The Originall, Increase, Moderne Estate, and Government of that City . . . inlarged by . . . A*[nthony] *M*[unday]. London, 1633.
———. *A Survey of London*. Ed. Charles Lethbridge Kingsfield. 2 vols. Oxford: Clarendon Press, 1908.
Sugden, Edward H. *A Topographical Dictionary to the Works of Shakespeare and his Fellow Dramatists*. Manchester: Manchester University Press, 1925.
Sullivan, J. P. *Martial: The Unexpected Classic*. Cambridge: Cambridge University Press, 1991.
Sweeney, John Gordon, III. *Jonson and the Psychology of Public Theater*. Princeton, N.J.: Princeton University Press, 1985.
Swinburne, Algernon Charles. *A Study of Ben Jonson*. London: Chatto and Windus, 1889.
Teague, Frances. *The Curious History of "Bartholomew Fair."* Lewisburg, Pa.: Bucknell University Press, 1985.
Thirsk, Joan, ed. *The Agrarian History of England and Wales*. 4 vols. Cambridge: Cambridge University Press, 1967.
Thomas, Keith. *Religion and the Decline of Magic*. Harmondsworth: Penguin, 1978.
Tillyard, E. M. W. *The Elizabethan World Picture*. New York: Vintage Books, n.d.
Trent, Christopher. *Greater London: Its Growth and Development Through Two Thousand Years*. London: Phoenix House, 1965.
Tricomi, Albert. *Anticourt Drama in England, 1603–1642*. Charlottesville: University of Virginia Press, 1989.
Trimpi, Wesley. *Ben Jonson's Poems: A Study of the Plain Style*. Stanford, Calif.: Stanford University Press, 1962.
Trinh, Minh-ha T. *Woman, Native, Other: Writing Postcoloniality and Feminism*. Bloomington: Indiana University Press, 1989.

van den Berg, Sara. *The Action of Ben Jonson's Poetry*. Newark: University of Delaware Press, 1987.
Watson, Robert N. *Ben Jonson's Parodic Strategy: Literary Imperialism in the Comedies*. Cambridge, Mass.: Harvard University Press, 1987.
Wayne, Don E. *Penshurst: The Semiotics of Place and the Poetics of History*. Madison: University of Wisconsin Press, 1984.
Whigham, Frank. *Ambition and Privilege: The Social Tropes of Elizabethan Courtesy Theory*. Berkeley: University of California Press, 1984.
———. "Reading Social Conflict in the Alimentary Tract: More on the Body in Renaissance Drama." *ELH* 55.2 (1988): 333–350.
Whipple, T. K. *Martial and the English Epigram from Sir Thomas Wyatt to Ben Jonson*. Berkeley: University of California Press, 1925.
White, Harold Ogden. *Plagiarism and Imitation During the English Renaissance*. Cambridge, Mass.: Harvard University Press, 1935.
Williams, Raymond. *The Country and the City*. New York: Oxford University Press, 1973.
Wilson, Edmund. "Morose Ben Jonson." In *The Triple Thinkers: Twelve Essays on Literary Subjects*. New York: Oxford University Press, 1948. 213–232.
Wiltenburg, Robert. *Ben Jonson and Self-Love: The Subtlest Maze of All*. Columbia: University of Missouri Press, 1990.
Womack, Peter. *Ben Jonson*. Oxford: Basil Blackwell, 1986.
Woods, Susanne. "The Context of Jonson's Formalism." In *Classic and Cavalier: Essays on Jonson and the Sons of Ben*, ed. Claude J. Summers and Ted-Larry Pebworth. Pittsburgh, Pa.: University of Pittsburgh Press, 1982. 77–89.
Zorzetti, Nevio. "The *Carmina Convivalia*." In *Sympotica: A Symposium on the "Symposion,"* ed. Oswyn Murray. Oxford: Clarendon Press, 1990. 289–307.

Index

Alchemist, The, 22, 53, 80, 81, 113, 148, 149–150, 171–173, 203
Althusser, Louis, 17
Anacreon, 101, 103
Anspaugh, Kelly, 151
Appleby, Joyce, 37, 38
Aristophanes, 160
Aristotle, 123
Armenters, Joan de, and William Thorney, 160
Athenaeus, 129–130
Aubrey, John, 95
Avicenna, 119

Bacon, Sir Francis, 200
Bakhtin, Mikhail, 8, 14–21, 23, 60, 143, 160, 167–168, 207; *Rabelais and His World*, 15, 16
Barbour, Richmond, 105, 108
Barish, Jonas, 33, 101, 110, 114, 121, 204
Barrow, Philip, 187
Barthes, Roland, 153, 183
Bartholomew Fair, 2, 3, 17, 57, 80, 82–83, 148, 170, 176, 189–200, 201, 203
Barton, Anne, 13–14, 58, 105, 118, 190, 196
Barton, Nicholas, 161
Bate, Jonathan, 124–125
Beier, Lucinda, 188–189
Berg, Sara van den, 2, 56, 64, 87, 177
Birt, Theodor, 35
Blissett, William, 73
Bogue, Ronald, 25, 177
Borges, Jorge Luis, 145–146
Bourdieu, Pierre, 20–21
Bristol, Michael, 16
Brown, Norman O., 13
Buckingham, George Villiers, Duke of, 126
Burckhardt, Jakob, 122
Burke, Kenneth, 35, 148–149
Burt, Richard, 18, 36, 67, 112
Busino, Orazio, 62

Camden, William, 177, 179
Campion, Thomas, 19
"Captayne Hungry, To," 56, 58–60, 84, 91, 147
Carson, Johnny, 175
Cary, Walter, 186–187
Case Is Altered, The, 137, 154, 172
Catiline, 94
Catullus, 74
Cave, Richard Allen, 204
Cecil, Sir Robert, 96, 97
Chapman, George, 19
Charles I, King of England and Scotland, 15, 103, 126, 127
Christian IV, King of Denmark, 96
Chute, Marchette, 113
Civilité manuals, 59–63
Closet for Ladies and Gentlewomen, A, 157
Conspicuous consumption, 92–99
Convivial behavior, 47–56
Conygrave, William, 157
Coryate, Thomas, 176, 177, 179, 200; *Crudities*, 176
Cotton, Sir Robert, 177
"Courtling, To," 94
Crapper, Thomas, 159–160
Crooke, Helkiah, 120, 186–188
Cummings, Alexander, 159
Curteys, Richard, 120
Cynthia's Revels, 57, 194, 204

Dali, Salvador, 202, 205
D'Arms, John, 51
Davis, Natalie Zemon, 38
Dekker, Thomas, 134–135, 178–186, 188; *Satiromastix*, 134, 135, 185
Deleuze, Gilles, and Felix Guattari, 4, 23–27, 36, 39, 47, 49–50, 67–68, 75, 85, 104, 105, 108–109, 116, 121, 150, 165–166, 172–173, 177, 201, 204–205; *Anti-Oedipus*, 23
Devil Is an Ass, The, 17

Dickens, Charles, 159
Digestion, 119–121
Discoveries, 78, 115, 117, 118–124, 176
Domitian, Emperor of Rome, 32, 51–52, 56
Donaldson, Ian, 14
Douglas, Mary, 20–22, 36, 112; *Purity and Danger*, 21
Drummond, William, of Hawthornden, 5, 6, 66, 82, 90, 183, 202, 203, 205
Dryden, John, 125; *An Essay of Dramatick Poesy*, 125
Duncan, Douglas, 8, 47–48, 87
Dutton, Richard, 131

Eastward Ho, 110, 179, 183
Edward I, King of England, 158
Eisenstein, Elizabeth, 30
Elias, Norbert, 46, 47, 59, 193; *History of Manners*, 46
Eliot, T. S., 133, 203
"Elizabeth, Countess of Rutland, To," 28
Elizabeth I, Queen of England, 120, 158, 173
Emesis, 186–189
Epicoene, 7, 57–58, 62, 113, 147, 170, 197
Epigrams, 1, 167
"Epistle to Master John Selden," 28
"Epistle to Mr. Arthur Squib," 83
"Epistle . . . to One that Asked to be Sealed of the Tribe of Ben," 77
Erasmus, Desiderius, 59–62, 157–158, 191; *De Civilitate Morum Puerilium*, 59, 191
Evans, Robert, 19, 32, 47, 86, 92, 96, 170–171, 177, 184
Everitt, Alan, 37, 38
Every Man in His Humour, 56, 80, 82, 170
Every Man out of His Humour, 61–62, 180–181, 184

"Famous Voyage, On the," 152, 159, 160, 161–166, 167, 172, 173, 190, 203
Felltham, Owen, 133
Ferenczi, Sandor, 153, 169
Ferguson, Arthur, 122
Ferrabosco, Alphonso, 6
"Fine Lady Would-Be, To," 94
Fish, Stanley, 29, 32, 91
Flandrin, Jean-Louis, 60
Fleet River, the, 158, 161–164, 167, 174–175
For the Honor of Wales, 17
Ford, John, 14
Foucault, Michel, 17, 85, 204

Freud, Sigmund, 8–14, 18, 19, 23, 153–154, 165, 168–169, 172, 173; *Civilization and Its Discontents*, 12; "The Disposition to Obsessional Neurosis," 12
Friedberg, Harris, 103
Fumerton, Patricia, 6–7, 77–78, 107–108
Fussell, Paul, 206–207

Galen, 119
Game at Chess, A, 1
Gilligan's Island, 42–43
Gognard, Roger, 2
Goldberg, Jonathan, 85, 99
Gondomar, Count, 1, 140
Goody, Jack, 84
Greenblatt, Stephen, 168
Greene, Thomas, 8, 26, 28–29, 54, 91, 101
"Gut, On," 84
Gypsies Metamorphos'd, The, 80, 81

Hall, John, 187
Hammill, Graham, 200–201
Harington, Sir John, 14, 96, 98, 150–152, 154–156, 157, 159, 161, 166–167, 173, 175; *The Metamorphosis of Ajax*, 150, 152, 154, 156, 157, 161, 167
Harrelson, Lowell, 174
Hawkes, Terence, 131–132
Haynes, Jonathan, 55, 86, 116, 134, 143–144, 170
Helgerson, Richard, 32, 45, 132, 167
Heminges, John, and Henry Condell, 117
Henry VIII, King, 5, 158
Herendeen, W. H., 131, 203
Herford, C. H., and Percy and Evelyn Simpson, 70, 113
Heydon, Sir Christopher, 161, 162, 164
Hill, Christopher, 4–5
Hipponax, 160
Hoeniger, F. David, 188
Horace, 51, 55, 56–57, 65, 101, 103, 136, 164, 194–195
Howell, James, 65–66

"Inigo Marquess Would-Be, To," 148
"Inviting a Friend to Supper," 1, 48, 87–92, 95, 98, 100

Jackson, Gabriele, 84
James I, King of England, and VI of Scot-

Index

land, 6, 15, 46, 84, 90, 95, 96, 98, 110, 126–128, 159, 173–174, 179
Johnson, Samuel, 131, 145
Jones, Ernest, 12, 153, 168, 169
Jones, Inigo, 6, 19, 125, 134, 176

Kelly, William, 24
Kibbit, John, 160

Lacan, Jacques, 5, 23, 108
Leges Convivales, 47–49, 57, 63, 67–79, 87, 90, 203, 205
Leggatt, Alexander, 4, 83, 202, 205
Leinwand, Theodore, 19
Leroi-Gourhan, André, 26, 27
Lewis, C. S., 204
Loewenstein, Joseph, 31–32, 64, 66, 88, 96, 125, 153, 206
Love's Triumph Through Callipolis, 103, 125
Lucan, 33
Lucian, 65, 74
Ludlow, Sir Henry, 160
Luther, Martin, 173

Magnetic Lady, The, 138
Malone, Edmond, 113
Manningham, John, 94–95
Marcus, Leah, 14–17, 19, 84, 110
Marotti, Arthur, 94
Marston, John, 19, 94–95, 176, 177, 188; *Histriomastix*, 178, 183; *The Malcontent*, 178, 183; *Sophonisba*, 179
Martial, 32–35, 42, 47–57, 59, 63–66, 74, 92, 97, 178–186
Marx, Karl, 90, 94
Masque of Blackness, The, 125
Masque of Queens, The, 28
Massumi, Brian, 121
Maus, Katharine, 8, 27, 94, 99, 162, 191
McCanles, Michael, 29, 205
McPherson, David, 97
Meagher, John, 128
Medine, Peter, 165
Middleton, Thomas, 1, 92–93; *The Changeling*, 21; *A Chaste Maid in Cheapside*, 93; *A Game at Chess*, 1
Miller, David Lee, 5
Milton, John, 110; *Comus*, 110
Mobro, The, 174–175
Montaigne, Michel de, 118, 176, 200
Murray, Oswyn, 50

Murray, Timothy, 130
"My Lady Covell, To," 83–84
"My Picture Left in Scotland," 83–84

Nashe, Thomas, 167
Neptune's Triumph for the Return of Albion, 7, 81, 120, 126–130
"New Crie, The," 147–148
New Inn, The, 7, 100–101, 103
Nichols, J. G., 84
Nietzsche, Friedrich, 108, 121

"Ode to Himself," 101–103
Orgel, Stephen, 125–126, 128
Ormskirk, 157
Orwell, George, 87, 99, 110
"Over the Door at the Entrance into the Apollo," 72–73, 75–77

Parker, Patricia, 196
Parr, Thomas, 157
Parrot, Henry, 133–134
Partridge, A. C., 114
Paster, Gail, 20, 22, 148, 149–150, 152, 171, 187, 190
Pearlman, E., 9, 11
"Penshurst, To," 56, 76, 99–100, 203
Persius, 195–196
Peterson, Richard, 8, 16, 25, 28, 87–88, 112, 115, 122–124, 206
Petronius, 87
Plato, 108
"Play-Wright, On," 130
Pleasure Reconciled to Virtue, 80, 81, 96, 142–143
Pliny, 106–107; *Natural History*, 106
Plutarch, 70–71
"Poet-Ape, On," 130
Poetaster, 40, 42–46, 57, 94, 176, 179–186, 189, 194, 199, 201
Porta, Giambattista, 158
"Proule the Plagiary, On," 130

Rabelais, François, 15–16, 88, 97; *Gargantua and Pantagruel*, 15
Raleigh, Sir Walter, 192
Ranum, Orest, 77
Revard, Stella, 64
Revel, Jacques, 61
Riddell, James, 163
Riddell, James, and Stanley Stewart, 112

Riggs, David, 6, 9–11, 14, 83, 90, 94, 113, 131, 154, 172, 182, 192
Rose, Mark, 38
Rowe, George, 44, 109, 167, 177–178, 183
Ruggle, George, 184

Scriverius, Peter, 97
Second Part of the Return from Parnassus, The, 117
Sedley, Sir Charles, 61
Sejanus, 94, 113, 179
Selden, John, 177
Sewage disposal, 155–161
Shakespeare, William, 14, 112–118, 131–132, 144–145, 156–157, 179, 187; *The Merchant of Venice*, 21
Shapiro, James, 119
Shelton, Thomas, 161, 162, 164
Shields, David, 67
Simon, André, 98
Siraisi, Nancy, 119–120
Slights, William, 78, 161
Smith, Bruce, 165, 167
Spencer, Gabriel, 205
Stallybrass, Peter, and Allon White, 14–19, 22, 90, 166, 190
Staple of News, The, 138–141, 190
Stone, Lawrence, 84, 98
Stow, John, 158; *The Survey of London*, 158
Stuart Prescott, 156–157, 158
Suetonius, 52

Sullivan, J. P., 33, 52, 53
Sweeney, John, 45
Swift, Jonathan, 169
Swinburne, Algernon Charles, 165

Tale of a Tub, A, 136–137
Teague, Frances, 3, 190
Thirsk, Joan, 84
Thomas, Keith, 160
Titus, Emperor of Rome, 32
"To My Booke-Seller," 29–39
"To the Memory of my beloved, the Author Mr. William Shakespeare," 136
Trimpi, Wesley, 68–69, 72, 74, 87, 165
Trinh, Min-ha, 154

Vicary, Thomas, 120
Volpone, 74, 98, 104–109, 113, 169–170, 172, 173, 184, 197, 203

War of the Theaters, 117, 178–186
Watson, Robert, 7, 192, 206
Wayne, Don, 76, 86, 98, 100, 104, 110
Whigham, Frank, 21–22, 61
Wilson, Edmund, 7, 8–9, 11, 13–14, 110, 152, 159
Winstanley, William, 95–96; *Lives of the Most Famous English Poets*, 95
Womack, Peter, 14, 31

Zorzetti, Nevio, 50–51, 54